Artificial Intelligence for Sustainable Energy Systems 2

Environmental Sustainability and Artificial Intelligence Set

coordinated by

Abhishek Kumar, Arun Lal Srivastav, Ashutosh Kumar Dubey

Artificial Intelligence for Sustainable Energy Systems 2

AI-Driven Innovations, Climate Intelligence, and Pathways to Net-Zero Energy

Edited by

Inam Ul Haq
Sanna Mehraj Kak
Anand Kumar Gupta
Muhammad Sher Ramzan

iSTE

WILEY

First published 2026 in Great Britain and the United States by ISTE Ltd and John Wiley & Sons, Inc.

ISTE Ltd
27-37 St George's Road
London SW19 4EU
UK

www.iste.co.uk

John Wiley & Sons, Inc.
111 River Street
Hoboken, NJ 07030
USA

www.wiley.com

Library of Congress Control Number: 2026933922

British Library Cataloguing-in-Publication Data
A CIP record for this book is available from the British Library
ISBN 978-1-83669-143-3

The manufacturer's authorized representative according to the EU General Product Safety Regulation is Wiley-VCH GmbH, Boschstr. 12, 69469 Weinheim, Germany, e-mail: Product_Safety@wiley.com.

Contents

Preface

The urgent need to transition toward low-carbon and sustainable energy systems has intensified global efforts to adopt intelligent technologies capable of addressing climate change, energy security and environmental resilience. As renewable energy sources expand across power generation, transportation and industrial sectors, complex challenges related to forecasting, optimization, system integration and policy planning continue to emerge. Artificial intelligence (AI), along with machine learning and deep learning techniques, has become a powerful enabler for transforming how energy systems are designed, managed and optimized.

This volume of *Artificial Intelligence for Sustainable Energy Systems* focuses on advanced AI-driven innovations that support clean energy transitions and climate-responsive solutions. It covers intelligent forecasting for solar and wind resources, hybrid optimization models, AI-enabled green hydrogen ecosystems, smart electric mobility, environmental intelligence and net-zero energy strategies. By combining technical developments with policy perspectives and future research directions, the book aims to provide researchers, engineers, decision-makers and students with actionable knowledge for building intelligent, resilient and sustainable energy infrastructures.

Inam UL HAQ
Sanna Mehraj KAK
Anand Kumar GUPTA
Muhammad Sher RAMZAN

April 2026

1

AI for Solar Energy Forecasting and Optimization

With the help of artificial intelligence (AI), we can forecast and optimize techniques for managing renewable energy sources, particularly solar energy. Systems that use AI produce better predictions while operating with enhanced efficiency. The natural operation of solar power systems depends on unpredictable energy output. The power output of solar systems depends on multiple environmental factors, which include cloud coverage, temperature, humidity levels and sunlight intensity. This chapter examines how AI technologies improve solar energy systems. AI enables more accurate solar power forecasting. These capabilities support improved energy planning, reduced grid instability, and optimal system performance in solar power systems integrated with energy storage and smart grids. The combination of long short-term memory (LSTM) and convolutional neural network (CNN) and ConvLSTM models within machine learning (ML) and deep learning (DL) frameworks delivers successful results for short-term and daily sunlight prediction. AI-based optimization systems enable battery management, power generation planning and energy demand response in modern power distribution networks. The current implementation of AI systems faces three main obstacles related to poor data quality, lack of or poor model interpretability and ethical deployment challenges. The development of sustainable and intelligent solar energy systems requires researchers to work on explainable AI, uncertainty quantification and real-time edge computing.

1.1. Introduction

Integrating renewable energy sources is crucial for managing climate change impacts. Among renewable sources, solar energy holds an incredibly positive outlook due to favorable economics, enticing incentives, energy self-sufficiency aspirations, technological advancements and a growing desire for energy independence. However, solar energy remains an

---

Chapter written by Sarika AGARWAL, Mamta NARWARIA, Rohit KUMAR and Savita SINGH.

intermittent and variable source of power. Thus, integrating solar power generation along with battery storage and demand response planning to optimize storage and usage is necessary for seamless power system integration. ML is helping to advance a growing list of applications including microgrids, electric vehicles and smart buildings, among others. In light of these advancements, a generalized solar energy forecasting model is illustrated in Figure 1.1 with the main driving factors for a few forecasting periods. This figure demonstrates an example of a solar energy forecast and interval of interest with a microgrid and weather input. The forecast output is either a projected value or a chart outlining available solar energy for the duration. Solar energy generation depends, primarily, on the level of irradiance.

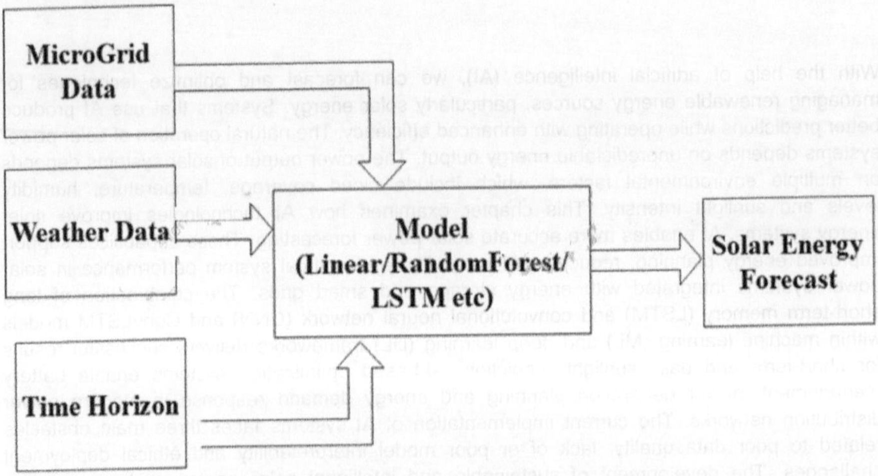

Figure 1.1. *Solar energy forecast model*

Weather information incorporation will enhance solar irradiance forecasting. Common meteorological drivers in the context of solar energy generation forecasting include cloud cover, wind speed, temperature, humidity and aerosol optical depth. Nevertheless, mixed-integer linear programming (MILP) optimization can remain tractable with low-complexity models: for example, a simple on–off decision. Four key performance criteria – mean absolute error (MAE), root mean square error (RMSE), Brier skill score (BSS) and continuous ranked probability score (CRPS) – help gauge the quality of different forecasting approaches, data inputs, training methods and technical solutions. Detailed specifications for these criteria across nowcasting, short-term and day-ahead horizons enable clear performance comparisons (Boussif et al. 2023)

1.2. Fundamentals of solar energy and forecasting

Solar energy is the most abundant source of energy available on Earth. The Earth receives 174 petawatts (PW) of incoming solar radiation in the upper atmosphere. Approximately 30% of this is reflected back to space and the rest is absorbed by the atmosphere, oceans and the landmasses. Solar energy comes in different forms. Photovoltaic (PV) energy is a direct conversion of solar energy into electricity using PV cells. Concentrating solar power (CSP) is the conversion of solar energy into thermal energy, which is then used to generate electricity. Both PV and CSP have distinct characteristics, and their analysis is performed using openly available and lightning-fast weather forecasts, depending on system requirements. Weather variables such as cloudiness, wind, temperature and relative humidity, derived from numerical weather prediction (NWP), are incorporated into the assessment (Ul Haq 2024). Typical weather data include cloud cover, wind speed, dry bulb yard temperature, relative humidity, precipitation, global solar radiation (insolation) and surface pressure. Solar energy varies on an hourly, daily, monthly and yearly basis and depends on local climate and geographical position. Solar energy utilization results in numerous environmental, economical and social benefits. Atmospheric pollution and green-house emissions are minimized and green technologies are enhanced. Water consumption of energy production is reduced. By optimizing the utilization of solar energy, the gap between energy supply and demand can be reduced. Solar modeling and forecasting technology can enhance the deep exploration and utilization of solar energy to a new level. Further, by jointly optimizing multiple energy sources of smart-integrated energy systems and promoting their cooperation, the integrated energy sources utilization efficiency can be maximized (Pinto et al. 2017).

1.2.1. *Solar resource characteristics*

Solar energy generation depends on a renewable resource: the solar irradiance incident on a converter surface. The available solar resource fluctuates with the geographic location of the installation, as well as both the time of the year and time of day. The precise spectral content of the solar irradiance is also an important factor. Solar energy enters the surface of the

Earth in the form of solar radiation, which is a combination of electromagnetic energy emitted from the sun, typically described by its spectral content that includes ultraviolet (UV), visible and infra-red (IR) wavelengths. The only planetary variable that may be considered regarding this spectrum is the orbital distance of the Earth from the Sun. The fundamental physical information of the solar irradiance is quantified, apart from the forecasting keys, waveform-type indicators (variability) and the effect of the atmospheric contributions (pollution), which contribute to diffuse irradiance and the level of solar shading (cloudiness). The value of direct normal radiation (DNI) of solar radiation also varies strongly due to the intermittency of day-night cycles, as well as weather (sunny versus overcast conditions). It is also affected by the variable presence of haze and particulate matter in the atmosphere that blocks out long wave IR energy during the night. Therefore, the accurate forecasting of solar irradiance performance plays an important role in sunny days for solar power generation, as it helps to understand the expected plant output and the effectiveness of an expansion investment. The foregoing solar irradiance characteristics are recognized as essential to development models that are able to predict with a reasonable degree of accuracy the expected level of energy output from PV or concentrating (CSP) systems connected to the grid (Pinto et al. 2017).

Solar resource characteristics involve evaluating the solar energy resource required by solar thermal and PV systems. This assessment may range from 1 h to several-day forecasts, covering the short-range, medium-range, and long-range time scales. Presently, various methods for forecasting solar radiation have been proposed, and emphasis has recently been placed on short-range forecasting, specifically on intra-hour and hourly meteorological prediction using site-based satellite data of geo-stationary satellites, supervised learning with actual sky images and deterministic model output statistics technique based on artificial neural networks, multiplicative ARMA and other statistical models. Terrain data using the built-in sun-movement model may also be utilized as additional resources to enhance prediction capability. Forecasts at the intra-hour and hourly level enable greater control over energy generation, optimal matching with the load requirement of the installation and discharging to the external power utility, thus balancing the charging and discharging and enhancing the economic benefit of the system. Improvements to the forecasting of solar irradiance, insolation, PV system energy output and solar thermal energy are therefore expected to yield economic benefits (Ul Haq et al. 2025c).

The solar irradiance incident on the Earth is subject to multiple influences, including diurnal patterns, seasonal cycles, geographic location, atmospheric composition and climatic conditions (Alanazi et al. 2017). A multitude of different sources of data and meteorological parameters are used to forecast solar irradiation, depending on the spatial and temporal scales adopted in the models. Various datasets, such as GLOBE, NCEP, NARR, ISD, and Era-Interim, as well as atmospheric data from sites such as JMA, NASA-JPL-NEO, and B-smes, provide enabling information to forecast solar irradiation, temperature, precipitation and wind speed. Forecasters have defined them as a combination to forecast the energy output of PV systems connected to the grid. Given the scarcity of actual long-term historical data, the proposed methodology is thus targeted to forecasting PV production at several locations simultaneously with significantly different climatic and seasonal conditions. The forecasted meteorological parameters are also extensively used to estimate models of energy production and relevant decision timetable, thereby facilitating comprehensive planning for PV production and system design.

1.2.2. *Weather data and meteorological variables*

Weather data refers to the collection of information that describes the condition of the atmosphere at a particular place and time. Meteorological variables are the specific measurable factors or parameters used in weather and climate studies shown in Table 1.1. They are the individual components of weather data, basically the scientific variables that describe atmospheric conditions.

These variables help scientists, energy planners and AI models in understanding and predicting the behavior of the weather. Weather data and meteorological variables are crucial to solar forecasting and renewable energy integration (Pinto et al. 2017). The most important is reliable records of sunshine duration and cloud cover; supplementary weather data like wind speed and temperature support filtering techniques in boosting the accuracy of forecasting methods.

Solar radiation consists of direct, diffuse and global components, each portion depends on a different set of atmospheric variables (Ul Haq et al. 2025c). The hourly global radiation observed at a site is modeled as a function of those components along with the sunshine duration, wind speed and temperature, provided as inputs for forecasting techniques.

Variable	**Meaning/description**	**Unit**
Temperature	Heat level of the air	°C or K
Humidity	Moisture content in air	%
Wind speed	How fast is the air moving	m/s or km/h
Wind direction	Direction from which the wind blows	°
Solar radiation/irradiance	Amount of sunlight energy received	W/m^2
Rainfall	Amount of precipitation	mm
Atmospheric pressure	Force exerted by air	hPa or mbar
Cloud cover	Fraction of sky covered by clouds	%

Table 1.1. *Meteorological variable used in weather studies*

Weather forecasting data form the basis of predictions related to solar energy generation, primarily supported by AI and ML techniques.

1.2.3. *Forecasting horizons and evaluation metrics*

The solar energy forecasting community is concerned with the formulation of relevant problems that can be solved through a data-driven approach. A well-defined problem statement determines the necessary data acquisition and the expected model performance of the solution, while providing a clear notion of success (Carriere et al. 2019). The two main applications of solar forecasting are resource evaluation and site selection, and power generation forecasting.

Solar forecasting systems can be grouped according to the time horizon into nowcast (a few seconds to minutes ahead), short-term (from minutes to a few hours ahead), medium-term (from hours to a couple of days ahead) and day-ahead (the full next day) (Ul Haq and Khanday 2025). The choice of horizon influences the number of meteorological drivers needed, the prediction methods and the validation approach (including the choice of metrics). The weather data required at each time horizon and the corresponding auxiliary input variables (lagged measurements of drivers and geographical coordinates) are summarized for the different levels of prediction (Pombo et al. 2022).

1.3. AI techniques for forecasting

Solar forecasting involves the prediction of future solar energy production based on available data and plays a crucial role in integrating solar technologies into the electrical grid optimally. Solar forecasting aims to predict either the solar irradiance or PV power output at a particular location and over a given time horizon up to several days in advance. In CSP installations, forecasting is also relevant, but research pertains to the forecast of heat generated from inputs to solar radiation. Time-horizon definition in forecasting solar energy remains variable across studies. Some researchers define "nowcasting" as a range of time horizons from seconds up to 1 h (Pinto et al. 2017).

From an operational viewpoint, commonly adopted definitions include a nowcast extending from a few seconds to 1 h ahead, a short-term forecast from 1 h up to 6 h and a medium-term forecast between 6 h up to 1 week ahead. A day-ahead forecast is defined as 24-h forecasts made at least 24 h in advance of the target date and time (Ul Haq and Khanday 2025).

The solar irradiance and PV power output are controlled by several meteorological variables such as cloud cover, wind speed, temperature, humidity and aerosol optical depth. The selection of input features and corresponding modeling approaches depends upon the desired forecasting horizon.

The short-term forecasting relies on the satellite imagery of cloud cover and short-term weather forecasts; images are commonly used as an input to models in this timescale. Intermediate forecasting uses the same variables at the higher timescales together with historical power trends but still in the presence of external meteorological drivers. Day-ahead forecasting generally works without satellite inputs but utilizes historical irradiance, PV power and meteorological data. Such use of cloud forecasts is highly inexact for timescales larger than the following day. Longer horizon models in general focus on trend and weather analysis instead.

Typically, various error metrics are relevant for different horizons. Nowcast evaluation depends heavily on the analysis of maximum and minimum irradiance values since these are the key quantities of interest for equipment sizing. Different metrics capture the timing of those peaks.

1.3.1. *Statistical and ML approaches*

Various techniques can be employed to forecast solar energy: linear regression, decision tree, random forest and XGBoost. When the data have a time-series pattern, algorithms such as Box–Jenkins autoregressive moving average (ARMA), Seasonal Auto Regressive Integrated Moving Average (SARIMA) and exponential smoothing are generally used for univariate forecasting. These models work fine for short-term predictions but face difficulties in generalization and capturing the effects of external variables (Pinto et al. 2017).

For multivariate data, approaches such as multiple linear regression, support vector machines (SVM) (Ul Haq and Khanday 2025) and tree-based methods such as random forest and gradient boosting constitute some of the most common methods. Ensemble methods can merge forecasts in a way that improves overall prediction precision because the prediction errors from the models individually can demonstrate overlapping or unique patterns. Although statistical methods have been the go-to approaches because they perform better with smaller datasets, extreme value situations and overall generalization, they have become increasingly inadequate with large and complex datasets. On the other hand, the use of ML techniques has been proven to be more beneficial in complex large-scale spatiotemporal datasets. These models utilize numerous additional predictor variables, such as weather and climate dynamics and time series, to extend prediction capabilities beyond basic sequences.

Consequently, there has been a lot of focus on different forms of DL and combined structures. CNNs can successfully pull out the pertinent details from satellite imagery as well as from sky camera footage. For spatiotemporal forecasting, a variety of models have shown a high level of success, including Recurrent Neural Networks (RNNs), LSTMs, and Temporal Neural Networks (TCNs) (Ul Haq et al. 2025a).

1.3.2. *Deep learning for spatiotemporal forecasting*

Forecasting spatiotemporal data involves working with historical data that are temporally and spatially referenced, and gathered from sensor arrays distributed in a region. For instance, multivariate time series forecasting, traffic forecasting, video frame interpolation and estimating rainfall are all examples that fit in this category. Recently, the development of certain types of DL models that can capture spatial and temporal relationships has surpassed the ability of traditional approaches and has become the preferred choice for the complex forecasting of spatiotemporal data. Forecasting solar irradiance for a single location is a good representative case because neighboring locations provide useful contextual information that is helpful for learning spatial relationships and correlations (Yu et al. 2024).

Conventional approaches to spatiotemporal forecasting have, to a large extent, viewed time series analysis and spatial analysis as independent tasks. This approach has a ceiling effect in terms of forecasting precision. State-of-the-art performance on a variety of practical applications has been seen with new architectures that combine spatial and temporal learning in a single cohesive framework (Boussif et al. 2023).

With respect to solar irradiance forecasting, the ability to capture the spatiotemporal features of the data simultaneously makes the ConvLSTM network architecture effective. Incorporating data from neighboring sites also enhances noise robustness. In a similar manner, fully convolutional recurrent neural networks (FCRNNs) identify varying patterns of irradiance using multi-scale spatial-temporal representations and utilize configured physical cloud–structure models to suppress overfitting (Goh et al. 2006).

Another promising approach integrates 2D CNNs with 1D LSTM layers, operating on a two-dimensional temporal–spatial–irradiance grid to jointly capture spatial and temporal dependencies, thereby enhancing the accuracy of day-ahead global horizontal irradiance (GHI) forecasting.

1.3.3. *Hybrid and ensemble methods*

Complementary algorithms are combined in hybrid forecasting strategies to increase accuracy and expand capabilities. Particularly appealing are stacking and blending, which make use of the same or different geographic locations without requiring fresh input data (El-Kenawy et al. 2022). By using physically meaningful equations to constrain inputs or outputs, physics-informed hybrids enhance system comprehension. Historical availability, computational resources, necessary forecasting horizons, temporal granularity (e.g. point versus sequence), the desired balance between data-driven flexibility and physical constraints, and the application context all influence the method selection.

1.3.4. *Uncertainty quantification*

Probabilistic forecasting of renewable energy generation, such as solar irradiance, is a growing field of research aimed at reducing the uncertainty of point forecasts and providing an additional valuable energy management tool (Iversen et al. 2014). In particular, many studies emphasize multi-step prediction, which estimates energy production across several future time intervals, thereby maximizing the use of available historical data. At the same time, it is essential to develop robust policies and strengthen the legal framework for intellectual property protection to ensure fair competition and safeguard the interests of domestic enterprises

1.4. Predicting solar energy output using a LSTM DL model

This experiment simulates the operation of actual smart grid solar forecasting systems. It illustrates how solar power generation can be predicted using AI, more especially a LSTM neural network, in conjunction with meteorological data. To predict the amount of solar energy produced in the upcoming hour, the model uses hourly data from the past, including solar irradiance, temperature, humidity, cloud cover, wind speed and previous power output. A dataset comprising these meteorological factors and the associated solar power output is first created or loaded by the code. To train the model, the data are then normalized and transformed into 24 hr sequences. Multiple layers make up an LSTM model, which is used to identify patterns in the data that change over time. It has been trained to reduce the discrepancy between expected and actual power levels. After training, the model forecasts solar energy for test data that have not been seen yet.

This chapter proposes an end-to-end solar power forecasting method that combines the LSTM model with meteorological variables. This method demonstrates how the LSTM network learns temporal patterns from the raw weather data after it has been preprocessed, scaled and converted into sequential inputs for training. It also demonstrates how the predictions that are produced are assessed for accuracy.

1.4.1. *Dataset*

For this experiment, we forecast the next hour's solar power output in kW, emulating the real-world applications of solar forecasting systems in smart grids. To make a forecast, the model uses the last 24 h of historical weather data including solar irradiance, temperature, humidity, cloud cover, wind speed and prior solar power values.

1.4.2. *Mode architecture and training*

It uses MinMaxScaler for normalization of all features, scaling their values between 0 and 1, in order to stabilize and speed up model training. Continuous hourly data are then converted into 24-h input sequences where each sample represents the past 24 h of weather data, while the corresponding target output is to predict solar power for the next hour.

A subsequent LSTM model was built, which is an architecture of neural networks for time series prediction. The LSTM layers in the model learn temporal patterns that capture how recent weather conditions tend to influence the upcoming hour of solar power generation. Dropout layers (each 20%) are included to avoid overfitting, while dense layers handle the final regression task of predicting power output (final power prediction).

The model was trained for up to 30 epochs using the Adam optimizer and the mean squared error loss function. EarlyStopping was used to automatically stop training when the validation loss stopped improving, with the goal of optimal generalization.

The dataset is split into 80% for training and 20% for testing. The model is allowed to train for a maximum of 30 epochs. EarlyStopping automatically stops the training when the model performance improvement diminishes. Finally, a model is used to predict next hour solar power from unseen test data, inverse-scaled back into real kilowatt units using the saved MinMaxScaler. Evaluation metrics such as RMSE and MAE are used to measure how well the predicted values match the actual solar power output. Steps used in solar energy prediction are depicted in Table 1.2 and Figure 1.2.

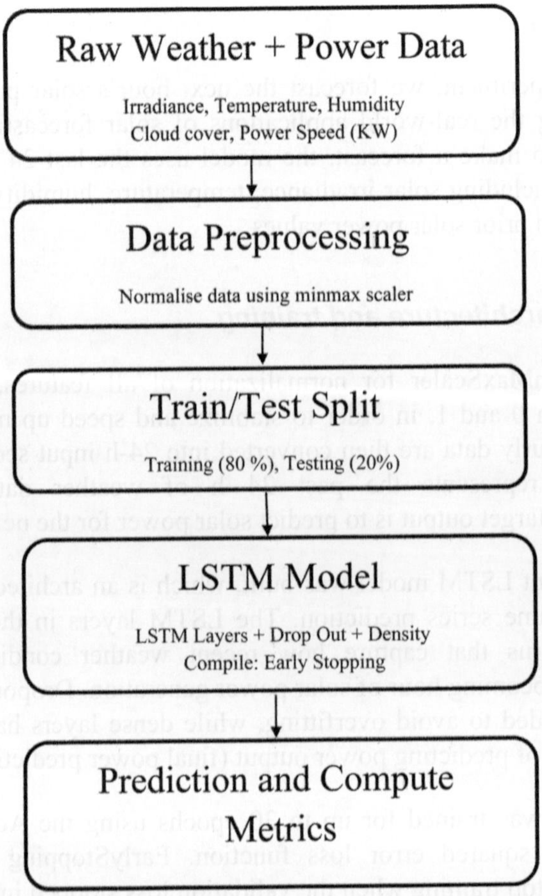

Figure 1.2. *LSTM model to predict energy steps*

Step	Operation	Purpose
1	Create realistic synthetic weather and power data	Mimic real solar plant data
2	Normalize and create 24-h sequences	Prepare time-series inputs
3	Build LSTM neural network	Learn time-based relationships
4	Train with early stopping	Optimize model on data
5	Predict solar power	Forecast next-hour generation
6	Evaluate and plot results	Measure accuracy (RMSE, MAE)
7	Save output CSV	Store results for analysis

Table 1.2. *Steps involved in predicting solar energy*

1.4.3. *Results*

During the training phase, the training loss (MSE) constantly decreases, which means that it is learning the underlying patterns in the data. The validation loss also decreased and stabilized, meaning that the model does not overfit at all and captures meaningful temporal relationships. Due to an EarlyStopping mechanism, training automatically stopped after about 7–10 epochs, which indicates the optimal balance in the balance between accuracy and generalization.

After training, the model was assessed using unseen test data, which consisted of 20% of the dataset. The model obtained an RMSE of 10.706 kW, which means that its prediction is on average 10.7 kW away from the actual values. The average magnitude of prediction errors (MAE), which is independent of direction, was found to be 7.1 kW. Given that the dataset contains noise, seasonal variations and random variations, these results guarantee good prediction accuracy.

Furthermore, the model's predictions appear to be stable and consistent, with no notable outliers, as indicated by the comparatively small difference between RMSE and MAE. The error results are shown in Table 1.3.

Error	**Value**
Root mean squared error (RMSE)	10.706 kW
Mean absolute error (MAE)	7.135 kW

Table 1.3. *Error results*

Figure 1.3 shows the actual and forecasted solar power outputs, demonstrating how the AI model tracks real output trends. The figure consists of two lines: the blue line indicates the actual solar power output, while the orange line reflects the predicted values of the model. Both lines follow a similar pattern, which, as expected, happens during the daytime when the generation of solar power is at its peak. There are slight differences during overcast conditions or at times of sunrise and sunset, mainly because of random variations in the synthetic data.

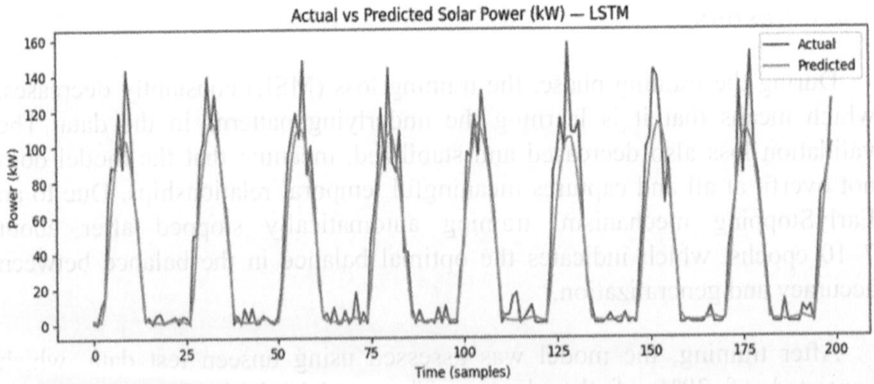

Figure 1.3. *Actual versus predicted solar power (kW). For a color version of this figure, see www.iste.co.uk/ulhaq/artificial2.zip*

The model showed great accuracy in the forecasting of solar power. It can be seen that most predicted values are very near to the actual ones, as portrayed by the almost complete overlap of both curves in the graph. With an RMSE of 10.7 kW and MAE of 7.1 kW, the errors in prediction were relatively small compared to the total power output range. This shows that the model is very reliable in predicting solar power generation on a short-term basis. Minor deviations are expected because of unpredictable variations in weather; however, the trend in prediction depicts the effectiveness of AI in predicting solar energy. These types of models are essential for energy dispatch improvement, battery storage management and smart grid stability in modern renewable power systems.

1.5. Applications and case studies

Solar energy possesses a high potential, but it is a variable energy source. Solar forecasting and optimization studies have witnessed a growing interest and extensive development in the solar energy community. AI can help achieve unprecedented results; hence, these developments hold a major promise for the future.

Case studies from various systems clearly illustrate the broad applicability and adaptability of the AI-driven technologies, accompanied by the imparting of findings from those initiatives to support further advancements and enable efficient and more effective exploration and utilization of such technologies elsewhere. Elements and examples from forecasting and optimization arenas are here highlighted to emphasize the opportunity space, elucidate tangible opportunities and signal the strategies to be pursued. Three representative system configurations are therefore highlighted, along with the inclusion of underlying core AI concepts, lessons learned and key considerations.

1.5.1. *Utility-scale PV forecasting*

Utility-scale PV generation has made a significant contribution to the renewable energy transition and is expected to be a major source of energy in the near future. Accurate prediction of solar power production can provide significant benefits to grid operators through improved energy management and planning.

Forecasting the electricity generated from utility-scale PV systems is highly dependent on site-specific factors such as geographical location and system characteristics and, importantly, on the solar irradiation forecast. Forecasting the solar irradiation is therefore central to PV generation forecasting (Ul Haq et al. 2025c, 2025d).

1.5.2. *Rooftop solar forecasting for building management*

Electricity consumption in intelligent buildings may be effectively shaped by rooftop PV systems equipped with energy management systems (EMSs), which forecast both solar generation and load.

An EMS leverages forecasting to prolong discharge time of energy storage and to charge batteries during low-usage hours (Yuan et al. 2021). A reliable PV generation forecast allows the delineation of time windows for diminishing peak load while considering additional factors such as the state of charge (SOC) of batteries used to further augment the dispatch scheduling problem.

Tight regulation is imposed by the utility on the building's hourly consumption; thus, demand should remain consistently below a stipulated value. Long forecasting horizons model the entire profile, which offers potential savings during charge or discharge periods; consequently, partial forecasts aggressively reduce peak electricity demand during time windows clearly identified beforehand (Ul Haq et al. 2025d). A combination of long-term and short-term forecasts support these objectives, where the former identifies daily patterns and the latter increases accuracy at specific time slots.

1.5.3. *Microgrids and remote communities*

The integration of renewable energy in isolated microgrids offers several benefits such as energy price stability, grid resilience under extreme weather conditions and environmental management. As isolated grids rely heavily on generators and battery systems, optimizing their operations is of great importance. Forecasting is essential for scheduling missions and assessing multiple parameters. In a microgrid, the global forecast of system behavior considers the joint state of batteries, the immersion of pollutants and comfort values. Through the installation of a centralized global forecasting system, both the forecast quality and local parameter interdependencies are guaranteed (Ul Haq et al. 2022).

1.6. Challenges, risks and ethical considerations

AI offers numerous opportunities to enhance decision-making in diverse domains. However, AI deployments can have unintended side effects on the social, economic and environmental facets of the world. Therefore, it is critical to contemplate the potential challenges and ethical considerations associated with AI techniques for solar energy forecasting and optimization. Some of the principal issues include the following:

– Data quality: available datasets can exhibit gaps, spatiotemporal mismatches, inaccuracies or biases, leading to flawed models. Rigorous data quality checks, innovative preprocessing for data harmonization and careful feature selection can mitigate these concerns (Robu et al. 2019).

– Model interpretability: the complexity of widely used AI models can hinder their understanding by stakeholders and limit trust in resulting decisions. Inductive explanations can elucidate the influence of selected features on predictions and empower stakeholders to evaluate models and inputs critically (Ul Haq et al. 2024).

– Privacy, security and reliability: AI models may unearth insights into proprietary business strategies or inadvertently disclose sensitive information. Robust security procedures, including oracles, differential privacy or data augmentation, can reduce the risk of information leakage.

– Environmental and social impact: AI methods typically necessitate extensive computation, which can have adverse effects on the planet and its inhabitants. Ensuring responsible use of resources, such as by dormant model preservation, alleviates these repercussions.

1.6.1. *Data quality and availability*

Data quality and availability play a pivotal role in solar forecasting (Sangrody et al. 2017). While advanced ML techniques can compensate for gaps or noise in the training data to some extent, strong generalization remains dependent on the reliability of the information, as reflected in training and validation performance. Selected datasets for solar forecasting must therefore possess high temporal and spatial resolution and a low level of missing data in the historical period relevant for learning the prevailing patterns. The following characteristics are essential for the available data: (i) a comprehensive set of relevant variables, (ii) sufficient station density to capture geographic distribution and ensure representative coverage of each target site, (iii) homogenous data quality across stations and (iv) operational continuity to avoid abrupt changes in statistical distributions (Alqudah et al. 2020).

Key meteorological variables influencing solar irradiance and PV power conversion include cloud cover, wind, surface temperature, relative humidity and aerosol optical depth (Ul Haq et al. 2025b). Cloud cover exerts the most significant direct impact on solar resource availability, serving as a primary drivers for statistical models based on either historical observations or NWP outputs. In locations where cloud cover data are not feasible for the time horizon required, wind speed profiles play a secondary yet important role. The results of time series and spatial analysis indicate that, although high-resolution wind speed has only a minor independent correlation with GHI, it is the most relevant worldwide variable for long-term temporal and spatial analysis of sunlight availability.

1.6.2. *Model interpretability and transparency*

Although advanced ML techniques are becoming mainstream for solar energy forecasting, the need for interpretability and transparency remains essential. Public confidence in these models is still threatened by unpredictable weather fluctuations and high deployment requirements. Furthermore, many stakeholders expect assurance regarding model soundness and predictions adhering to basic meteorological laws because the electricity sector is highly regulated. Model explainability makes it easier to identify areas for improvement and improves comprehension of input–prediction relationships (Bamisile et al. 2022).

To improve transparency, a variety of explanation techniques are available, such as generating synthetic observations, identifying important temporal patterns or spatial regions and attributing input features (Yang et al. 2024). These methods can assist in determining whether unphysical approximations predominate and whether models make accurate predictions under truly representative circumstances. Certain methods might make it possible to adjust the trade-off between interpretability and fidelity in a flexible way (Letzgus 2022).

1.6.3. *Privacy, security and reliability*

Data-driven modeling and forecasting of renewable energy production are susceptible to various risks related to privacy, security and reliability. These risks may arise from the nature of the data being collected from geographically dispersed weather stations or physical assets, or from the collection of overhead imagery. A single system failure or breach, be it at the data source or at the modeling, processing or control layer, could lead to incorrect forecasts that can jeopardize the long-term viability of automated decision-making. Threats of tampering, leakage or failure are inherent in any setup that depends on data collection, movement or processing.

Privacy and security risks demand particular attention if residential PV systems, rooftop or building-integrated solar assets, or on-site energy storage are included in the forecast models. At these locations, any data captured could be deemed sensitive, such as output measurements, consumption behavior or surrounding meteorological indicators. By relying on a well-structured but synthetic multi-site dataset to prevent privacy and security concerns from ever materializing, the risk of operation or appearance of privacy-preserving models being introduced does not go away.

Collecting overhead imagery from different cameras can further exasperate privacy concerns, especially when residential properties are captured. Access to this information could compromise property security and allow for undesirable practices. In some jurisdictions, certain applications may fall under personal data protection regulations such as the General Data Protection Regulation (GDPR) in the European Union (Venkataramanan et al. 2023). Consequently, considerable effort must be directed into establishing a robust computation procedure before residential data are stored and removing any perspectives of these sites even at the aggregation level using systematic principles.

1.6.4. *Environmental and social impacts*

Concerns about equity and sustainability arise from algorithmic decision-making. Although many ML frameworks encourage temporarily exempting sensitive datasets, autonomous learning systems do not guarantee algorithmic decoupling from social aspects. System design, algorithmic selection and data choice are critical, particularly when human agency and social systems are impacted, such as human exploitation in algorithmic trading. Environmental and social considerations also influence autonomous energy systems, including forecasts for planning and control.

Despite technological advancements in solar PV and electricity storage development, research emphasizes econometrics and statistical modeling over systems with known physics. Most atmospheric and light-based environmental phenomena exhibit predictable physical patterns. When computational resources allow energy forecasting, models can remain grounded in established physical principles, improving accuracy through reduced reliance on training. For PV systems operating alongside integrated storage, logistic curves describing scheduling fall naturally into classical planning. Long-term storage installations can follow established macroeconomic behavior. Forecasts of solar illumination support diverse financial planning tasks beyond simple consumption, with residual forecasts aiding projection of obligation netting for generation-import, generation-export and generation-usage systems (Ul Haq et al. 2025c).

1.7. Future directions and research opportunities

The transition to solar energy generation is urgently required to combat climate change. Solar energy generation is inherently intermittent, limiting its contribution to the energy supply. Solar energy generation must be accurately forecasted to maintain the balance between supply and demand, yet most areas have only limited historical data to train and validate forecasting models. Accordingly, practitioners have turned increasingly to AI, notably, ML and DL, to forecast solar generation for grid operation (Macq et al. 2016). Forecast horizons vary from minute-ahead to day-ahead and can be characterized by their level of difficulty, focus on spatial versus temporal factors, the forecast lead time and data length compared to the forecast horizon (Engel and Engel 2022). AI system design must meet technical requirements such as robustness, while forecasting also supports the economic dispatch of storage-charging schedules for various hybrid configurations. The combination of power generation often determines priority. Nonetheless, solar-generation forecasts can deliver substantial socioeconomic benefits with limited data.

Despite the variety of environments, conditions, configurations, priority policies and other factors, research papers record numerous experiences, making case studies valuable for practitioners to leverage both technical and domain knowledge from different contexts. Twelve utility-scale solar energy generation forecasting case studies were conducted to develop, evaluate, and deploy operational forecasting systems for photovoltaic (PV) power. These systems provide temporal and spatial aggregation, enable hybrid grid integration, and support from-scratch estimation, while demonstrating the reusability and high accuracy of two-time-scale stacking models. Detailed design choices, evaluation procedures, baseline comparisons and continuously integrating modern approaches demonstrate that even basic combinations with either standard or solar-compatible feature engineering can outperform direct-power methods. As one-third of worldwide electricity comes from roof-mounted panels, rooftops have gained increasing attention for solar-generation forecasting, especially to accommodate distributed generation across different grid and regulatory frameworks. Forecasts for single- or multi-unit generation systems support both energy estimation and operational demand management in building-related applications.

The microgrid and zone-rural communities associate hybrid support, and resilience with disturbances, remain crucial in many regions. Internally, these applications collect, store, scrutinize and exploit data with or without cloud services. For solar energy supply forecasting or pricing anticipation, low documentation, public landmark and systematic procedure income generating frameworks monitor, predict or guarantee/top price under selection, retrieval and recording.

1.8. Conclusion

AI techniques for solar energy forecasting and optimization have matured considerably in recent years, a trend likely to continue. Although solar energy delivers significant environmental benefits, integrating variable solar generation into existing power systems poses considerable technical challenges. Accurate, reliable forecasts of solar power availability, therefore, play a vital role in facilitating the transition to clean energy.

AI-driven solar forecasting addresses the challenge of accurately predicting the instantaneous PV output of solar energy generation systems (Bamisile et al. 2022). Solar forecasting applies to all power systems integrating PV generation, from large utility-scale installations to small rooftop or building-integrated systems.

Problem statements, atmospheric data inputs, target operating specifications and stakeholders vary; early work targeted utility-scale systems, while recent approaches address much broader applications at multiple scales (Ul Haq et al. 2025c). AI techniques can also optimize the operation and economics of solar energy systems subjected to uncertain forecasts, thereby enhancing their value to grid operations, customers and owners of generation facilities (Engel and Engel 2022).

Solar forecasting projects the amount of output expected from PV generation systems. As the environmental factors directly impact output, the forecasting approaches draw on a wide range of meteorological information. Solar irradiance is the amount of solar energy reaching Earth's surface and is a key variable controlling PV output. In general, solar generation forecasting takes into account the forecasted evolution of several meteorological drivers, including atmospheric conditions, to model the expected generation of the solar power system.

1.9 References

Alanazi, M., Mahoor, M., Khodaei, A. (2017). Two-stage hybrid day-ahead solar forecasting. In *North American Power Symposium (NAPS)*. IEEE.

Alqudah, M., Djokic, T., Kezunovic, M., Obradovic, Z. (2020). Prediction of solar radiation based on spatial and temporal embeddings for solar generation forecast. arXiv Preprint. arXiv220608832.

Bamisile, O., Cai, D., Oluwasanmi, A., Ejiyi, C., Ukwuoma, C.C., Ojo, O., Mukhtar, M., Huang, Q. (2022). Comprehensive assessment, review, and comparison of AI models for solar irradiance prediction based on different time/estimation intervals. *Scientific Reports*, 12(1), 9644.

Boussif, O., Boukachab, G., Assouline, D., Massaroli, S., Yuan, T., Benabbou, L., Bengio, Y. (2023). Improving day-ahead solar irradiance time series forecasting by leveraging spatio-temporal context. *Advances in Neural Information Processing Systems*, 36, 2342–2367.

Carriere, T., Vernay, C., Pitaval, S., Kariniotakis, G. (2019) A novel approach for seamless probabilistic photovoltaic power forecasting covering multiple time frames. *IEEE Transactions on Smart Grid*, 11(3), 2281–2292.

El-Kenawy, E.S.M., Ibrahim, A., Bailek, N., Bouchouicha, K., Hassan, M.A., Jamil, B., Al-Ansari, N. (2022). Hybrid ensemble-learning approach for renewable energy resources evaluation in Algeria. *Computers, Materials & Continua*, 71(3), 5837–5854.

Engel, E. and Engel, N. (2022). A review on machine learning applications for solar plants. *Sensors*, 22(23), 9060.

Goh, S.L., Chen, M., Popović, D.H., Aihara, K., Obradovic, D., Mandic, D.P. (2006). Complex-valued forecasting of wind profile. *Renewable Energy*, 31(11), 1733–1750.

Iversen, E.B., Morales, J.M., Møller, J.K., Madsen, H. (2014). Probabilistic forecasts of solar irradiance using stochastic differential equations. *Environmetrics*, 25(3), 152–164.

Letzgus, S. (2022). XAI for transparent wind turbine power curve models. arXiv Preprint. arXiv221012104.

Macq, A., Mercier des Rochettes, L., Martin-Carron, L., Cristi, N., Gleizes, M.-P., Bernon, C. (2016). A use of artificial intelligence for improving pv array performance (empirical approach). In *Proceedings of the 32rd European Photovoltaic Solar Energy Conference and Exhibition (EU PVSEC 2016)*, Munich, 1978–1981.

Pinto, T., Marques, L., Sousa, T.M., Praça, I., Vale, Z., Abreu, S.L. (2017). Data-mining-based filtering to support solar forecasting methodologies. *ADCAIJ Adv. Distrib. Comput. Artif. Intell. J.*, 6(3), 85–102.

Pombo, D.V., Bindner, H.W., Spataru, S.V., Sørensen, P.E., Bacher, P. (2022). Increasing the accuracy of hourly multi-output solar power forecast with physics-informed machine learning. *Sensors*, 22(3), 749.

Robu, V., Flynn, D., Andoni, M., Mokhtar, M. (2019). Consider ethical and social challenges in smart grid research. *Nature Machine Intelligence*, 1(12), 548–550.

Sangrody, H., Sarailoo, M., Zhou, N., Tran, N., Motalleb, M., Foruzan, E. (2017). Weather forecasting error in solar energy forecasting. *IET Renewable Power Generation*, 11(10), 1274–1280.

Ul Haq, I. (2024). Diagnosis of neurological disease using bioinspired algorithms. In *Bio-Inspired Optimization for Medical Data Mining*, Srivastava, S., Anand, A., Kumar, A. et al. (eds). John Wiley & Sons, Hoboken, NJ.

Ul Haq, I. and Khanday, A.M.U.D. (2025). Exploring the role of explainable AI in women's health: Challenges and solutions. In *Explainable Artificial Intelligence in the Healthcare Industry*, Kumar, A., Kumar, T.A., Das, P. et al. (eds). John Wiley & Sons, Hoboken, NJ.

Ul Haq, I., Kumar, N., Koul, N., Verma, C., Eneacu, F.M., Raboaca, M.S. (2022). Machine learning techniques for result prediction of one day international (ODI) cricket match. In *The International Conference on Recent Innovations in Computing*. Springer, Singapore.

Ul Haq, I., Kaur, G., Rather, A.H. (2024). Fruit leaf classification using transfer learning for automation and industrial applications. In *Deep Learning Techniques for Automation and Industrial Applications*, Rathore, P.S., Ahuja, S., Burri, S.R. et al. (eds). John Wiley & Sons, Hoboken, NJ.

Ul Haq, I., Khanday, A.M.D., Shah, H.A., Rufai, S.Z. (2025a). Enhancing water security through automation: Case studies and technical advancements in water quality management. In *Computational Automation for Water Security*, Dubey, A.K., Srivastav, A.L., Kumar, A. et al. (eds). Elsevier, Amsterdam.

Ul Haq, I., Kumar, A., Rathore, P.S. (2025b). Machine learning approaches for wind power forecasting: A comprehensive review. *Discover Applied Sciences*, 7(10), 1139.

Ul Haq, I., Malhotra, J., Rawat, V., Kumari, J., Kaur, G. (2025c). Machine learning approaches for early detection of cervical cancer: A comparative study of classification models. In *Targeted Chemotherapy with Personalized Immunotherapy: An AI Approach*, Kumar, A., Das, P., Rathore, P.S. et al. (eds). John Wiley & Sons, Hoboken, NJ.

Ul Haq, I., Nandal, V., Uppal, H. (2025d). Blockchain applications in aviation securing transactions, streamlining operations, and improving passenger experience. In *Blockchain in the Tourism Industry: A New Era of Secure and Transparent Travel Solutions*, Kumar, A., Abreu, A., Batta, P. et al. (eds). Springer, Cham.

Venkataramanan, V., Kaza, S., Annaswamy, A.M. (2023). DER forecast using privacy-preserving federated learning. *IEEE Internet of Things Journal*, 10(3), 2046–2055.

Yang, R., Hu, J., Li, Z., Mu, J., Yu, T., Xia, J., Li, X., Dasgupta, A., Xiong, H. (2024). Interpretable machine learning for weather and climate prediction: A review. *Atmospheric Environment*, 338, 120797.

Yu, M., Huang, Q., Li, Z. (2024). Deep learning for spatiotemporal forecasting in earth system science: A review. *International Journal of Digital Earth*, 17(1), 2391952.

Yuan, R., Dinh, N.T., Pipada, Y., Pourmouasvi, S.A. (2021). Optimal activity and battery scheduling algorithm using load and solar generation forecast. arXiv Preprint. arXiv211202827.

2

Integrating ANN, SVM and GA for Optimized Wind Resource Assessment and Energy Management

Artificial intelligence (AI) is essential in improving the performance of wind power systems, especially regarding site selection and optimization of energy. AI technologies such as artificial neural networks (ANNs), support vector machines (SVMs) and genetic algorithms (GAs) are being used with growing frequency to process large amounts of meteorological and geospatial data. ANN models are particularly useful for forecasting wind velocity and electrical power production with consideration of past data, whereas SVM is deployed in classification and regression functions as a measure of the environmental impact and suitability of the site. GA is the optimal method for turbine positioning and layout to maximize energy and reduce waste. These are AI-based models that allow proper estimation of the wind resources, minimize uncertainty in location selection and assist in predictive maintenance in order to increase the reliability of the system. In addition, AI and smart grid systems are highly compatible, and real-time monitoring, fault detection, as well as energy delivery forecasting, enable efficient power dispatch and lower operational costs. The combination of ANN, SVM and GA wind energy systems helps in generating cost-effective energy sustainably, and supports the transition toward cleaner energy solutions.

2.1. Introduction

The growing global energy requirements and the desperate need to reduce the negative impacts of climatic degradation have redirected energy research to renewable and sustainable sources (Ohalete et al. 2023). Within this group, wind energy has come up as one of the most reasonable and largest growing sources of clean energy. Use of wind to generate electricity also

---

Chapter written by Vikrant SHARMA and Salliah SHAFI.

offers the benefit of decreasing reliance on fossil fuels as well as helping to decrease greenhouse gases emissions and ensure environmental sustainability (Ul Haq et al. 2025c).

As per the latest reports from international energy agencies, global installed wind energy capacity is growing at a rate of over 10% per year, highlighting its increasing contribution to the energy mix of many countries (International Energy Agency 2024). This growth notwithstanding, optimal efficiency and reliability of wind energy systems are still complex issues with multiple compositional factors, especially the highly unpredictable and unstable nature of wind resources, and the compounding factors of terrain, atmospheric and turbine design dependence. The performance of wind energy systems largely depends on three important factors, which are proper site selection, effective turbine layout planning and efficient energy management.

Conventional methods of measuring wind resources are meteorological data over the long-term and empirical models that do not frequently consider the nonlinear interactions of atmospheric factors. In addition, these traditional models are not adaptive and do not predict different geospatial and climatic circumstances.

To avoid these deficiencies, researchers started getting acquainted with AI processes that can learn through sophisticated data, discover hidden patterns and provide reasonable decision-support systems to maximize the system (Ul Haq 2024). Use of AI has transformed the renewable energy sector by enabling intelligent automation, prediction and real-time optimization. Techniques such as artificial neural networks (ANNs), support vector machines (SVMs), and genetic algorithms (GAs) are capable of addressing complex nonlinear and multidimensional problems, making them particularly effective in the context of wind energy applications. All these AI methods have their own benefits and, when combined, can significantly improve the performance and stability of wind energy systems (Ul Haq and Sharma 2026). ANN can replicate the information processing abilities of the human brain and therefore is very appropriate when studying large meteorological and operational data. ANN models can be trained to learn complicated mappings between their input variables (wind speed (WS), direction, temperature and atmospheric pressure) and their output variables (power generation or energy loss (Ul Haq and Khanday 2025). Adaptive learning enables them to forecast the WS, power output and energy scheduling with accuracy.

According to various studies, ANN-based predictive models have proved to be more accurate and generalize better than the traditional statistical and regression models. Also ANN can be continually improved by retraining on new data and is therefore suitable in constantly changing wind environments where the climatic conditions vary very swiftly (Ul Haq et al. 2026a). Another profitable AI solution is SVM that is generally used to perform regression and classification in wind power systems.

Compared to ANN that carries out learning through repetitive training, SVM represents hyperplanes that best define the classes of data, meaning that it is suitable for working with a high-dimensional dataset with little overfitting. According to wind resource assessment, the SVM may be applied to categorize potential sites depending on environmental or land use restriction and categories of wind potential. It also facilitates the use of regression in making predictions of WS and energy required that contribute importantly in establishing the feasibility and viability of a site. Second, SVM models are highly robust to noise and can work with sparse data, a useful feature when working with incomplete meteorological data (Ul Haq et al. 2025a).

GAs are also a different category of AI methods based on biological evolution theory including selection, crossover and mutation. GAs can be effectively applied in resolving optimal problems that are complex in nature with multiple conflicting goals to be compromised. When used in wind energy, GAs may study the location, spacing or direction of turbines, ensuring that the impact of wakes is minimized and as a result, the total yield of the wind is maximized (Singh et al. 2026). It may also be used to optimize operations plans such as maintenance plans, energy dispatch plans and integration of the hybrids with other renewable sources. Adaptability of the search nature of GAs allows them to settle to solutions of global optimality that withstand the local minima fixed points that are a significant problem for conventional optimization methods (Ul Haq et al. 2026b). Although all these AI methods contribute separately to the development of various wind energy management features, their combination creates a synergistic model that establishes the benefits of each method.

The ANN-SVM-GA hybrid model has the advantages of ANN prediction power, SVM analysis and GA optimization in the development of an overall and intelligent decision-making system. It is an integrated model that can be used to better evaluate wind resources, optimize the layout of turbines and manage energy at the system scale. Predictive maintenance can also be supported by such integration in order to detect faults and performance degradation early and decrease downtimes and maintenance (Ul Haq et al. 2025d). Moreover, AI-based wind energy systems and smart grid technologies are converging, which creates further opportunities for real-time monitoring, adaptable load balancing and energy forecasting. AI algorithms can analyze the operational conditions to predict energy demand and work with power dispatch, using the data from sensors, IoT devices and meteorological stations to analyze data and predict the situation. This combination improves the stability of the grid, minimizing the amount of energy wasted because of different power sources being variable and enabling easy integration of the renewable sources into the already existing energy infrastructure (Ul Haq et al. 2026c).

The integration of AI is the basis of not only technological development but also economic and environmental sustainability. By clever optimization, it improves the use of returns on investment, keeps land use effective and lowers the level cost of energy (LCOE). Furthermore, better control and predictability will reduce dependency on backup fossil fuel systems and therefore carbon emission will be greatly reduced. Through offering useful insights into future energy prediction and investment decision-making, the AI-based models enhance national and global efforts directed at reaching both carbon neutrality and the sustainable development goals (SDGs) (Ul Haq et al. 2022).

Combining ANNs, SVMs and GAs provides a whole package of successful wind resource evaluation and energy control technologies. Integrating ANNs, SVMs and GAs offers a comprehensive framework for effective wind resource assessment and energy management. This hybrid approach enhances intelligent automation and operational efficiency by tackling key challenges in prediction, classification and optimization. The present study explores the implementation of this integrated AI model, emphasizing its potential to improve overall energy system reliability, reduce uncertainties in site selection and optimize wind energy performance. By advancing renewable energy technologies through intelligent modeling, this research aims to contribute to the global transition toward a sustainable, clean and resilient energy future.

The main objectives of this chapter are to develop a hybrid ANN–SVM–GA framework for accurate wind resource assessment and energy management; enhance the forecasting accuracy of WS and power output using ANN models optimized through GA-based hyperparameter tuning; classify and evaluate potential wind farm sites using SVM regression and classification techniques based on meteorological and topographical data; optimize wind turbine layout and configuration through GA to maximize energy yield and minimize wake losses and environmental impact; and integrate hybrid AI framework with smart grid systems for real-time energy dispatch, load balancing and predictive maintenance. The segmentation of this chapter is as follows: section 2.2 is a literature review. Methodology is discussed in section 2.3, with the results and discussion in section 2.4; finally, the conclusion and future work are provided in section 2.5.

2.2. Literature review

Wind energy has become an essential part of the global renewable energy policy in a sector where the need to liberate energy sources is demanded with urgency along with the necessity to prevent the further climate change. Within the last 20 years, studies on wind energy have made significant progress in the main areas of wind resource evaluation, turbine placement optimization, energy prediction and predictive maintenance (Lipu et al. 2021). These areas have seen a rise in the use of AI techniques such as ANNs, SVMs and GA to solve these challenges related to nonlinear, unpredictable and data-rich systems. Research constantly proves that intelligent computational approaches are better than the conventional empirical and statistical constructs of accuracy, adaptability and scalability. ANN has been widely applied for predicting WS and power output due to their nonlinear prediction capabilities when modeling complex relationships with the various meteorological variables.

Compared to the classical autoregressive and persistence models, initial research findings showed that multilayer perceptron (MLP) and backpropagation-based ANNs provided significantly improved prediction accuracy. Based on the same framework, other studies came later with more elaborate neural networks such as recurrent neural networks (RNN) and radial basis function (RBF) networks that learn temporal behavior with better results in the short- and long-term prediction of WS (Kumar et al. 2025c).

Mapping wind resources and estimating wind energy yield has also been achieved using ANN models. Scholars have come up with models that can forecast the power generation of all forms of turbines based on meteorological parameters such as WS, direction, temperature and air pressure. ANN is a flexible algorithm, and therefore it can easily accommodate any imperfections that real-world wind data can present due to missing or noisy values. Moreover, the combination of ANN with optimization methods such as GAs and particle swarm optimization (PSO) can be used to fine flow network parameters in order to reduce the rates of training errors and overfitting and attain greater levels of prediction accuracy. ANN has also been used in wind farm fault diagnosis and predictive maintenance beside forecasting. ANN is able to predict the occurrence of anomalies and possible failure by analyzing vibration data, temperature data and operation data, which in turn lowers the maintenance costs and also minimizes the downtime. These functions render ANN an important element in the creation of intelligent and self-learning wind energy systems (Dhaka et al. 2024). SVMs constitute the other formidable AI methods of modeling wind energy systems, particularly in activities that are associated with classification, regression and pattern recognition. As opposed to ANN, which utilizes iterative learning, SVM operates by constructing optimal hyperplanes that partition data into classes with maximum margins. This feature contributes to the effectiveness of SVM in high-dimensional and limited-sample data sets, which are typical in research related to meteorology and geography (Selvaraj et al. 2025).

Support vector regression (SVR) has been used to develop the nonlinear relationship between meteorological factors and output energy in forecasting WS. Research has demonstrated that SVM is better than the conventional linear regression and decision tree models in that it has better generalization powers and resistance to noise. Hybrid SVM-based models have in addition been designed to combine both the stability of SVM and learning of neural networks. As an example, ANN-SVM hybrid architecture can also be used in

WS prediction, where ANN is employed to extract features and SVM to perform the last prediction, which increases the precision and decreases the computational cost (Song et al. 2024). Environmental impact assessment and site suitability analysis have also been done using SVM. Such models are also used in the identification where wind farms should be established, categorizing geographical areas using determinants like terrain elevation, roughness of the surface and the vicinity to urban centers. Also, SVM-related methods have been found to be effective in both fault classification and turbine performance monitoring. In the example of sensor data, SVM can be used to compare sensor data to consider patterns such as vibrations, power variations and acoustic emissions in order to differentiate between normal and mal-adjusted turbine operation. This will allow fault to be identified early, increasing the reliability and safety of the wind power systems (Shafi et al. 2025).

GAs based on the principle of natural selection are a type of evolutionary optimization algorithms. GAs have been eminent in the wind energy industry by offering solutions to dilemmas concerning the design of wind farms and installation of turbines. Turbine placement is a key issue for the overall performance of a farm because improper turbine placement may result in power loss due to wake generation. GAs have been extensively used to optimize the locations of turbines to reduce the effects of turbine wakes and maximize land utilization and power output. Its capability to handle multi-objective and nonlinear constraints makes it particularly suitable for solving such complicated engineering problems (Ul Haq et al. 2024). Spatial optimization and predictive model parameter adjustment have been done with the help of GAs.

As an example when applied to ANN or SVM, hyperparameters such as learning rate, kernel parameters and size of hidden layers can be optimized by using GAs. This leads to an increase in the level of prediction and convergence speed. Also there have been GA applications to hybrid renewable systems for example, wind–solar microgrids, to schedule when to run and when not to run as well as optimization of control. All these applications emphasize the flexibility of GAs in addressing the operational and structural problems in wind energy systems (Togun et al. 2025).

GAs have a second related use in the field of economic and multiobjective optimization. Researchers use GAs to optimize allocation of resources in high scale wind farms, as well as to optimize energy production in accordance with environmental constraints and minimize the cost of energy. Due to its capability to explore a large solution space and identify near-global optima, GAs are is a powerful tool for strategic decision-making in wind power development. Recent research highlights the increasing tendency toward combining several AI methods in order to capitalize on their complementary capabilities.

The hybrid approach of ANN, SVM and GAs has demonstrated great potential for achieving reliable, accurate and efficient wind energy management. Such frameworks optimize system parameters and settings using GAs, while SVM and ANN are employed for classification and regression tasks, with ANN serving as the primary predictive model for estimating WS and power output (Simankov et al. 2024). Hybrid AI has been used to design the turbine layout, their placement as well as to evaluate the wind resources. These systems enable the optimization of energy generation by combining maximization and predictive modeling approaches to reduce uncertainty in both energy production and system operation. Predictive maintenance, fault detection and real-time monitoring have been optimally performed using hybrid models in combination with smart grid and Internet of Things (IoT) technologies. These smart designs will support the easy integration of renewable energy sources into the current power systems, increase the stability of energy and allow flexible control systems (Ul Haq et al. 2025b).

Even though significant progresse has been made in demonstrating the use of AI in different areas of the wind energy system, research has shown that the full potential of ANN, SVM and GA application is yet to be explored. The majority of the current studies concentrated on single or two combinations of methods and, as such, have a reduced capacity to provide holistic optimization to forecasting, classification and control spheres. There is an urgent need to have integrated frameworks to realize the potential of these techniques in resource assessment and energy management. In addressing this gap, the current work suggests a hybrid ANN-SVM-GA model, which utilizes smart data-driven approaches to streamline operational efficiency, optimize turbine placement and enhance forecasting accuracy (Zhao et al. 2022).

2.3. Methodology

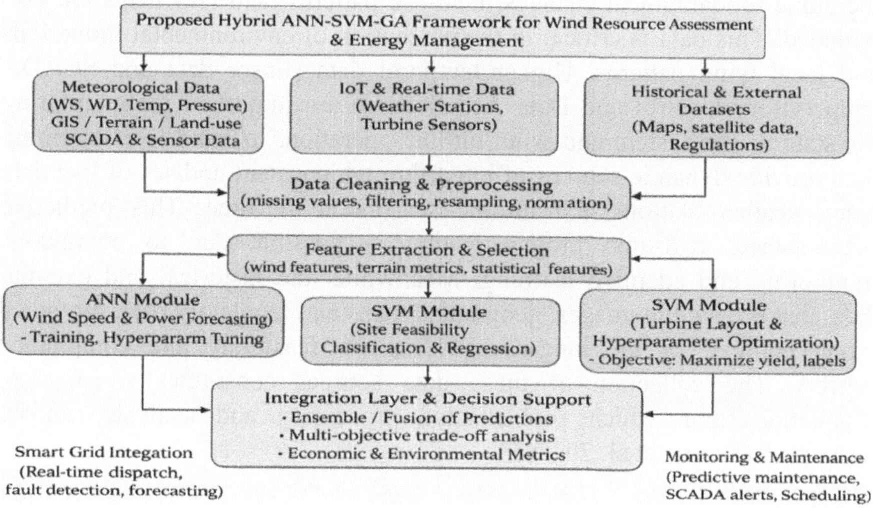

Figure 2.1. *Smart hybrid framework for wind energy forecasting and optimization*

2.3.1. *ANN-SVM-GA framework energy management hybrid ANN-SVM-GA framework wind resource evaluation*

GAs, SVMs and ANNs are combined in the proposed hybrid framework in Figure 2.1 to improve the efficacy and excellence of energy administration and wind resource evaluation. The smart grid platform was developed to assist real-time decision making at the framework level, in a smart grid environment by integrating data-driven intelligence with optimization and predictive analytics. Through the aid of varied assets of data such as historical data, IoT-powered real-time streams and meteorological data, it creates an all-encompassing wind energy forecasting, viability analysis and performance enhancement apparatus.

2.3.2. *Data acquisition layer*

The first phase of the framework is gathering data that comes in the form of many varied foundations. It mainly takes into account three types of historical and external data, real-time streaming data based on IoT, and meteorological information. The meteorology data (met) consists of vital parameters, which are temperature, air pressure, wind direction (WD) and WS. Moreover, the data involving geographical and topographical attributes including topographical changes, land-use patterns, and GIS maps are also included. This data is critical in the perception of environmental limitations and local wind patterns. Higher temporal data (Ensor data and SCADA (Supervisory Control and Data Acquisition)) are important for monitoring the state of the system and wind turbine operation. IoT and live streaming data provide dynamic sources of input through constant updates of live data from weather stations and turbine sensors at all time. This predictive maintenance, real-time prognostication is possible due to continuous monitoring and adaptive learning. Meanwhile, the historical and external data, that is, satellite images, geographic maps and regulatory data, provide a larger context for the long-term WDs, site feasibility and compliance aspects. The collection of these data sources constitutes a complete foundation upon which sophisticated processing and analysis can be performed (Kumar et al. 2025a).

2.3.3. *Data cleaning and preprocessing*

The second phase involves data cleaning and preprocessing to ensure the quality and accuracy of the input data. Since data collected from multiple sensors and sources often contains noise, inconsistencies, and missing values, several preprocessing techniques are applied, including filtering, re-sampling, normalization, and interpolation. Filtering is used to eliminate the potential presence of outliers and inaccurate readings, which may cause models to be inaccurate, and any missing values are handled either through statistical or predictive methods. Normalization and resampling make the two features equal, and resampling makes all the time points of data collected on different days equal to the machine learning algorithm, respectively. Altogether, this preprocessing stage converts raw data into a readable, consistent and predictable format making the results of any prediction model more reliable and accurate (Razak et al. 2025).

2.3.4. *Feature extraction and selection*

The following step is feature extraction and selection, which aims at deriving meaningful and representative features out of processed data. Some of the extracted features are wind-related (average speed, gust patterns and directional variability), topographical (elevation, slope and surface roughness) and statistical features (mean, variance and correlation). The most important and non-redundant features are selected using feature selection methods, typically based on GA. These selected features enable the model to minimize overfitting and complexity while enhance generalization. This phase provides a strong foundation for subsequent model training and prediction in the ANN and SVM modules (Ohalete et al. 2023).

2.3.5. *ANN Python module*

Following the feature extraction and selection stage, the ANN Python module utilizes the selected features – including wind-related (average speed, gust patterns, and directional variability), topographical (elevation, slope, and surface roughness), and statistical (mean, variance, and correlation) features – as inputs for model training.

The ANN is designed to capture complex nonlinear relationships between these input features and target variables such as wind speed and power output. By leveraging its capability to model high-dimensional data, the ANN enhances predictive accuracy and supports robust wind resource assessment.

The model is trained using the optimized feature set to ensure improved generalization performance while minimizing overfitting.

2.3.6. *SVM modules*

The framework uses two SVM modules both with different yet complementary functions. The initial SVM module is concerned with site feasibility classification and regression. It then uses the extracted features to evaluate the possible sites where wind turbines can be located by analyzing wind potential, topography limitations and the environments, among other factors. In its operation, this module implements the analysis of regression analysis to estimate the output of energy that results from individual sites using kernel-based learning, and categorizes sites into feasible and non-viable sites on the basis of identified patterns (Smart et al. 2025). The second SVM module is dedicated to hyperparameter optimization and turbine design optimization. It uses the concept of GA to optimize the placement and configuration of turbines to achieve the best possible energy production under spatial, environmental and regulatory restrictions. Its optimization goals are power generation, reduction of losses and the environmental impact. With GA incorporated with SVM, it is possible to efficiently explore a large and difficult search space to guarantee optimal layout of wind farms and operating conditions. The two SVM modules, in combination, are efficient and reliable at both the macrolevel, determining site selection, and the microlevel, determining the configuration of turbines.

2.3.7. *Integration layer and decision support system*

The architecture includes the integration layer and decision support system as the central part of the system that integrates the results of ANN and SVM modules. This layer uses the ensemble learning methods to provide a combination of the results of various models that guarantee success and correct results. Voting or weighted averaging are the fusion methods employed in order to make decisions based on the different forecasts. Multi-objective trade-off analysis of the integration layer also allows trade-off between factors, which can be maximizing energy yield, and minimizing cost and the environmental effect. It also calculates economic and environmental indicators to assist the decision-makers in assessing the profitability and long-term sustainability of various energy management strategies (Ukoba et al. 2024). By means of this decision-support mechanism, operators and policymakers are able to make evidence-based, efficient and environmentally friendly decisions.

2.3.8. *Smart grid integration*

Platform is a technology that can be incorporated easily into the smart grids to aid in forecasting, fault-detection and real-time dispatch of energy. Using the high levels of predictability of ANN and SVM modules, the system will be able to predict changes in wind energy generation and modify the grids functions. As the smart grids can be integrated with the entire energy network, they make the energy network more stable and resilient since it allows the allocation of energy in a dynamic way, controlling storage efficiently and balancing loads effectively both ways. In addition, predictive analytics will help make early faults and schedule maintenance, minimize downtime and enhance operational efficiency in general.

2.3.9. *Monitoring and maintenance*

The last stage of the framework is maintenance and monitoring. The system monitors the health and performance of turbines on a continuous basis using SCADA alerts and predictive models. Predictive maintenance algorithms can be used to identify a possible problem before it happens and reduce maintenance expenses and unforeseen downtimes. The ability to schedule and provide alerts will guarantee that interventions are done at the right time, which in turn will increase the overall reliability of operations. This type of feedback loop allows the system to be self-improving and adaptive, as the system is always updating and improving its learning models based on changing operational and environmental conditions.

2.4. Result and discussion

The highly promising result that was obtained with the implementation of the proposed hybrid ANN–SVM–GA framework was the successful performance in wind resource assessment and energy management optimization. The integrated system showed a marked difference in various aspects compared to the conventional methods: accuracy in prediction, reliability of the site selection and the efficiency of turbine layout. With the help of real-time meteorological and IoT-based data, the ANN component reasonably predicted WS and power output with less error margins, which guaranteed more accurate energy scheduling and dispatch. This enabled the framework to respond well to the shifting environmental conditions, thus improving the reliability of the energy output.

The SVM module was instrumental in classification and regression enabling the accurate selection of wind farm locations based on topographical and environmental influences, including elevation, surface roughness wind variability. The regression model produced site-specific estimates of energy yields, which were used to support informed decision-making during feasibility studies.

In addition, the genetic algorithm (GA) component effectively optimized the turbine layout, maximizing overall energy production while minimizing turbine inefficiencies. The optimization process factored in on a number of constraints such as the land use, the effect on the environment and cost effectiveness, which underscores the talent of GA in coming up with globally optimized solutions in a multifaceted search space.

The decision support system and integration layer were important for integrating the predictive results of the ANN and SVM models and providing a balanced result for the energy yield, cost-effectiveness and sustainability of the environment. The forecasting outcomes of the ensemble-based fusion were more reliable and strong enough, which actually minimizes the shortcomings of each model separately. The hybrid framework, which was implemented together with smart grid systems, facilitated real-time load balancing, fault detection and efficient energy dispatch. Moreover, predictive maintenance algorithms were able to effectively predict when performance would deteriorate, causing considerable cuts in turbine maintenance and downtime. These results suggest that combining machine learning and optimization algorithms will lead to an intelligent, self-adaptive and data driven system of energy management to improve the overall grid reliability.

In addition, the model assists in minimizing uncertainty in site selection and embedding improved forecasting accuracy, reducing the LCOE and supporting the environmental objectives in generating a cleaner form of energy. The experiment also found that AI hybrid models are superior to conventional statistical and empirical models, particularly during dynamic meteorological conditions. The ANN-SVM-GA system has shown great scalability and versatility that is suitable for large wind farms and multi-source renewable energy systems.

However, some restrictions were noted with respect to working with highly volatile streams of data, where it was found that temporal discontinuities had an impact on the accuracy of short-term predictions. A solution to this problem, may be to incorporate deep reinforcement learning or fuzzy logic systems, which would facilitate flexibility in case of uncertain situations.

On the whole, the hybrid framework is a great improvement to the intelligent automation of wind power infrastructure. It is a scalable and sustainable system solution, that will contribute to the global transition toward smart-clean and resilient energy infrastructure.

2.5. Conclusion and future work

The combination of ANNs, SVM and GAs is an effective hybridization of the wind resource assessment and energy management. This method leverages SVM for site viability classification and regression, GAs for optimizing turbine layout and operating conditions, and ANN for power generation and speed-based wind forecasting. These elements enhance the accuracy of the forecasting, optimize the turbine setup and permit the dispatch of energy in smart grids. This is a hybrid method that improves the reliability of the system, minimizes the uncertainty regarding site selection and encourages the generation of energy at relatively low costs and with a sustainable nature. On the whole, the research will be helpful in the creation of smarter, evidence-based policies on how renewable energy systems can be optimized. Future studies to improve the hybrid ANN SVM GA model and the hybrid algorithms with other AI approaches (deep reinforcement learning and fuzzy logic) would address the growing uncertainty in the environment. The system could be enhanced by adding real-time IoT and satellite data streams to enhance the accuracy and adaptation of the system to dynamic conditions. In addition, the model should be expanded into hybrid renewable systems, for example, wind–solar or wind–hydro, to improve grid flexibility. Last but not least, the proposed architecture can be reinforced by increased field testing and cloud-based deployment, making it sufficiently robust, scalable and applicable to international smart energy networks.

2.6. References

Dhaka, P., Sreejeth, M., Tripathi, M.M. (2024). A survey of artificial intelligence applications in wind energy forecasting. *Archives of Computational Methods in Engineering*, 31(8), 4853–4878.

International Energy Agency (2024). World Energy Outlook 2024. Report, IEA Publications [Online]. Available at: https://www.iea.org/weo.

Kumar, K., Prabhakar, P., Verma, A. (2025a). Innovative approaches to wind power forecasting: A comprehensive review. *Clean Energy Technologies*, 1(1), 17–44.

Kumar, K., Prabhakar, P., Verma, A. (2025b). Advancements in wind power forecasting: A comprehensive review. *Journal of Electronics and Electrical Engineering*, 4, 298–322.

Kumar, K., Prabhakar, P., Verma, A., Saroha, S., Singh, K. (2025c). Advancements in wind power forecasting: A comprehensive review of artificial intelligence-based approaches. *Multimedia Tools and Applications*, 84(10), 8331–8360.

Lipu, M.S.H., Miah, M.S., Hannan, M.A., Hussain, A., Sarker, M.R., Ayob, A., Saad, M.H.M., Mahmud, M.S. (2021). Artificial intelligence based hybrid forecasting approaches for wind power generation: Progress, challenges and prospects. *IEEE Access*, 9, 102460–102489.

Ohalete, N.C., Aderibigbe, A.O., Ani, E.C., Ohenhen, P.E., Daraojimba, D.O., Odulaja, B.A. (2023). AI-driven solutions in renewable energy: A review of data science applications in solar and wind energy optimization. *World Journal of Advanced Research and Reviews*, 20(3), 401–417.

Razak, T.R., Ismail, M.H., Darus, M.Y., Jarimi, H., Su, Y. (2025). Artificial intelligence in renewable energy: A systematic review of trends in solar, wind, and smart grid applications. *Research and Reviews in Sustainability*, 1(1), 1–22.

Selvaraj, J., Muthuramalingam, L., Karthikeyan, V., Karthick, A., Sathiyaseelan, V. (2025). Optimizing wind energy integration: A review of forecasting techniques and emerging trends. *Archives of Computational Methods in Engineering*, 1–26.

Shafi, S., Ahmad, S., Ansari, G.A., Abdeljaber, H.A.M., Alanazi, S., Nazeer, J. (2025). Cuckoo-inspired algorithms for selecting features in the prediction of diabetes using machine learning models. *SN Computer Science*, 6(7), 860.

Simankov, V., Buchatskiy, P., Kazak, A., Teploukhov, S., Onishchenko, S., Kuzmin, K., Chetyrbok, P. (2024). A solar and wind energy evaluation methodology using artificial intelligence technologies. *Energies*, 17(2), 416.

Singh, A., Haq, I.U., Jain, N., Kumar, R., Rather, M.A., Masoodi, F.S. (2026). Hybrid quantum–classical learning architectures for 6G/7G edge intelligence. In *Deep Quantum Neural Networks: AI for 6G/7G Communication Systems*, Kumar, A., Rathore, P.S., Juárez-Ramírez, R. (eds). Springer, Singapore.

Smart, E.E., Olanrewaju, L.O., Usman, J., Otaru, K., Umar, D. (2025). Artificial intelligence (AI) in renewable energy forecasting and optimization. *Renewable Energy*, 10, 11.

Song, D., Tan, X., Huang, Q., Wang, L., Dong, M., Yang, J., Evgeny, S. (2024). Review of AI-based wind prediction within recent three years: 2021–2023. *Energies*, 17(6), 1270.

Togun, H., Basem, A., Dhahad, H.A., Mohammed, H.I., Biswas, N., Homod, R.Z., Chattopadhyay, A., Sharma, B.K., Niyas, H., Alhassan, M.S., Paul, D. (2025) Artificial intelligence in renewable energy: Comprehensive insights into challenges, opportunities, and future trends. *Journal of Thermal Analysis and Calorimetry*, 151, 1–31.

Ukoba, K., Olatunji, K.O., Adeoye, E., Jen, T.C., Madyira, D.M. (2024). Optimizing renewable energy systems through artificial intelligence: Review and future prospects. *Energy and Environment*, 35(7), 3833–3879.

Ul Haq, I. (2024). Diagnosis of neurological disease using bioinspired algorithms. In *Bio-Inspired Optimization for Medical Data Mining*, Srivastava, S., Anand, A., Kumar, A. et al. (eds). John Wiley & Sons, Hoboken, NJ.

Ul Haq, I.U. and Khanday, A.M.U.D. (2025). Exploring the role of explainable AI in women's health: Challenges and solutions. In *Explainable Artificial Intelligence in the Healthcare Industry*, Kumar, A., Kumar, T.A., Das, P. et al. (eds). John Wiley & Sons, Hoboken, NJ.

Ul Haq, I and Sharma, N. (2026). AI and quantum-driven IoT frameworks for sustainable 6G/7G smart homes. In *Deep Quantum Neural Networks: AI for 6G/7G Communication Systems*, Kumar, A., Rathore, P.S. and Juárez-Ramírez, R. (eds). Springer, Singapore.

Ul Haq, I.U., Kumar, N., Koul, N., Verma, C., Eneacu, F.M., Raboaca, M.S. (2022). Machine learning techniques for result prediction of one day international (ODI) cricket match. In *The International Conference on Recent Innovations in Computing*. Springer, Singapore.

Ul Haq, I.U., Kaur, G., Rather, A.H. (2024). Fruit leaf classification using transfer learning for automation and industrial applications. In *Deep Learning Techniques for Automation and Industrial Applications*, Rathore, P.S., Ahuja, S., Burri, S.R. et al. (eds). John Wiley & Sons, Hoboken, NJ.

Ul Haq, I.U., Khanday, A.M.D., Shah, H.A., Rufai, S.Z. (2025a). Enhancing water security through automation: Case studies and technical advancements in water quality management. In *Computational Automation for Water Security*, Dubey, A.K., Srivastav, A.L., Kumar, A. et al. (eds). Elsevier, Amsterdam.

Ul Haq, I.U., Kumar, A., Rathore, P.S. (2025b). Machine learning approaches for wind power forecasting: A comprehensive review. *Discover Applied Sciences*, 7(10), 1139.

Ul Haq, I.U., Malhotra, J., Rawat, V., Kumari, J., Kaur, G. (2025c). Machine learning approaches for early detection of cervical cancer: A comparative study of classification models. In *Targeted Chemotherapy with Personalized Immunotherapy: An AI Approach*, Kumar, A., Das, P., Rathore, P.S. et al. (eds). John Wiley & Sons, Hoboken, NJ.

Ul Haq, I.U., Nandal, V., Uppal, H. (2025d). Blockchain applications in aviation securing transactions, streamlining operations, and improving passenger experience. In *Blockchain in the Tourism Industry: A New Era of Secure and Transparent Travel Solutions*, Kumar, A., Abreu, A., Batta, P. et al. (eds). Springer, Cham.

Ul Haq, I.U., Singh, A., Jain, N., Rather, M.A., Masoodi, F.S. (2026a). Quantum convolutional neural networks for intelligent spectrum management in 6G/7G. In *Deep Quantum Neural Networks: AI for 6G/7G Communication Systems*, Kumar, A., Rathore, P.S., Juárez-Ramírez, R. (eds). Springer, Singapore.

Ul Haq, I.U., Yousuf, A., Masoodi, F.S. (2026b). Integrating blockchain and metaverse for next generation smart healthcare networks. In *Blockchain Enabled Metaverse for Smart Wireless Sensor Networks*, Kumar, A., Rathore, P.S., Moreira, F. (eds). Springer, Cham.

Ul Haq, I., Kak, S.M., Ul Islam, M. (2026c). Emerging trends in blockchain metaverse for intelligent sensor network applications. In *Blockchain Enabled Metaverse for Smart Wireless Sensor Networks*, Kumar, A., Rathore, P.S., Moreira, F. (eds). Springer, Cham.

Zhao, E., Sun, S., Wang, S. (2022). New developments in wind energy forecasting with artificial intelligence and big data: A scientometric insight. *Data Science and Management*, 5(2), 84–95.

3

Next-Generation Renewables: AI Applications in Green Hydrogen Production and Marine Energy Harvesting

As the world transitions toward sustainable energy, next-generation renewable energy technologies have become increasingly important, particularly the generation of green hydrogen and the utilization of marine energy. Green hydrogen, a product of the electrolysis of water with renewable energy, is a versatile carbon-free energy carrier for transportation, industrial applications and storage energy. Marine energy, such as tidal and wave power and offshore wind systems, off the potential for uninterrupted and predictable power generation, which remains largely underexploited. Artificial intelligence (AI) emerging as a groundbreaking technology advancing these sectors by enhancing efficiency, reducing costs and enabling predictive maintenance. Machine learning (ML) algorithms can dynamically regulate electrolyzer operation, forecast hydrogen production optimize the energy input from variable renewable sources. Similarly, AI-based modeling and real-time analytics can be applied to forecast the tidal flows, wave patterns and offshore wind variability with high accuracy and optimize energy capture and system resilience. Moreover, AI is applicable in environmental impact assessment, resource allocation and smart grid integration, thereby supporting a sustainable and reliable energy supply. In this chapter, recent AI-driven solutions in green hydrogen and marine power systems will be discussed, along with examples, challenges and research perspectives. Combined with state-of-the-art computational intelligence and renewable technologies, these approaches have the potential to accelerate the global transition toward a low-carbon energy future.

3.1. Introduction

The 21st century has seen a revolution on an international scale as the technological advances have become faster, and the environmental concerns and the growing feeling of urgency regarding sustainable development have

Chapter written by Pardeep KUMAR, Sanjeev KUMAR and Mohammad Badruddoza TALUKDER.

become more apparent. The sustainability issues have swept the global agenda and become an asset in the creation of policies, corporate strategy, and community action. The implementation of sustainable practices into the realm of tourism as one of the largest and the fastest growing spheres of the world economy has not only become appealing but also a necessary requirement for retaining natural and cultural reources for future generations (Hassan and Kumar 2024). National economies are heavily dependent on tourism as it creates jobs, stimulates local growth and cultural exchange; however, uncontrolled growth and development of the tourism industry is commonly linked to environmental degradation, commercialization of the culture and social imbalance. Therefore, the need to monitor, evaluate and manage tourism operations in a sustainable way has become the most significant concern. Sustainable tourism is a concept that emerged due to the growing awareness that tourism, despite its profitability, causes a lot of pressure on the natural environment, the local culture and infrastructure (Shash et al. 2025). Excessive consumption of water and energy, generation of waste, release of carbon dioxide by way of transport and overcrowding of historic and natural destinations are only a few of the recorded impacts of unsustainable tourism. To address such issues, governments, researchers and industry stakeholders have turned to technology as a necessary enabler of sustainability. One of the most promising technological developments in this respect is the Internet of Things (IoT) since it enables the collection, analysis and real-time making of decisions to monitor the environment and manage the resources in tourism destinations (Boopathy et al. 2025).

Data that may be shared between devices that have sensors, software and a network connection enabling them to fetch and transmit data are termed the IoT. In the context of sustainable tourism IoT technologies can be used to change the destinations management system to offer real-time data on visitor flows, the environmental state, energy use and the amount of waste. As an example, IoT-based sensors can be used to check the quality of air and water in tourist destinations, traffic flow in the sensitive locations, or can be used to find ways to cut down on the consumption of energy in hotels and transport infrastructures. The destination managers will use these intelligent systems to make effective decisions that will be cost-effective besides conserving the environment (Leandro et al. 2024). The IoT is therefore very important in the process of ensuring that the development of tourism aligns with the principles of sustainability that encompass environmental conservation, social inclusiveness and economic sustainability. The IoT has been the focus of sustainable tourism monitoring due to the urgent need for correct, continuous and integrated data systems that are able to facilitate policy and practice (Zhang et al. 2025). The initial techniques that were employed in monitoring the effects of tourism, such as manual surveys and periodic environmental surveys, are normally time consuming, costly and subject to human error. In addition, they cannot offer the real-time information that is required for proactive management. Conversely, IoT-based systems provide an active and automated system through which the stakeholders can monitor the key sustainability indicators accurately in real-time. This is required in the context of climate change when the reaction to environmental risks, like the outburst of pollution or habitat disturbance, may be timely and lead to the long-term prevention of ecological damage (Thorson et al. 2022). In this way, the IoT can be regarded as a shift in the conceptualization and application of sustainable tourism.

More active unification of digital technologies and sustainability plans is the most probable global trend in the so-called smart tourism destinations. They are locations that take advantage of the use of information and communication technologies (ICTs) in improving the quality of the visitor experiences beyond making them sustainable. In order to have efficient tourism system management, smart tourism destinations include technologies like IoT, AI, big data analytics and blockchain. By implementing the IoT into the sustainable tourism process, policy makers have put themselves in a position to develop smart systems that are able to exert control over environmental performance and visitor behavior independently (Dehankar and Das 2025). For example, the use of IoT waste containers with sensors to inform the government about the lack of capacity to prevent littering the natural environment, and smart energy meters can assist hospitality providers to minimize carbon footprints. This approach enables the IoT to support efficient operations while promoting environmental sustainability and responsibility.

The primary aim of the current research is to examine the opportunities and significance of IoT in the context of sustainable tourism through efficient monitoring and control of environmental impacts. The research involves determining which IoT applications enhance the collection and analysis of the environmental information as well as how to use this environmental information, to influence the sustainability of the tourism policies and practices (Shayo et al. 2025). It also tries to define the problems and opportunities that come along with the implementation of IoT technologies in tourism ecosystems in the presence of factors such as data privacy, infrastructure readiness, stakeholder engagement and financial viability. In this way, the study will be geared toward delivering a conceptual model of the role of the IoT in realizing the objective of sustainability in tourism destinations. Speaking more precisely, the research is directed toward the assessing the possibility of the IoT technologies optimizing the process of decision-making that will deliver evidence-based and real-time data on the primary environmental indicators. The parameters that will be monitored include air and water quality, waste production, energy and visitor utilization (Fayemi et al. 2025). The adaptive management strategies that guarantee the efficiency of the resources and minimize ecological footprints can be implemented with the assistance of the IoT systems due to continuous observation. In the case of high level air pollution at a heritage site, the local authorities can limit the number of vehicles on the road or encourage alternative means of transportation that are less polluting, such as cycling or walking. In the same way, smart water management systems would be able to identify water leaks or overuse of water within hotels and resorts, which would promote the sustainable use of water. These illustrations show how the IoT can be turned into the facilitator of responsible tourism practices that will be of benefit to the environment and the local community (Kumar et al. 2026).

The study has vast coverage aspects on monitoring sustainable tourism. It also involves natural and cultural attraction, hospitality and transport industry and community participation. The research acknowledges that sustainability does not only entail environmental protection, it also entails addressing socioeconomic and cultural issues. Therefore IoT-based solutions are expected to embrace all the dimensions including visitor satisfaction, cultural preservation and even equal resource distribution (Ziarati et al. 2024). The use of IoT in rural or heritage-based tourism destinations to maintain intangible cultural heritage, where the behavior of visitors can be tracked and digital storytelling projects can be supported to promote responsible tourism is one such application. IoT sensors and buoys may also be installed on the coastline and in the sea in underwater tourism to assess changes in the water quality and marine biodiversity, which could be of great use in conservation. The applications demonstrate the broad potential of the IoT in facilitating sustainability objectives across various forms of tourism (Jafri et al. 2023). This study adds to the already existing literature on the interaction of technology and sustainability in the tourism sector. It explains how the IoT can be applied to align the policy objectives with reality through measurable actionable insights. The development of sustainable tourism can be linked to the interactions between the different parties involved, such as government agencies, private enterprises, tourists and locals, the IoT is the platform utilized to guarantee the communication between them and the exchange of data (Kumar et al. 2024). As an example, tourists will be notified about the scale of congestion in real-time, environmentally friendly travel or conservation areas in the vicinity, fostering awareness and responsible attitudes. At the same time, the information supplied by the IoT will be able to help the authorities and businesses optimize the distribution of resources, enhance service delivery and track adherence to the sustainability objectives.

Moreover, the research could be used in implementing the world sustainability strategy, including the United Nations Sustainable Development Goals (SDGs), Goal 11 (Sustainable Cities and Communities), Goal 12 (Responsible Consumption and Production) and Goal 13 (Climate Action). The IoT-based tourism practices can be used directly to achieve these goals to facilitate effective utilization of resources, minimize emissions and foster sustainable lifestyles. More importantly, in an era where information-based governance is emerging as a new reality, the capability of creating plausible information about the environment through the IoT is required in effective policy-making. Such data can be used by policymakers to develop evidence-based interventions, establish the progress and establish accountability in sustainability programs. The second IoT application in sustainable tourism is to build resilience (Atilhan et al. 2021). The tourism industry has been noted to be vulnerable to climatic changes, pandemics and natural calamities. The IoT systems can be used to create resilience through the incorporation of early warning systems, predictive analytics and adaptive management tools. The IoT climate sensors can forecast extreme weather conditions as an indicator, and the destinations can take precautionary measures to ensure the safety of the visitors and the ecosystem. In the same manner, the IoT can be employed in health emergencies to track the number of visitors and monitor social distancing, as was the case in the COVID-19 pandemic. The IoT therefore contributes to sustainability, in addition to enhancing the adaptive nature of tourism systems uncertain world (Dewangan et al. 2024). Nonetheless, there are no obstacles to the implementation of the IoT in tourism surveillance. Problems with the high cost of implementation, technical competence, cybersecurity threats and data privacy concerns will be adequately handled. In addition, the IoT solutions are not popular in less developed countries because there is no digital infrastructure. Thus, the necessity to address these impediments through policy frameworks, capacity-building and public–privacy partnerships is also introduced in the current research. To make sure that the IoT is an engaging and ethical instrument of sustainability, governance, transparency and stakeholder involvement are to be considered.

To sum up, the chapter has highlighted the fact that the use of the IoT in sustainable tourism monitoring is a radical practice of ensuring there is a balance between economic growth and environmental and social well-being. It converts traditional tourism management practices into modern and evidence-based sustainability practices. The study will help stakeholders to be more sustainable, smart and robust in their tourism systems by providing a step-by-step analysis of the IoT applications, benefits, challenges, and future prospects in tourism. The data that are received in the course of this study can be used by policy makers, tourism planners and technological developers to create systems that can utilize the full potential of the IoT without undermining the ethical and ecological values at the heart of sustainable development of tourism.

3.2. Next-generation renewable energy systems: introduction

The global energy environment is changing at a very high rate on the basis of the urgent need to cut down on greenhouse gas emissions, increase energy security and transition to resilient and sustainable energy systems. Conventional energy production based on fossil fuels has contributed to climate change, air pollution and ecological imbalance. The shift to next-generation renewable energy technologies that will not only lead to clean and sustainable power generation, but also to increased efficiency, scaling and integration with contemporary digital technologies, including AI, the IoT and advanced analytics has already occurred (Praveena et al. 2024). Some of these inventions that are currently becoming significant breakthroughs in the study and use of renewable energy include green hydrogen production and the exploitation of the sea energy. Those sectors that are difficult to electrify, including heavy industry, transport, and maritime operations, can be decarbonized by these technologies, which also contribute to a stable and diversified energy mix. The hybridization, storage and smart grid connectivity can be identified as the difference between the next-generation renewable systems and the previous renewable technologies. Unlike the old solar or wind systems, which are dependent on natural resources, which are not always available, the new systems such as green hydrogen and marine energy are designed to be more stable and flexible (Imran Khan et al. 2022). They can store excess energy, co-exist with other renewable energy sources and provide general power in cases where there is fluctuating energy demand. The 2050 carbon neutrality agenda across the globe has only boosted the investments and innovation in these regions as countries consider achieving net-zero emission and energy independence through the adoption of clean technologies.

One of the most promising technologies that will be able to penetrate the renewable energy industry is the generation of green hydrogen. This form of energy can be used in the production of electricity, transportation, industrial processes and household applications. Green hydrogen is produced through the electrolysis of water, whereby the electricity generated is obtained through renewable energy sources, including solar, wind or hydro energy. It is an eco-friendly process as it does not generate carbon dioxide as opposed to the conventional hydrogen production process, which utilizes natural gas or coal to divide the molecules of the water into oxygen and hydrogen. The primary advantage of green hydrogen is that it is easy to store and transfer renewable energy. It enables the intermittent renewable energy to be converted into storage to be used when the sun or wind is not present (Dhiraj et al. 2023).

Recent advances in the technologies of electrolyzers, such as proton exchange membranes (PEMs) and alkaline and solid oxide electrolysis cells (SOECs), have significantly improved efficiency, cost-effectiveness and scalability of hydrogen generation. The fusion of AI and ML algorithms has also been revolutionary in simplifying the tasks of electrolysis, predicting system failures and the balance of inputs and outputs of energy to ensure full efficiency. In addition, the energy hub can be hydrogen plants that are fueled with renewable energy, which connects the electric, gas and transport sectors. Cross-sectoral integration generates a circular, sustainable energy economy that minimizes waste and maximizes resource use (Nakano et al. 2017). Green hydrogen can play a significant role in the decarbonization of industry, which has traditionally used fossil fuels such as steel, cement and chemical production. In one instance, instead of metallurgical coke, hydrogen can be used in the steel-making process or as a feedstock in the ammonia- and methanol-making chemical industries. Hydrogen fuel cells also offer a potential alternative in the transportation sector, in heavy-duty vehicles, heavy-duty ships and aircraft, where it is not possible to electrify the vehicle by battery due to the weight and range limit. Countries like Japan, Germany and Australia have been leading in the establishment of hydrogen infrastructure, which is to establish hydrogen refueling stations, hydrogen pipeline and hydrogen storage facilities to support the hydrogen-based economy (Serban and Lytras 2020).

Despite these developments, high production cost, few storage facilities and lack of infrastructure are still problems. Scaling-up green hydrogen technologies and achieving cost parity with fossil fuels is the key to further research, which makes policies and international cooperation possible. Similarly to the popularity of green hydrogen, marine power generation is another field of the next-generation renewable systems. The ocean covers over 70% of the earth's surface and has enormous potential energy that is unexploited in the form of tidal energy, waves and offshore wind. Using these resources gives a consistent and uninterrupted source of renewable energy that complements the other intermittent sources. One of the marine energy technologies is a tidal energy system that is used to produce electricity by using the kinetic energy of moving water due to the tides through underwater turbines. These systems are highly predictable as the tides are repeated over the lunar cycles, which implies that there is consistency in power production. Similarly, wave energy converters make use of the mechanical energy of the surface waves and transform it into electrical energy through hydraulic or mechanical systems (Wang et al. 2021). The energy of the waves in the coastal regions is also abundant and can be utilized to contribute significantly to the overall world energy, assuming that the technological and cost obstacles can be addressed.

Technologically, there is a need to develop effective and sustainable materials to support the electrolysis process and marine energy. The long-term sustainability requirement is the erosion resistance material, energy saving turbine and cheap cost of maintenance. On the economic front, the huge scale implementation is hindered by the huge capital investments and unpredictable returns. It will need to use financial incentives, subsidies and relationships between the government and the businesses to reduce investment risks and promote innovation. The policy tier must be able to establish a sequence of integrated regulatory frameworks that can assist in supporting hybrid renewable frameworks, grid interoperability and international energy exchange on the international scale (Zeng et al. 2020). Conversely, the opportunities of innovation and cooperation are the challenges. The integration of hydrogen production with marine and offshore wind power has provided a solution to the decentralized production of carbon-free power. The efficient flow of energy and the transparency can be ensured by the implementation of smart grids and AI-directed systems and blockchain-based energy trading systems. In addition, the global transition to carbon neutral has led to the emergence of additional markets regarding the export of renewable technology, the creation of new jobs and the sustainable development of the economy. Research and pilot projects along with knowledge sharing can also be used to involve academic and industrial associations in contributing to technological breakthroughs (Higashikawa et al. 2024).

Finally, green hydrogen and marine energy harvesting represent the next generation of renewable energy systems, leading the way into a sustainable and resilient energy future. They will not be able to integrate successfully unless it is not only technologically innovative but also changes are made to energy production, distribution and consumption. These new technologies have the potential to change the global energy paradigm offering cleaner, more secure and fair global energy based on renewable resources, as the nation's endeavor to achieve their climate targets. The path to this future is not smooth it is fraught with complicated issues, and perspectives–economic, environmental and societal – which makes it a process of international importance.

3.3. AI for renewable energy systems

AI has emerged as a game changer for renewable energy systems streamlining operations, supporting decision-making and the transition toward sustainable energy systems. Renewable energy sources such as solar, wind, hydro- and bioenergy are slowly integrating into power system, thereby significantly increasing the complexity of their management. AI and ML are effective instruments for processing large amounts of data, forming predictions, increasing performance and energy consumption efficiency. These technologies have been instrumental in solving the intermittency issue, providing grid stability, demand and supply predictions, and reducing maintenance expenses (Higashikawa et al. 2024). The implementation of AI and renewable energy systems will be a step toward smarter, cleaner and more reliable global energy infrastructure. Table 3.1 shows how AI can be used in renewable energy systems.

AI application area	**Renewable energy type**	**Purpose/function**	**AI techniques used**	**Key benefits**
Energy forecasting	Solar, wind, hydro	Predict power generation and resource availability	Machine learning (ML), neural networks (NN), support vector machines (SVMs)	Improved forecasting accuracy, grid stability
Predictive maintenance	Wind, solar, bioenergy	Detect equipment faults and schedule maintenance	Deep learning (DL), decision trees, anomaly detection	Reduced downtime, lower maintenance cost
Energy optimization	Solar, wind, hydro	Optimize energy conversion and distribution	Reinforcement learning (RL), genetic algorithms (GA)	Increased efficiency, minimized energy loss
Smart grid management	All renewables	Balance supply-demand and automate grid operations	Fuzzy logic, AI-based control systems	Enhanced grid reliability, load balancing
Resource assessment	Wind, marine, solar	Identify optimal sites for installation	Data analytics, clustering, GIS-based AI	Cost-effective site selection, maximum yield
Energy storage management	Solar, wind	Optimize battery charging/discharging cycles	Predictive modeling, time-series analysis	Extended battery life, energy availability
Environmental monitoring	Hydro, marine, wind	Assess ecological impacts and sustainability	Computer vision, sensor data analytics	Eco-friendly operation, regulatory compliance

Table 3.1. *Applications of artificial intelligence in renewable energy systems*

AI enables the analysis of mass data from renewable energy systems using advanced algorithms that can determine patterns and make more precise predictions within a shorter timeframe compared to the traditional computational models. One of the most critical concerns in renewable energy generation is variability since solar energy is influenced by the weather and daylight, and wind energy is influenced by the speed and direction of the wind. These changes can be forecasted with high accuracy by predicting AI-based models and allow energy producers to organize the optimization of generation and storage. AI technologies are capable of forecasting solar radiance and wind patterns through the analysis of meteorological data, satellite images and real-time sensor data, to balance the production of energy to match the demand of energy consumption (Afridi et al. 2022). This will reduce the level of wasted energy, eliminate grid congestion and enable easier integration of renewables into national electricity systems.

ML plays a key role in energy optimization as it uses the data to continuously learn about the working process and become more efficient with time. ML algorithms applied to solar power systems are capable of calculating the tilt angle of the panels to maximize energy production, optimize sunlight intensity, temperature factors and eliminate faults. Similarly, wind farms have AI predictive maintenance systems that anticipate turbine failures long before they occur. Vibration analysis, optimization of blade angle and health monitoring of gears are some of the uses of AI in enhancing reliability and extending the equipment lifespan. Predictive maintenance can also reduce downtimes and operational costs that render renewable energy more cost effective. The systems are able to dynamically react to varying environmental conditions and system behaviors that are produced by the ability of AI to learn from data and lead to a self-improving energy ecosystem (Alkahtani et al. 2023). Another significant use of AI in renewable energy is also in predictive modeling and decision-making. Renewable energy systems produce masses of sensor, smart meter and weather forecasting data. This information is then fed into the AI-based predictive models to model the patterns of energy production and consumption, predict the peak load periods and provide the optimal energy storage or distribution model. As an example, AI-based models can forecast when a solar farm is going to generate the highest energy and manage the energy storage systems. The models also help the grid operators to balance the demand and supply by forecasting the power demand in real-time, therefore averting power failure or instability the grid. AI-led predictive analytics are useful in making smarter investment choices according to the market trends, identifying lucrative places to build renewable energy infrastructure and giving forecasts of the energy demand scenario in the future depending on the growth of the population and industrialization.

The grid operations and energy trading have also been altered by the use of data-driven decision-making in the management of renewable energy. The smart grids, which will be powered by AI, will be in a position to regulate the flow of energy and redirect the energy in case of failures, as well as decentralized energy sources, for example, rooftop solar or small wind turbines. AI assists in identifying anomalies, thwarting cyberattacks on grid infrastructure and real-time stability. The AI models of the energy trading markets forecast the price of electricity, optimized the bidding strategy and forecast the income of the renewable power producers. AI enables the stakeholders to make knowledgeable, efficient and sustainable choices because it provides them with real-time awareness of the dynamics of energy (Abdul Baseer et al. 2023). These smart systems, are founded on AI algorithms and calculation techniques. The artificial neural networks (ANNs), support vector machines (SVMs), reinforcement learning (RL) and deep learning (DL) are some of the techniques that are commonly used in renewable energy applications. ANNs have been modeled after the human brain and are primarily applied in solar and wind energy predictions because of their ability to model nonlinear relationships that are complex and exist between the input parameters, such as temperature, humidity, wind speed and energy production. ANN models are trained on past data, and therefore, they have the ability to predict for both the short-term and long-term with high accuracy, which is required by grid balancing and energy trading. The other powerful ML method applied in energy forecasting, fault detection, and anomaly detection processes is SVMs which are applied in classification and regression problems. They are especially useful in terms of determining the areas of inefficiency in operation and streamlining energy conversion processes.

RL is another potentially useful AI methodology that can be used to make the energy systems learn the most appropriate control policies through trial and error. In renewable energy systems RL optimizes the charging and discharging of batteries, dynamic grid control and demand-side management. The algorithm enhances energy efficiency and loss reduction strategies through iterative interaction with the environment and the feedback. One example is a hybrid renewable energy system that integrates solar, wind, and energy storage. Reinforcement learning (RL) algorithms assist in determining how much energy should be stored, utilized, or discharged at any given time based on current system conditions and predicted future demand. It is a separate decision-making authority that minimizes human intervention and maximizes the efficiency of operations (Dewangan and Kumar 2024). ML, in its turn, enables the management of renewable energy in a more effective way, DL is one of its subdivisions, which enables the identification of complex patterns in large amounts of data. Convolutional neural networks (CNNs) and recurrent neural networks (RNNs) are particularly applicable in the analysis of image-based and time-series data respectively. Cracks, dust or shading issues on solar panels are checked using CNNs based on drone images, but the velocities or power requirement of the wind is forecasted with the assistance of RNNs in time-series forecasting. These frameworks can process large amounts of sensor data from, drones and satellites to provide real-time analysis and predictive control (Kumar et al. 2025). This has been improved with the continuously increasing computational power and cloud storage to support the capacity of AI models to process multi-dimensional data more efficiently to support a smarter renewable energy infrastructure.

In addition, AI is also significant in bringing together distributed energy resources (DERs) and microgrids. Decentralization is becoming more popular today in the current power systems where households and businesses have the ability to generate their own power by placing rooftop solar panels or small wind turbines. Such distributed resources are managed by AI machines, which predict the generation trend, regulate power distribution and aligning local grids with the central grid, ensuring an even and stable energy supply even when the main grid is unstable.

The other outcome of AI is energy sharing among prosumers (producers and consumers) and this enables prosumers to exchange energy with their peers in energy markets that are mediated by blockchains. These innovations clean energy more accessible and contribute to more sustainable and resilient energy communities.

3.4. Application of AI in hydrogen green production

Artificial intelligence (AI) has emerged as a transformative technology in energy systems, and green hydrogen production is no exception. Among the most promising approaches for decarbonizing energy systems and reducing reliance on fossil fuels is green hydrogen, which is produced through the electrolysis of water using renewable energy sources. However, its large-scale deployment faces several challenges, including high operational costs, inefficiencies, variability in renewable energy supply, and maintenance issues. These processes can be streamlined with the help of the AI technologies, such as ML, DL and predictive analytics, to improve yield and operational cost-effectiveness (Ahmed et al. 2024). The production and utilization of hydrogen in industry are evolving with the assistance of AI in optimizing the electrolysis process, predictive maintenance, energy input control and intelligent forecasting.

This implies that optimizing the electrolysis process using AI is the foundation of optimizing hydrogen production efficiency. The art of splitting water into hydrogen and oxygen with the assistance of an electric current is called electrolysis and it is highly sensitive to alterations in voltage, temperature and quality of the input energy. Traditional control systems tend to be founded on fixed models that fail to respond dynamically to the changing conditions especially when the source is renewable like solar or wind. Alternatively, AI models can process real-time sensor data (voltage, current density, temperature, etc.) and continuously optimize electrolysis parameters. AI may be applied to find optimal currents, temperatures and electrode arrangements to achieve the highest hydrogen yield with minimal energy loss (Agwu et al. 2025). In addition, AI can also be trained in the operational trends to determine the most efficient operating windows for the different kinds of electrolyzers, such as alkaline, PEM or solid oxide electrolyzers. This is an optimizing dynamic operation, whereby the electrolysis system is optimally operating even with varying renewable energy input that results in reduced energy consumption and operation cost (Alhussan et al. 2023).

In addition, predictive maintenance and fault detection of hydrogen production plants also may be implemented with the help of AI. The conditions in the electrolyzers, pumps, valves, sensors and compressors are harsh and lead to wear and corrosion and degradation of the components over time. The old ways of maintenance that are more responsive or time-based fail to anticipate faults and therefore generate costly downtimes and even hazards. Predictive maintenance systems, which are based on the combination of AI and IoT sensors, monitor the equipment state and control parameters such as vibration, temperature, pressure and electrical characteristics. Machine learning (ML) algorithms can be applied to anticipate abnormal patterns and predict potential machine failures in advance. For example, AI models trained on historical operational data can detect early indicators of electrode degradation or membrane fouling. These models identify subtle signs of deterioration long before they lead to a significant decline in system performance. This type of predictive capability allows maintenance personnel to perform certain operations at the right time in order to minimize the number of interruptions and extend the life of the equipment. In addition, root-cause analysis can be performed by AI-based fault detection systems, giving the engineer an understand of where the inefficiencies have been introduced and enabling corrective actions to be implemented in the long-term, which increases the overall reliability of the system.

Energy input control and yield forecasting are also highly significant aspects where AI is changing the production of hydrogen. Since green hydrogen is reliant on renewable energy sources that are intermittent in nature, there is a need to regulate the energy input to ensure that the production remains constant. AI algorithms are able to analyze the trends of renewable energy production, weather prediction and energy prices in the market to schedule the hydrogen production in the case of surplus renewable energy. An example is the use of predictive models to predict solar and wind energy variation and modify the electrolysis process to maximize the utilization of renewable electricity. In addition, AI is capable of balancing energy storage and hydrogen generation, ensuring that the excess renewable energy is stored as hydrogen during the maximum energy production time and hydrogen production is minimal when the energy levels are low. Thereby, AI increases the efficiency of production, not to mention grid stability and optimization of the energy market.

The next important task, where AI can be applied, is yield forecasting, which enables the producers to estimate the production of hydrogen with reference to a set of parameters in the environment and during operation. The data on electrolysis plants, renewable energy and from environmental sensors is synthesized, and AI models are capable of estimating the amount of hydrogen that should be produced daily, weekly or monthly. These are significant forecasts, which are applied in supply chain management, warehousing and demand fulfillment in industry or transport. The use of yield forecasting can also be used to make financial and operational decisions in large-scale hydrogen plants since it helps in predicting profitability and production risks. AI-based analytics allow companies to recreate various scenarios under which they will be operating, taking into account the effects of their energy consumption and simplify the resource allocation process. This intuition is more potent and cost-effective in the long-term of the production process (Rezk et al. 2023). In addition to the industrial activities, AI is also relevant in research and development to improve hydrogen technologies. Simulation-based modeling with the help of AI can be used to perform virtual experimental modeling of new materials, electrode and electrolyzer designs, before researchers undertake physical modeling. DL can learn complex chemical reactions, reduce catalyst blends and predict how electrolyzers will act in different conditions in the future. These lessons can be applied to reduce the cost of the experiment and shorten the innovation of hydrogen technology. In addition, AI is involved in adjusting green hydrogen to align with broader energy systems, including transportation, storage and fuel cells. Through the utilization of the whole hydrogen value chain, such as production to consumption, AI transforms hydrogen into a prospective component of the global clean energy system.

The future of AI application in green hydrogen generation is promising, and data analytics, automation and digital twins development are underway. As the hydrogen production systems continue to become more digital, AI enables the use of the so-called self-educating, autonomous plants, which are capable of making decisions in real-time and will not need a human operator. These intelligent systems will monitor all production activities such as energy input, and storing logistics will be the most efficient and secure. Further, AI will enhance the interoperability of hydrogen plants and renewable grids and make coordination and energy exchange possible. This is a combination that is required to realize the full potential of green hydrogen as a center of the global net-zero plan. AI will assist in changing to a clean, sustainable hydrogen economy by reducing the consumption of energy, streamlining the costs of operations and making the systems more reliable. A summary of the application of AI in green hydrogen production is provided in Table 3.2.

Application area	AI techniques used	Key benefits	Industrial examples
Smart electrolysis optimization	Machine learning, reinforcement learning	Maximizes hydrogen yield, reduces energy loss	Siemens energy, H2Future project
Predictive maintenance and fault detection	Neural networks, anomaly detection	Reduces downtime, improves equipment lifespan	Toshiba hydrogen plant, shell hydrogen projects
Energy input management	Predictive analytics, forecasting algorithms	Balances renewable input and production demand	European offshore hydrogen projects
Yield forecasting	Time series analysis, deep learning	Predicts hydrogen output, supports supply chain planning	Japan's AI-based hydrogen facility
Industrial implementation and research	Digital twins, simulation models	Accelerates innovation, reduces R&D costs	Global hydrogen research programs

Table 3.2. *Summary of AI applications in green hydrogen production*

3.5. AI in marine energy harvesting

The integration of AI into marine energy systems has revolutionized the exploration of tides, waves and offshore winds, their harvesting and management. Marine energy could potentially satisfy the global requirements for clean energy since it is one of predictable and the most abundant renewable energy resources. The varying environmental conditions, complex hydrodynamic interactions and high cost of operation has however been a long-term issue with efficient energy production (Delgado-Alvarado et al. 2025). After the introduction of AI technologies, specifically ML, DL and data-driven optimization, the improvement of efficiency, predictive capabilities and sustainability in marine energy harvesting has a solid solution. Not only do these intelligent systems enhance the precision of prediction and control of energy production, but also contribute to reducing maintenance and environmental impacts, which makes marine energy more applicable on a large scale.

The uses of AI-based models are largely associated with forecasting tidal and wave patterns, streamlining the work of offshore wind and managing marine systems in real-time. The availability of resources in the case of tidal and wave energy plays a critical role in determining the effectiveness of energy conversion. The traditional physical models are limited due to the application of complex hydrodynamic equations and high computation power. On the other hand, AI models, such as RNNs, long short-term memory (LSTM) networks and CNNs, can predict wave height, frequency and energy flux with remarkable precision using vast numbers of ocean buoys, satellites and sensors. The models rely on past and real-time information to forecast the alterations in the tidal cycles and generate more stable power production (Albarakati 2025). Regression models based on ML have been applied to predict the velocity of tidal currents and the energy content of waves several hours or days in advance to allow operators to plan energy storage and grid integration more effectively.

The offshore wind energy industry has also seen AI applied to optimize the placement of turbines, load balancing and fault prediction. High winds, salt water corrosion and weather extremes are typical factors in offshore wind farms that can affect the performance and durability of equipment. It is possible to empower energy producers with AI-based optimization techniques, such as genetic algorithms, particle swarm optimization (PSO), and RL, to determine the best turbine configurations for maximizing energy output and minimizing wake and mechanical load effects. Moreover, AI-based predictive maintenance can detect anomalies in turbine operation due to vibration, temperature and acoustic indicators (Yu et al. 2025). Such intelligent systems can identify the first indications of wear or trouble and fix them quickly, saving time. Optimal blade pitch and yaw control in real-time can also be found using DL algorithms. To harness the maximum amount of energy the turbine must be able to adapt to the changing wind direction. Hence, AI assists in improving the equipment's lifespan, reliability and energy efficiency in offshore wind installations.

In real-time monitoring and control systems AI can be applied to demonstrate the transformative value. Marine energy systems in a harsh and unpredictable environment, whereby they must be constantly monitored and controlled dynamically. Sensors and the IoT (IoT) are AI-driven devices mounted on turbines, platforms and seabed structures to provide real-time information about the ocean currents, temperatures, salinity and mechanical performance. This data is transmitted to centralized control platforms that analyze and interpret them with the help of AI algorithms and make immediate decisions. ML models can automatically adjust the energy output, run power conversion systems and balance the loads among different energy sources. The RL technique enables such systems to learn the most appropriate operational strategies over time that results in increased efficiency in performance with minimal human interventions. Also, the AI-controlled systems can be applied to grid integration, as they can predict energy generation in advance, thereby maintaining the balance between supply and demand. Both AI and IoT can offer a solution to ensure that the marine energy activities are smarter and more resilient to environmental uncertainties. The combination of AI and marine energy technologies also enables the combination and integration of larger renewable systems. When used alongside smart grids, AI can integrate the flow of energy from marine sources with other renewable energy sources such as solar and wind. Predictive analytics enables operators to make energy dispatch plans, which ensure grid stability even in the face of changing environmental conditions. Also, AI algorithms are able to forecast the demand and supply of energy in coastal regions, which enables dynamic pricing and load control. These intelligent systems are required in order to achieve effective, carbon neutral energy systems that can vary according to the requirements and natural variations.

The advantages of AI application in marine energy harvesting are enormous and yet there are multiple challenges. Higher quality datasets that are labeled are scarce, especially in remote marine environments. The sea environment is also very harsh, and it is difficult to sustain sensors and communication systems that are required to gather data. Moreover, AI models cost a great deal of computing resources and knowledge in marine engineering and data science. Others are data security, transparency and model interpretability, particularly in cases where the decisions made pertain to environmental conservation and the general population's resources. Therefore, there should be concerted efforts among scientists, policymakers and industry participants to come up with unified structures, open data repositories and regulatory measures that will ensure that AI is implemented responsibly.

However, the future of AI in marine energy harvesting is bright. New technologies in the form of digital twins, or the virtual replicas of marine systems, can be simulated in real-time and optimized and predicted through simulation-based control. With AI in conjunction with robotics and autonomous underwater vehicles (AUVs), the company will be able to conduct real-time inspections, maintenance and data collection of inaccessible underwater places. Moreover, explainable AI (XAI) may ensure transparency and confidence in the decision-making processes which is environmental and operational evaluations. Such technologies lead to a future where AIs-based marine global energy systems will be autonomous, sustainable and efficient ensuring carbon neutrality.

In conclusion, the introduction of AI to the marine energy harvesting sector can be described as a groundbreaking trend in renewable energy research and practice. Tidal energy systems, wave energy systems and offshore wind energy systems can be enhanced with AI to improve efficiency, reliability and sustainability by predicting, optimizing, monitoring and protecting the environment using smart algorithms. As the global requirement for clean and resilient energy increases, AI is at the forefront of the growing potential of marine energy and minimizing the adverse effect on the environment. AI, along with digital technologies, IoT systems and smart grids, is a new move in renewable innovation, which is environmentally responsible, technologically advanced and economically sustainable.

3.6. AI-intensified systems interaction with smart grids

The global energy situation is radically changing due to twin issues of sustainability and technological innovativeness. As countries continue to accelerate their electricity transformation to renewable energy sources such as solar, wind and hydroelectric power the conventional centralized power grid system is being transformed into dynamic, decentralized, intelligent systems called smart grids. It is a contemporary infrastructure, founded on digital technologies, real-time data processing and automated control systems to control the complicated flow of electricity between producers and consumers. Nevertheless, increased incorporation of intermittent renewable energy sources poses new problems to grid stability, optimization of energy storage and computer security (Hlalele 2025). AI has played one of the most significant roles in this transition increasing efficiency, resilience and intelligence in smart grids. Smart grids that are AI enhanced can also learn and adapt to large datasets, forecast demand and supply variability, and control power distribution, without human intervention to a large extent. In contrast to the traditional grid systems that are established on fixed rules and manual decision-making, AI brings flexibility in terms of intelligence that has the capability of handling real-time information of smart meters, sensors, weather forecasts and energy markets (Vinoth Kanna and Shibi 2025). This will enable grid operators to forecast consumption, predict failures and dynamically allocate resources in line with the predictive consumption patterns. Introducing AI into smart grids will be a paradigm shift to responsive, proactive and prescriptive management, and, therefore, the energy systems will be more sustainable, cost-effective and resilient to disruptions.

Supply intermittency is one a fundamental issues for renewable energy systems. Solar energy and wind energy are generated depending on the environmental conditions that are never constant and predictable. To mitigate this problem, batteries in energy storage systems, pumped hydro and thermal storage are required to match generation and consumption. AI helps to make storage systems more efficient using intelligent forecasting, optimization algorithms and control strategies. AI systems can optimize the time to store or release the energy by analyzing the real-time data on weather patterns, energy demand and market prices.

For example, when the renewable energy production is high, and the demand is low, AI algorithms can command the system to fill batteries with the surplus energy (Anwar and Kumar 2025). On the other hand, when the demand is high and the production is low, the stored energy can be utilized without the supply reliability causing an issue. This will not only reduce energy wastage, it also reduces reliance on fossil-based back-up systems, which in turn leads to decarbonization.

In addition, AI-driven predictive analytics has the potential to enhance the lifespan of an energy storage system. Traditional energy storage control problems mostly take the shape of over-charging, under-utilization or premature wear and tear of batteries. The battery health can be predicted using ML models and other forms of AI models to optimize the charge-discharge cycle and increase the lifespan. For example, the RL algorithm can use real-time feedback to adjust the storage parameters to maximize energy retention and minimum wear. These capabilities in systems are synonymous with reduced expenses and increased reliability, which are necessary for mammoth adaptation to renewable energy systems.

Aside from applications in storage, AI is a new solution for energy distribution optimization. The energy flows in smart grids are no longer one-sided: consumers to the power plants, it is now a two-way flow, and consumers have become prosumers, who produce, store and sell energy to the grid. The gird is developed in the form of a sophisticated web of microgrids and DERs that should be synchronized. This complication can be solved with AI algorithms, which redirect the energy toward the areas of greatest need. AI can forecast a surge of demand in certain regions and reroute power before it runs out. In the same breath, AI systems can automatically optimize local generation and consumption over microgrid networks and can isolate parts of the grid on faults to avoid system-wide failures. This intelligent management level is beneficial in terms of optimizing operation and minimizing the transmission losses and decentralization of the energy ecosystems.

The improved systems that incorporate AI also aid in grid stability and load balancing, which is important in ensuring that power is provided without failure. Traditional grids load balance by arranging the generation power based on the consumption history. This method is not, however, applicable to grids, which are largely composed of variable renewable sources. AI brings on board real-time elasticity of predictive load forecasting and demand–response. Consumption patterns of millions of smart meters can be studied with ML to forecast the short-term and long-term patterns of demand with a level of accuracy that is just awe inspiring. Short-term demand forecasting makes neural networks and DL models some of the most useful applications of AI for load balancing since the grid operators can actively adjust the generation time and energy flows minimizing the risk of overloads or blackouts. With the data given by the weather stations, social events and energy markets, AI can predict consumption spikes in a minute. AI models can anticipate an increase in electricity use in the middle of a heatwave or a vacation and increase supply as required. In addition, AI can be used to assist automated demand response (ADR) systems that encourage consumers to adjust their energy demand during peak times. Smart appliances (e.g. thermostats and electric vehicle chargers) can communicate with the grid through AI-enabled platforms to automatically control their functionality and reduce grid load and energy costs for customers.

Predictive maintenance is also another area of AI in smart grids. The old maintenance plans are usually time based and that is what contributes to the unwarranted check-ups or failures. AI changes this model by enabling condition-based and predictive maintenance which continuously monitors grid elements. The sensors that monitor the electrical performance of transformers, substations and transmission lines are used to monitor temperature, vibration and electrical performance. These data streams are processed using ML algorithms to identify anomalies that will indicate possible equipment failure. This will enable the maintenance teams to work before a fault arises in order to reduce the downtimes and extend the life of the system. It is not only possible to make the energy infrastructure cheaper by operating with the assistance of AI-based predictive maintenance, but also to increase to the overall safety and resilience of the energy infrastructure.

Nevertheless, with the increased connectivity of smart grids and the use of data, the issue of the cybersecurity and data protection has taken center stage. Digitalization of the grid creates the possibility of cyberattacks that can include data breaches, unauthorized access and malware attacks that may interfere with the power supply or sensitive information. Cybersecurity measures are AI based, which means that the level of security is high as the traffic on the network is monitored constantly, anomalies are detected and a response to the threats is provided in real-time. For example, AI-based intrusion detection systems apply ML algorithms to distinguish between legitimate and malicious actions. Upon finding suspicious behavior, the system is capable of isolating the affected nodes automatically to curb the propagation of cyberattacks in the grid.

Moreover, AI also helps in dynamic defense against emerging threats. Traditional cybersecurity policies rely on a collection of norms, which are unlikely to be applicable for preventing novel vectors of attacks. On the contrary, AI can learn about past events and alter its defense mechanisms. DL and adversarial training techniques enable AI models to identify more sophisticated threats that traditional systems can fail to identify. This is particularly important for smart grids that must be able to persist and maintain their data intact even after being attacked.

In addition to cybersecurity, data management can also be considered a pillar of AI-enhanced smart grids. A tremendous amount of data is generated by sensors, meters and IoT devices, which requires proper collection, storage and analysis. The AI-powered data management platform can filter, organize and analyze this information in real-time, ensuring that only relevant information is relayed to the control centers. Federated learning and edge computing is increasingly gaining popularity in order to reduce latency and guarantee data privacy. Edge-based AI has data processing capabilities at the edges of the devices as opposed to centralized transfer of data, and it minimizes the susceptibility to cyber threats. Meanwhile, federated learning allows AI models to be trained using a single device, yet they do not share raw data, which enhances performance and privacy. The use of AI is also important in making decisions based on data about renewable grids. Due to the heterogeneous source of data (e.g. weather predictions, market trends, and consumption data), AI will be capable of generating actionable insights into stakeholders. This will help policy makers develop dynamic pricing schemes that will increase energy conservation. In utilities this helps optimize schedules and investment planning. It provides consumers with a clearer overview of their energy usage encouraging them to conserve energy with the help of smart devices and personalized recommendations.

AI and smart grids also communicate to allow the decentralization of grids and peer-to-peer energy trading – in which households and businesses can trade surplus renewable energy with one another with the assistance of blockchain-based systems. The AI algorithm has the ability to pair buyers and sellers in real-time and optimize the deal of demand, price and location. Innovation enhances local energy resilience, minimizing losses during transmission to consumers and making consumers active members of the energy ecosystem.

Although AI and smart grids have transformative potential, numerous challenges can be encountered during integration – including the necessity for effective data governance models, the ethical aspect of algorithmic decision-making and the overly high computational demands of AI models. Moreover, AI-enhanced grids can only be employed in situations where the data quality is high and communication infrastructure is stable. Developing countries may face the challenge of less connectivity and bad technical skills hindering mass implementation. These issues demand cooperation between governments, energy companies and technology suppliers in order to establish standardized protocols, invest in digital infrastructure and support employee training.

To sum up, AI-based systems and the implementation of smart grids can be listed as one of the pillars of the global shift toward a sustainable and intelligent energy future. AI will make smart grids efficient in a more complex environment by optimizing the storage and distribution of energy, providing grid stability and enhancing cybersecurity. The collaboration between AI and renewable energy has not only boosted the functionality of operations but also broad-scale sustainability objectives, such as carbon neutrality, energy equity and environmental protection. With the ever-expanding energy ecosystem, future power systems will be built upon AI-enabled smart grids, which will underpin autonomous, adaptive and resilient power systems, creating a smarter and cleaner planet.

3.7. Challenges and limitations

Even though AI and ML are exceptionally promising in terms of creating renewable energy systems, significant challenges and limitations still hinder their large-scale adoption and full efficiency. These problems are related to fields such as technical, computational, data, economic and policy. As the renewable energy systems grow more interconnected and data-intensive, these constraints are becoming increasingly significant so that AI-driven innovations can provide the desired outcome in terms of efficiency, sustainability and reliability. The major challenges include the technical and computational ones, which are associated with the introduction of AI into renewable energy systems. The systems of AI and ML demand a high level of hardware and high-intensity computing to process large volumes of real-time data from various renewable energy sources. These renewable systems include solar farms, wind turbines and smart grids that generate terabytes of data daily with the help of sensors, meters and foretelling devices. Massive amounts of data need to be processed and analyzed with the use of powerful computing infrastructures and sophisticated algorithms that would be capable of making real-time decisions. Many operators of renewable energy particularly in developing nations lack the computer power and technical expertise to execute and support such systems.

In addition, AI models are typically trained on large, high-quality datasets to improve the accuracy of predictions and control decisions. However, renewable energy data can often be complex, incomplete, or inconsistent due to variations in sensor performance, communication issues, and environmental factors. Nonlinearity in the production of renewable energy adds to the complexity of computation, as it depends on the weather, seasonal changes and geographic position. The greatest technical issue is to create robust AI models that can be extended to other sources of renewable energy and locations. Moreover, AI is not so readily applicable to the established energy systems since the existing infrastructure was not originally created to be executed in digital and automated form. The additional issues that face smooth implementation are compatibility issues, latency of data and network vulnerability.

Another aspect that is problematic is the low explainability and transparency of most AI models used in renewable energy. Neural networks and DL are strong, but tend to be black box, and engineers and policymakers might not be able to understand the reasoning behind an AI-based decision. Such opacity can lead to distrust or misunderstanding in systems where decision-making directly affects grid stability, safety, and regulatory compliance, which are critical aspects of modern energy systems. The lack of explainability reduces accountability and slows the adoption of AI-based control mechanisms, particularly in policy-regulated or safety-sensitive environments.

In addition, several technical barriers are closely associated with data quality and standardization issues in renewable energy applications. AI algorithms rely on consistent, high-quality, and well-structured datasets to generate accurate predictions and effective optimization strategies. In practice, however, renewable energy data are often fragmented and non-standardized. Data are collected from multiple sources, including different types of sensors, weather stations, grid operators, and regional agencies, each using different data formats, sampling rates, and measurement protocols. This heterogeneity complicates data integration and may introduce errors or biases in AI-based analyses. Furthermore, inconsistent equipment calibration, missing data points, and delays in data transmission can further reduce data reliability.

The other major problem is that the renewable energy industry does not have universally accepted data collection and sharing standards. In most organizations, operational data may be regarded as proprietary and is not readily available to research and cross-industry collaboration. Absence of common data ecosystems implies that AI models are not able to leverage large heterogeneous data to facilitate valuable learning and generalization.

Data privacy and cybersecurity are also a problem that complicates the process of data sharing between stakeholders. Taking into consideration that energy networks are becoming increasingly digitized, AI systems can also be attacked by cyberattacks. Any breach of data integrity or unauthorized interference to AI controlled energy controls can have a significant impact on grid stability and national security.

Besides the technical and data challenges, barriers to the growth of AI in renewable energy are also presented by economic and policy factors. The creation of AI-controlled energy management infrastructure is also expensive as it requires the allocation of money toward new technologies and computer equipment, clouds and experienced specialists. Many of the renewable energy firms, especially the small and medium ones or those operating in an emerging economy, cannot justify such costs without immediate returns. The high price of AI systems at the initial stage of its development, as well as the absence of promises of success, is a negative aspect hindering its implementation in resource-constrained environments. In addition, the energy markets tend to fluctuate in terms of prices and regulations, and AI investments cannot be planned in the long-term.

The rapid technological development of AI in renewable energy does not come with policy and regulatory frameworks either. Little to no guidelines exist on the ethical use of automated energy systems, data regulation and responsibility in AI in most countries. The uncertainty surrounding the regulation of the use of AI in grid control, forecasting, and energy trading is the cause of hesitation among investors and operators. The technical capacity of governments and other regulatory bodies to inspect and accept AI-based energy projects is also an impediment to innovation. To make it even more difficult, the international cooperation and exchange of technologies is complicated by the fact that the national policies and regulatory standards differ across regions.

Another limitation to development is that there are few incentives or supportive policies for those incorporating AI into renewable systems. Physical infrastructure development is more significant to several governments than the digital transformation in the energy sectors. The use of AI-based technologies cannot become commonplace without funding, tax benefits or the presence of a partnership between the government and the business sector. In addition, AI in renewable energy can only be economically viable when the data at hand is adequate and when the operation is on a large scale – since large companies can efficiently utilize AI due to the economies of scale, but small ones will incur disproportional costs. This offers a skewed playing field for the renewable energy market and limits the inclusive growth of smart energy systems.

The other side of the challenge is the knowledge gap and human resource. AI-based renewable energy systems require expertise in many areas: data science, power engineering, control systems and environmental modeling. The absence of experts who have expertise in the field of energy management and AI development is the reason why innovations are restrained and the implementation is sluggish. The only solution to this gap is undertaking continuous training, interdisciplinary training and industry-academia collaboration. In order to make sure that adoption of AI is not limited to technologically advanced nations, sufficient capacity-building programs are required to bridge the global gaps in the development of renewable energy.

The growing dependence on AI also poses the problem of computational energy consumption and sustainability, ethically and environmentally. Big AI models consume a great deal of electricity, which is typically supplied by non-renewable sources. It is ironic that, on the one hand, AI will increase the optimal use of renewable energy, and, on the other hand, its computational footprint can cancel some of the advantages, unless it is considered in a sustainable way. To ensure the ecological integrity of AI-driven solutions, green computing must be applied, that is, renewable energy is involved in the operation of the data centers, and the efficiency of algorithms is increased.

On the whole, the possibilities of AI in renewable energy systems are enormous, yet its implementation is full of numerous issues that are interrelated. These barriers are technical in nature, such as computational constraints, explainability and integration complexity making the adoption hard. Data-related problems like data quality, data fragmentation and non-standardization influence the reliability of AI models. Economic and policy constraints also restrict scalability, and they are expensive, not incentivized and supported by policies. In order to deal with these limitations, global policy making, industry leaders, researchers and technology developers are required. The precursors of responsible and efficient AI application in renewable energy can be the creation of universal data structures, investment in digital infrastructure, encouraging cross-sector relationships and the creation of adaptive policies. Only these issues can be solved systematically and, in this way, the world will be able to explore the full potential of AI in order to create cleaner, smarter and more sustainable energy systems in the future.

3.8. Future research directions

As the renewable energy industry becomes increasingly dynamic, the role of AI is becoming more prominent in the development of next-generation technologies, including green hydrogen production, intelligent grid systems, and marine energy technologies. AI and renewable technologies make the working process more efficient, founding an entirely new energy paradigm on automation, flexibility and sustainability. However, when much positive change has already been made, there are still untapped opportunities, and they need particular research, technological development and policy alignment. The future research directions for the field are concentrated on developing new AI-based models for renewable innovation, the appearance of digital twins and autonomous energy systems, and the need for interdisciplinary collaboration, besides powerful policy frameworks to ensure that it is deployed in a sustainable way.

The future of AI-based innovation in the sphere of renewable energy is in the creation of models. The current generation of AI systems that are primarily based on general ML and DL algorithms has demonstrated promising opportunities for streamlining the renewable processes and forecasting the behavior of systems. Nevertheless, these systems usually require large amounts of labeled data and also come with the challenges of uncertainty and dynamism in the dynamic environments of renewable energy systems. The development of more advanced AI models, such as self-supervised learning, transfer learning, and generative AI, which can be effective with limited amounts of data and are constantly able to adjust to new circumstances of operation, should be the focus of future research. Self-learning models that are capable of deducing the intricate interactions of energy would be capable of controlling power flows between the solar, wind and hydrogen systems on their own to ensure optimal grid stability. Generative AI would be in a position to simulate various renewable energy possibilities, anticipating variations in the demand and recommend efficient investment or storage alternatives. Moreover, quantum ML has the potential to change the quality of calculations, in which more complicated renewable systems can be optimized quicker. The second possible pathway is XAI, which makes energy choices more transparent and understandable, contributing to a higher level of human trust and acceptance of the policy. With the increase in renewable systems, it is important to create explainable and adaptive AI systems to assist decision-making particularly in areas that are safety critical, such as hydrogen storage or offshore energy generation.

The other significant area of future research and innovation is the digital twins and autonomous energy systems. A digital twin is a simulated version of an actual energy system that continuously monitors it with sensors, responds to it with AI and predicts the performance. By using digital twins in the case of renewable energy, it is possible to reproduce wind farms, solar plants or hydrogen production plants to discover how to optimize it and anticipate the degradation of the system before it occurs. Future research should be oriented toward the creation of fully integrated digital twins, which may comprise a single renewable energy system with AI-based control systems. Such systems would be in a position to automatically arrange the renewable sources, load balancing and maximize energy storage and distribution without human involvement. The hydrogen sector can apply digital twins to the electrolysis process in various environments and operating conditions to identify the efficiency and lifespan of the components and the maintenance requirements. The combination of AI-based digital twins, IoT sensors and edge computing can be used to support real-time decision-making at a site level and reduce latency and enhance the reliability of operations. In addition, establishing self-driven energy systems, in which AI agents manage entire renewable ecosystems, will transform the manner in which the future energy grids operate. These systems will be dynamically receptive to the alteration in the environment, change in demand and conditions in the grid by altering energy production, storage and distribution. Research should be conducted to improve the interoperability of systems, cybersecurity and scalability to be in a position to ensure that digital twins and autonomous functions are safe in other renewable infrastructures.

Policy support and interdisciplinary collaboration also play a critical role in ensuring that AI-driven renewable energy systems achieve their potential. There is no way to successfully introduce intelligent renewable technologies without cooperation between environmental professionals, economists, data scientists and engineers. AI research on renewable energy cannot remain in the technological environment; it is increasingly engaged with environmental ethics, social equity and policy regulation. As a case in point, despite the fact that AI can be applied to optimize renewable systems, the amount of data and computing resources required can become a source of sustainability concerns on its own. Therefore, researchers must find energy-efficient AI models that can be in accordance with environmental goals. Future research should also focus on it to come up with a standard practice of data-sharing and interoperability systems that can enable different stakeholders to collaborate with one another, including governments, industries and research institutions. Interdisciplinary research programs can enable innovations in predictive modeling, grid integration and policy evaluation in such a way that the technological advancements are facilitated by a well-developed governance framework.

The encouragement of policies is among the key aspects contributing to the direction of the ethical and fair use of the AI in renewable energy systems. The development of regulatory frameworks that promote transparency, accountability and information privacy in AI applications should be prioritized by governments and international organizations. Policy must also promote research into AI-based renewable technologies through funding, research grants and industry-academia partnerships. Moreover, digital energy infrastructures should be scaled up by promoting public–private partnerships and creating open innovation ecosystems. Regulatory agencies must also establish safety standards and certification systems for autonomous energy systems and digital twins to offer operational security and engender trust in the population. A comprehensive policy framework that coordinates the incentives for innovation with ethics will be significant in guiding AI applications toward sustainable and inclusive energy transitions.

Another new research direction is the integration of AI and blockchain and other decentralized technologies to enhance transparency, data security and energy trading systems. AI systems constructed on blockchain would allow individuals and communities to purchase and sell surplus clean energy through decentralized systems, which would allow them to trade renewable energy peer-to-peer. With the assistance of AI, these transactions can be optimized as they are able to predict demand, stabilize prices and distribute energy fairly. These inventions will transform the energy economy and consumers will become active members in the renewable ecosystem.

Furthermore, the data transfer requirements can be reduced by integrating AI with edge computing and federated learning, which enables privacy-preserving analytics, which is also worth considering in the example of energy facilities that must work with drastic data security regulations.

Increased focus on hybrid renewable systems will also be reflected in the future, as AI will be used to organize the integration of solar, wind, hydro and hydrogen systems into single smart grids. This type of smart grid will require more advanced AI programming capable of managing the interdependence of different energy sources, storage facilities and consumption patterns. Research should therefore be directed toward the multi-agent AI systems, which can be trained to learn how to collaborate and make joint decisions in order to optimize the overall performance of the grid. The establishment of standardized data and open-source simulation software in the study of AI in renewable energy will promote innovation, transparency and collaboration worldwide.

Education and capacity-building programs will further improve the future of AI in renewable energy. The world is urgently in need of a new generation of interdisciplinary background engineers, data scientists and energy managers due to the changing technologies. Colleges and research centers should identify ways of incorporating renewable energy engineering, computer science and data analytics into courses. These educational programs will ensure that the new researchers will be capable of designing, implementing and controlling AI-powered renewable solutions in a responsible manner.

Finally, the future studies of AI implementation to renewable energy should be more independent, transparent and sustainable. New AI models will be more flexible and smart, digital twins will be able to optimize and simulate in real-time, and transversal collaboration will help to bridge the technology and policy gap. These guidelines, when combined, will determine the next phase of the global clean energy revolution. The combination of AI and renewable energy systems will see the world moving through a quicker path of becoming a carbon-neutral future with innovation and ethical integrity and regulation.

3.9. Conclusions and recommendations

The introduction of AI into the sphere of renewable energy can be considered a new step toward attaining sustainability, energy efficiency and environmental conservation in every corner of the world. The past decade has seen great developments in the energy industry, which have been influenced by the development of data analytics, automation and smart decisions. AI technologies, in particular, ML, DL and predictive analytics, can facilitate the most effective renewable energy production, distribution and consumption. The intersection of AI and technologies, including the IoT, big data analytics, digital twins and blockchain, has also expanded the prospect of controlling complex energy networks and switching to decentralized, resilient and low-carbon systems.

One of the key enabling factors of the global transition toward sustainable energy, as envisioned in the Paris Agreement and the United Nations Sustainable Development Goals, is the strategic application of artificial intelligence (AI) in renewable energy systems. The global transition to clean energy not only requires technological innovation but also coordinated efforts among governments, industries, and communities. AI can provide this coordination since it can derive insights based on the data to increase the transparency, accountability and resource distribution in the energy systems. AI-based analytics can also assist policy makers to find the most efficient decarbonization paths, calculate the cheapest renewable energy combinations and evaluate the trade-offs of major energy-generating projects on environmental health. This is one of the reasons for improving clean energy transition and remaining economically competitive and socially equitable at the same time.

The fact that the AI-enabled energy transition will potentially result in the democratization of energy access is one of the important implications of the AI-enabled energy transition. The distributed AI-based systems can be decentralized where the management and generation of the energy can be decentralized, and the communities are able to produce and use the renewable energy locally. Such decentralized energy ecosystems not only reduce the dependence of the centralized power grids but also enable rural and underdeveloped regions to access cheap and renewable energy. The strategic importance of AI in smart grids, demand-side management and optimization of microgrids ensures the efficiency of the distribution of energy resources, minimizing grid instability and transmission losses. As the degree of digitalization increases, renewable energy markets will be encouraged to become more transparent and efficient with the introduction of AI-based energy trading services based on blockchain technology.

Nonetheless, the implementation of AI into renewable energy systems on a large scale has a number of strategic issues related to it. Data security, ethical issues and carbon footprint associated with AI models training should be considered carefully to ensure that the technological progress is aligned with the notion of sustainability. The issue of privacy and governance arise due to the dependence of the big datasets, particularly when the energy systems are interconnected within and across regions and sectors. Moreover, the disparity in access to AI infrastructure and knowledge can lead to the inequality of the benefits of energy digitalization between developed and developing nations. Therefore, the global cooperation and capacity-building processes should assist in technological progress to ensure that the processes of AI-driven energy transformation are inclusive, equitable and sustainable.

To sum up, AI is an innovator and a prototype for re-inventing the future of renewable energy. Its prospects for converting data into actionable intelligence maximize energy production, proactively manage system and use efficiency – all of which are necessary for realizing a low-carbon future. Nonetheless, coordinated efforts at the technological, institutional, and societal levels are essential for realizing this potential. The future of sustainable energy will depend not only on technological innovation but also on the inclusive and ethical application of these innovations. AI should therefore be informed by sustainability-oriented models of governance and should be accountable, transparent and provide equal benefits. The trick to the effective combination of AI and renewable energy will be to find the balance between the creation and preservation, that is, use technology to enhance human and environmental welfare, rather than industrial efficiency. AI will be instrumental in helping to make smarter decisions, adaptive infrastructure and resilient energy infrastructure that will be capable of serving a sustainable and thriving global future as countries aim to achieve ambitious carbon reduction targets.

3.10. References

Abdul Baseer, M., Almunif, A., Alsaduni, I., Tazeen, N. (2023). Electrical power generation forecasting from renewable energy systems using artificial intelligence techniques. *Energies*, 16(18), 6414. doi: 10.3390/en16186414.

Afridi, Y.S., Ahmad, K., Hassan, L. (2022). Artificial intelligence based prognostic maintenance of renewable energy systems: A review of techniques, challenges, and future research directions. *International Journal of Energy Research*, 46(15), 21619–21642. doi: 10.1002/er.7100.

Agwu, O.E., Alatefi, S., Alkouh, A. (2025). Modelling the future of cleaner energy: Explainable artificial intelligence model for green hydrogen production rate estimation. *Cleaner Engineering and Technology*, 27, 101040. doi: 10.1016/j.clet.2025.101040.

Ahmed, R., Shehab, S.A., Elzeki, O.M., Darwish, A., Hassanein, A.E. (2024). An explainable AI for green hydrogen production: A deep learning regression model. *International Journal of Hydrogen Energy*, 83, 1226–1242. doi: 10.1016/j.ijhydene.2024.08.064.

Albarakati, A.J. (2025). Blue energy intelligence: A hybrid wavelet-AI model for sustainable marine energy harvesting and hydrological signal monitoring via IoT systems. *Journal of Circuits, Systems and Computers*, S0218126626420028. doi: 10.1142/S0218126626420028.

Alhussan, A.A., El-Kenawy, E.S.M., Saeed, M.A., Ibrahim, A., Abdelhamid, A.A., Eid, M.M., El-Said, M., Khafaga, D.S., Abualigah, L., Elbaksawi, O. (2023). Green hydrogen production ensemble forecasting based on hybrid dynamic optimization algorithm. *Frontiers in Energy Research*, 11, 1221006. doi: 10.3389/fenrg.2023.1221006.

Alkahtani, H., Aldhyani, T.H.H., Alsubari, S.N. (2023). Application of artificial intelligence model solar radiation prediction for renewable energy systems. *Sustainability*, 15(8), 6973. doi: 10.3390/su15086973.

Anwar, A. and Kumar, S. (2025). Leveraging AI to achieve sustainability goals in TVET: A multifaceted approach. In *Integrating AI and Sustainability in Technical and Vocational Education and Training (TVET)*, Sorayyaei Azar, A., Kant Gupta, S., Taherdoost, H., Alhamaty, F. (eds). IGI Global Scientific Publishing, Hershey, PA. doi: 10.4018/979-8-3373-1142-5.ch002.

Atilhan, S., Park, S., El-Halwagi, M.M., Atilhan, M., Moore, M., Nielsen, R.B. (2021). Green hydrogen as an alternative fuel for the shipping industry. *Current Opinion in Chemical Engineering*, 31, 100668. doi: 10.1016/j.coche.2020.100668.

Boopathy, G., Jayakumar, K., Suresh, C., Srinivasan, V. (2025). Harnessing artificial intelligence for a greener future in solar, wind, and hydrogen. In *Leveraging AI for Innovative Sustainable Energy: Solar, Wind and Green Hydrogen*, Hammouch, H. and Razzak Janjua, L. (eds). IGI Global, Hershey, PA. doi: 10.4018/979-8-3373-0045-0.ch017.

Dehankar, P. and Das, S. (2025). AI-driven approaches for next-gen solar cells. In *Innovations in Next-Generation Energy Storage Solutions*, Mhadhbi, M. (ed.). IGI Global, Hershey, PA. doi: 10.4018/979-8-3693-9316-1.ch005.

Delgado-Alvarado, E., Morales-Gonzalez, E.A., Gonzalez-Calderon, J.A., Peréz-Peréz, M.C.I., Delgado-Maciel, J., Peña-Juarez, M.G., Hernandez-Hernandez, J., Elvira-Hernandez, E.A., Figueroa-Navarro, M.A., Herrera-May, A.L. (2025). Recent advances of hybrid nanogenerators for sustainable ocean energy harvesting: Performance, applications, and challenges. *Technologies*, 13(8), 336. doi: 10.3390/technologies13080336.

Dewangan, S. and Kumar, S. (2024). Enhancing fraud detection in finance through AI and machine learning. In *Utilizing AI and Machine Learning in Financial Analysis*, Darwish, D. and Kumar, S. (eds). IGI Global, Hershey, PA. doi: 10.4018/979-8-3693-8507-4.ch014.

Dewangan, S., Kumar, S., Tyagi, P.K. (2024). Transforming hospitality and tourism with AI and innovative technologies. In *Impact of AI and Tech-Driven Solutions in Hospitality and Tourism*, Talukder, M.B., Kumar, S., Tyagi P.K. (eds). IGI Global, Hershey, PA. doi: 10.4018/979-8-3693-6755-1.ch004.

Dhiraj, A., Kumar, S., Rani, D. (2023). Social and emotional learning: Keys to the success of e-learning. In *Technology-Driven E-Learning Pedagogy Through Emotional Intelligence*, Sharma, P.C., Bansal, R., Singh, R. (eds). IGI Global, Hershey, PA. doi: 10.4018/978-1-6684-7639-0.ch008.

Fayemi, O.E., Atofarati, E.O., Kanu-Uchenna, O.R., Enweremadu, C.C. (2025). Seawater electrolysis for hydrogen production: Challenges, innovations, and future pathways. *International Journal of Green Energy*, 1–22. doi: 10.1080/15435075.2025.2572703.

Hassan, S.C. and Kumar, S. (2024). Safe green hydrogen: Production and storage as an emerging source of energy for sustainable future. In *Advancements in Renewable Energy and Green Hydrogen*, Raboaca, M.S., Djohra, S., Moussaoui, O., Mihaltan, T.C., Koussa, M. (eds). IGI Global, Hershey, PA. doi: 10.4018/979-8-3693-1014-4.ch008.

Higashikawa, K., Kiss, T., Kitaguchi, H., Hirano, N., Hayashi, K., Muyeen, S.M. (2024). Superconducting cable with energy storage function and its potential for next-generation power system compatible with large-scale renewable energy installation. *Superconductor Science and Technology*, 37(11), 115015. doi: 10.1088/1361-6668/ad7efb.

Hlalele, T.S. (2025). Smart grid enhancements: AI approaches for sustainable power transmission. In *2025 IEEE Conference on Technologies for Sustainability (SusTech)*. doi: 10.1109/SusTech63138.2025.11025752.

Imran Khan, M., Asfand, F., Al-Ghamdi, S.G. (2022). Progress in technology advancements for next generation concentrated solar power using solid particle receivers. *Sustainable Energy Technologies and Assessments*, 54, 102813. doi: 10.1016/j.seta.2022.102813.

Jafri, N., Tahir, M., Ahad, A. (2023). The role of artificial intelligence in solar harvesting, storage, and conversion. In *Solar Energy Harvesting, Conversion, and Storage*, Khalid, M., Walvekar, R., Panchal, H., Vaka, M. (eds). Elsevier, Amsterdam. doi: 10.1016/B978-0-323-90601-2.00010-6.

Kumar, S., Talukder, M.B., Tyagi, P.K. (2024). The impact of artificial intelligence on improving efficiency in service and implementing best practices in service marketing. In *AI Innovations in Service and Tourism Marketing*, Nadda, V., Tyagi, P.K., Singh, A., Singh, V. (eds). IGI Global, Hershey, PA. doi: 10.4018/979-8-3693-7909-7.ch004.

Kumar, H., Aswathy, V.K., Kumar, S. (2025). Converging realms of social health, domestic workers, and telemedicine landscape: Challenges and prospects. In *Organizational Sociology in the Digital Age*, Özbek, M.F. and Christiansen, B. (eds). IGI Global, Hershey, PA. doi: 10.4018/979-8-3693-7398-9.ch010.

Kumar, A., Sharma, G., Dewangan, A.K., Yadav, A.K. (2026). Green hydrogen production from renewable energy resources: Current status and future perspective. In *Next Generation Renewable Thermal Energy Harvesting, Conversion and Storage Technologies*, Yadav, D., Awasthi, M.K., Kumar, A. (eds). Elsevier, Amsterdam. doi: 10.1016/B978-0-443-33184-8.00027-5.

Leandro, G.S.M., Kumar, S., Jacinto Da Gama, M., Carvalho, H., Leandro, E. (2024). Circular economy practices in the hotel sector in Luanda, Angola: Challenges and future perspectives. In *Dimensions of Regenerative Practices in Tourism and Hospitality*, Tyagi, P.K., Nadda, V., Kankaew, K., Dube, K. (eds). IGI Global, Hershey, PA. doi: 10.4018/979-8-3693-4042-4.ch004.

Nakano, S., Arai, S., Washizu, A. (2017). Economic impacts of Japan's renewable energy sector and the feed-in tariff system: Using an input–output table to analyze a next-generation energy system. *Environmental Economics and Policy Studies*, 19(3), 555–580. doi: 10.1007/s10018-016-0158-1.

Praveena, K., Jain, A., Arun, V., Kaliyaperumal, G., Khan, I., Pahwa, S., Alkhafaji, M.A. (2024). A review on next-generation solar solutions: Pioneering materials and designs for sustainable energy harvesting. *E3S Web of Conferences*, 505, 02004. doi: 10.1051/e3sconf/202450502004.

Rezk, H., Olabi, A.G., Abdelkareem, M.A., Alahmer, A., Sayed, E.T. (2023). Maximizing green hydrogen production from water electrocatalysis: Modeling and optimization. *Journal of Marine Science and Engineering*, 11(3), 617. doi: 10.3390/jmse11030617.

Serban, A.C. and Lytras, M.D. (2020). Artificial intelligence for smart renewable energy sector in Europe – Smart energy infrastructures for next generation smart cities. *IEEE Access*, 8, 77364–77377. doi: 10.1109/ACCESS.2020.2990123.

Shash, A.Y., Abdeltawab, N.M., Hassan, D.M., Darweesh, M., Hegazy, Y.G. (2025). Computational methods, artificial intelligence, modeling, and simulation applications in green hydrogen production through water electrolysis: A review. *Hydrogen*, 6(2), 21. doi: 10.3390/hydrogen6020021.

Shayo, G.M., Mpelwa, M., Elimbinzi, E., Shao, G.N. (2025). Toward sustainable hydrogen production from renewable energy sources: A review. *Bulletin of the National Research Centre*, 49(1), 67. doi: 10.1186/s42269-025-01361-z.

Thorson, J., Matthews, C., Lawson, M., Hartmann, K., Anwar, M.B., Jadun, P. (2022). Unlocking the potential of marine energy using hydrogen generation technologies. Technical Report No. NREL/TP-5700-82538, National Renewable Energy Laboratory. doi: 10.2172/1871531.

Vinoth Kanna, I. and Shibi, B. (2025). AI-driven smart energy management systems for optimized renewable energy utilization in urban smart grids. Preprint. doi: 10.21203/rs.3.rs-6326251/v1.

Wang, X., Rincon, J.D., Li, P., Zhao, Y., Vidal, J. (2021). Thermophysical properties experimentally tested for NaCl-KCl-$MgCl_2$ eutectic molten salt as a next-generation high-temperature heat transfer fluids in concentrated solar power systems. *Journal of Solar Energy Engineering*, 143(4), 041005. doi: 10.1115/1.4049253.

Yu, Y., Yang, Q., Ji, F., Zhou, W. (2025). Research advances in energy management and harvesting technologies for autonomous profiling floats. *Frontiers in Marine Science*, 12, 1598701. doi: 10.3389/fmars.2025.1598701.

Zeng, Q., Lai, Y., Jiang, L., Liu, F., Hao, X., Wang, L., Green, M.A. (2020). Integrated photorechargeable energy storage system: Next-generation power source driving the future. *Advanced Energy Materials*, 10(14), 1903930. doi: 10.1002/aenm.201903930.

Zhang, D., Pan, W., Lu, H., Wang, Z., Gupta, B., Oo, A.M.T., Wang, L., Reuter, K., Li, H., Jiang, Y., Karuturi, S. (2025). Prospects of AI in advancing green hydrogen production: From materials to applications. *Applied Physics Reviews*, 12(3), 031335. doi: 10.1063/5.0281416.

Ziarati, T., Hedayat, S., Moscatiello, C., Sappa, G., Manganelli, M. (2024). Overview of the impact of artificial intelligence on the future of renewable energy. In *2024 IEEE International Conference on Environment and Electrical Engineering* and *2024 IEEE Industrial and Commercial Power Systems Europe (EEEIC/I&CPS Europe)*. doi: 10.1109/EEEIC/ICPSEurope61470.2024.10751553.

4

Mapping the Research Landscape of AI in Electric Vehicles: A Bibliometric Analysis of Foundations and Emerging Trends

The intersection of artificial intelligence (AI) and electric vehicles (EVs) represents a transformative milestone in the evolution of sustainable transportation and smart mobility systems. AI technologies are increasingly being integrated into EV design, manufacturing, operation and infrastructure, enabling advancements in energy efficiency, autonomous driving, predictive maintenance and intelligent charging solutions. This chapter examines the current research landscape on AI applications in EVs, mapping both established trends and emerging directions in the field. Employing a bibliometric method of analysis, data were retrieved from two major academic databases, Scopus and Web of Science (WoS), to ensure comprehensive coverage of scholarly output. The analysis identifies the most influential authors, institutions and journals contributing to the discourse, while also revealing the thematic evolution of research topics over time. Furthermore, the findings highlight the interdisciplinary nature of investigations, with contributions spanning engineering, computer science, environmental studies and transportation research. Emerging research clusters indicate growing interest in areas such as AI-driven battery management systems, vehicle-to-grid (V2G) optimization and deep learning (DL) for autonomous EV navigation. By mapping the intellectual and thematic structure of the field, this study provides valuable insights for academics, practitioners and policymakers, guiding future research directions and fostering innovation at the intersection of AI and electric mobility.

4.1. Introduction

Sustainable transportation plays a significant role in dealing with environmental challenges. By 2050, the transportation sector is projected to

Chapter written by Nivedita JHA, Rakhi ARORA and Sonal PUROHIT.

account for 21% of total CO_2 reductions, according to the IEA research (Ul Haq et al. 2025b). In response to climate change and to reduce CO_2 emissions, novel mobility and transportation systems are required (Geels 2012). EVs have emerged as a new transportation system for addressing environmental and health problems.

The limited availability of non-sustainable energy sources, such as coal, oil and gas, coupled with the detrimental effects on the environment and health, has led to a massive growth in EVs in recent years. The growth and diffusion of EVs is seen as an outcome of several factors, such as the rising consumer interest in sustainable transportation, new charging infrastructure and the potential for innovation (Ul Haq et al. 2024). Although EVs have many benefits for sustainable transportation, issues with charging times, range anxiety and the long-term viability of battery manufacturing and recycling procedures still exist (Ahmed et al. 2021).

The intermittent and erratic nature of renewable energy resources poses challenges of incorporating them for EV charging (Ul Haq et al. 2022). AI or algorithms supporting models have implications in the field of EVs and associated infrastructures, including charging stations, smart grids and EV battery design and management. The AI models mimic natural thinking, perception and action, and thus have the potential to advance and develop EV technologies and more intricate power and transportation systems. By utilizing machine learning (ML) and DL, AI can assist in optimizing EV performance by managing the battery, maintenance and distribution systems, thereby improving efficiency, reliability and safety (Ul Haq et al. 2025d).

The convergence of AI and EVs has thus evolved as a game changer in the transportation and energy sector (Jahangir et al. 2019). AI-powered EVs mark a turning point in technological innovation, policy formation and sustainable engineering as countries work toward decarbonization and intelligent transportation (Ul Haq et al. 2025a). The convergence of AI with EVs offers benefits such as increased efficiency, autonomy, enhanced vehicle design, battery management, traffic optimization, user experience and energy grid interactions. Given these benefits, scholars have shown significant interest in the area of AI and EVs, leading to a growing body of research across various disciplines, ranging from science and engineering to environmental and social science. The rapid rate of innovation has created a vast and dispersed academic environment in which academics, business executives and politicians must discover foundational works, significant contributions, institutional networks and new trends. Bibliometric analysis provides a strong, data-driven lens to evaluate the development, organization and course of this multidisciplinary field of study to manage this complexity (Shamszadeh et al. 2019; Ul Haq and Khanday 2025).

In order to map the field's intellectual structure and theme trajectories, this chapter lays the groundwork for an extensive bibliometric investigation of AI in EVs. This study offers a macroscopic perspective of the knowledge landscape by utilizing various bibliometric techniques, such as keyword co-occurrence, co-authorship networks, citation analysis and thematic clustering, and drawing from Scopus and WoS as two important scientific databases. It shows where study gaps and potential future opportunities may be found, how scholarly interest has changed over time and which subdomains are gaining traction. The objectives of this chapter are as follows:

1) to identify the foundational literature, key authors, journals, countries and leading institutions shaping the AI-EV nexus;

2) to uncover the thematic evolution and interdisciplinary nature of the field;

3) to explore intellectual structure and conceptual linkages through factorial analysis;

4) to highlight emerging research trends and propose potential directions for future inquiries.

In addition to improving our comprehension of the current state of research, this bibliometric analysis' methodical mapping of the academic landscape acts as a strategic road map for encouraging creativity and cooperation in the AI-driven development of electric mobility.

4.2. Methodology

Descriptive research design, adopted in this chapter, investigates the research landscape on the connection between AI and EVs through bibliometric methods. This analysis provides a detailed framework for explaining data from authenticated academic databases. This study has determined the influencing authors, trends, themes and thematic clusters explored based on existing literature of AI applications in EVs.

The data were obtained from two scientific databases, Scopus and WoS, and bibliometric analysis was performed on the collected data to achieve the objective of this chapter. The data were searched on June 4, 2025, using the keywords "AI" OR "Artificial Intelligence" AND "Electric vehicle" OR "Electric Vehicles" OR "EV". Initially, a total of 18,001 documents were found, including 15,094 from WoS and 2,910 from Scopus. Further, this search was limited to "Journal Articles" published in "English" in the "Business Management" area. In this initial screening, a total of 67 articles were received, 26 from WoS and 41 from Scopus. The criteria for searching and selecting articles are shown in Table 4.1.

The merging tool in bibiloshiny was used to merge the data downloaded from WoS and Scopus in BibTex and CSV formats, respectively. It generated an integrated bibliometrix file containing 59 articles and removed duplicate documents. The time span of these documents was from 2008 to 2025, and they were processed in RStudio (version 4.5.1). Biblioshiny in the Bibliometrix R package was used for the visualization and analysis of the documents. This analysis generated dendograms, thematic evolution plots and collaboration maps in a graphical manner.

The following techniques were used for analyzing and achieving the objectives of this study:

1) Descriptive analysis was used to identify the foundational literature, most relevant authors, journals and leading institutions.

2) Co-occurrence analysis categorized research themes based on their relevance and density in existing publications on AI applications in EVs.

3) Factorial analysis was used to explore intellectual structure and conceptual linkages.

4) Citation and impact analysis was used to identify influential authors and documents.

Table 4.1 exhibits the selection and exclusion criteria of the research articles.

Search criteria	Total No. of documents obtained	
Database hunt: Scopus and Web of Science	18,001	
Hunt date	June 4, 2025	
Hunt term	"AI" OR "Artificial Intelligence" AND "Electric vehicle" OR "Electric Vehicles" OR "EV"	
Subject area: "Business, management and accounting."	**Rejected**	**Accepted**
	17,613	388
Document type: "Articles"	318	70
Language selection: limited to English only	3 (non-English)	67
Duplicates removed	8	59

Table 4.1. *Search criteria and articles selection.*
Source: created by authors

4.3. Analysis and discussion

The study conducted by Ul Haq et al. (2025c) was an influential study in the field of AI in EVs on how AI can be used to predict wind power for continuous electric supply. The authors discovered the use of AI algorithms in smart transportation and effective energy management. The sustainable mobility of vehicles at present shows the transformational shift in EVs using AI (Aboelezz et al. 2023). Previous studies have explored the inspirational role of AI in EVs adoption, infrastructure, energy consumption, effective battery management, etc. Countries like China, Germany and the United States have significantly contributed to the market of EVs with government support and more innovative technology for a sustainable ecosystem. The companies use AI and ML models to optimize performance and operational efficiency in forecasting EV demand, maintenance management, EV charging power stations and the supply chain (Jahangir et al. 2019). AI's catalyst role in the transportation sector has been expressively addressed in the existing literature to determine customer behavior and demand for EVs based on algorithm models for safer journeys. Blockchain technology also supports the enhancement of EV data security and supply chain management (Capocasale et al. 2025). Thus, AI's intelligent system helps users make real-time decisions (Kahlen et al. 2024). This chapter identifies the most productive authors, journals, countries, affiliations and keywords through bibliometric analysis and discussion. Further discussion is also exhibited on co-occurrence networks and factorial analysis, and relevant themes in AI applications in EVs are identified.

4.4. Most relevant authors

The list of prolific authors with several published articles is presented in Table 4.2 and diagrammatically shown in Figure 4.1. As the number of articles published on the select theme is very low, a gap exists for further research explaining the AI-EV nexus. Through bibliometric analysis, it has been found that out of 59 documents and 221 authors and co-authors (Table 4.2), Gust G, Ketter W, Kim N and Schroer K have published two articles each. In contrast, Abdelrahman M, Aboelezz A, Ahmadian A, Ajay DJ, Akram A and Akram S have published one article each related to AI in EVs. Ul Haq (2024) conducted a study on "Designing electricity distribution networks: The impact of demand coincidence" (Gust et al. 2024) and analyzed the impact of increased electricity demand coincidence for EVs. The authors introduced a model using algorithms to optimize electricity distribution network designs and long-term investments by strategic operators in these cost-effective networks. The findings of this study offered a generalized solution for planning electricity distribution networks: "When new devices with coinciding demand, such as photovoltaic systems or charging stations for electricity vehicles, are connected to a distribution network, network planners can use DNRP-LSDC model to stress-test existing network infrastructures". The other study is published by Ketter et al. (2023) on "Information Systems Research for Smart Sustainable Mobility: A Framework and Call for Action". This study highlighted a technological shift related to AI-based EVs in the transportation sector. This study proposed information systems (ISs) research on designing real-time coordination mechanisms for smart, sustainable mobility ecosystem decisions such as "time horizons, modes of mobility, budget constraints, sustainability constraints, etc.". Similarly, the other authors have explored ML-based decision support systems for forecasting EVs' power requirements, factors affecting the purchase and adoption of EVs, the impact of policies and subsidies on battery pricing, supply chain, etc. These influential works of the prolific authors have significantly contributed to the existing knowledge on AI in EVs, and also provide further scope for research directions in this area for future scholars.

Sr. No.	Authors	Articles
1	Guest G	2
2	Ketter W	2
3	Kim N	2
4	Schroer K	2
5	Abdelrahman M	1
6	Aboelezz A	1
7	Ahmadian A	1
8	Ajay D J	1
9	Akram A	1
10	Akram S	1

Table 4.2. *Most relevant authors and number of articles published. Source: created by authors*

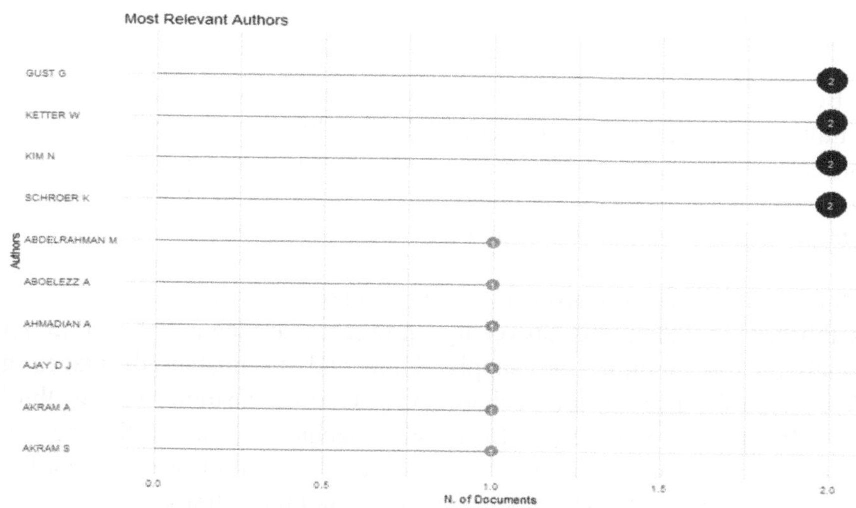

Figure 4.1. *Most relevant authors and the number of documents. Source: obtained from Biblioshiny*

We applied Lotka's law to assess the distribution of authors' productivity (Table 4.3). The results exhibited an acute deviation between theoretical and observed values, indicating a low recurrence (1.8%) in the author's contribution to the field. This contrasts Lotka's theoretical prediction, which suggests that 20% of authors should contribute two papers and the remaining 80% should publish one paper in this area. This variation in the observed and theoretical values suggests that research in this area is still fragmented and needs expert attention.

Documents written	No. of authors	Proportion of authors	Theoretical
1	217	0.982	0.8
2	4	0.018	0.2

Table 4.3. *Lotka's law. Source: obtained from Biblioshiny*

4.5. Most relevant affiliations

Bibliometric analysis was done on the affiliations of the contributing authors with organizations, presented in Table 4.4 and Figure 4.2.

Beijing Jiaotong University in China was identified as the leading institution, with the most publications. Through bibliometric analysis, it was also determined that the most cited country was China. The researchers of this university have focused on the nexus between AI and EVs, the growth of transportation systems, smart mobility and sustainability.

Lovely Professional University was in second place, with six publications. Established in India, this university showcases academic interest in AI models for cost optimization, supply chains and sustainable advantages in EVs. Karlsruhe Institute of Technology, a German institute, was in third place. It has five publications focusing on technology, innovative battery systems and the integration of companies and the government with regard to EV policy implications. The other universities and institutions mentioned are also advancing their knowledge in sustainable transportation, AI, EVs, challenges and policy implications.

Sr. No.	Affiliation	Articles
1	Beijing Jiaotong University	7
2	Lovely Professional University	6
3	Karlsruhe Institute of Technology	5
4	Shenzhen University	5
5	University of the Ryukyus	5
6	Chalmers University of Technology	4
7	Department of Electrical Engineering	4
8	Istanbul Technical University	4
9	Peking University Shenzhen Graduate School	4
10	Harbin University of Commerce	3

Table 4.4. *Most relevant affiliations and number of articles published. Source: created by authors*

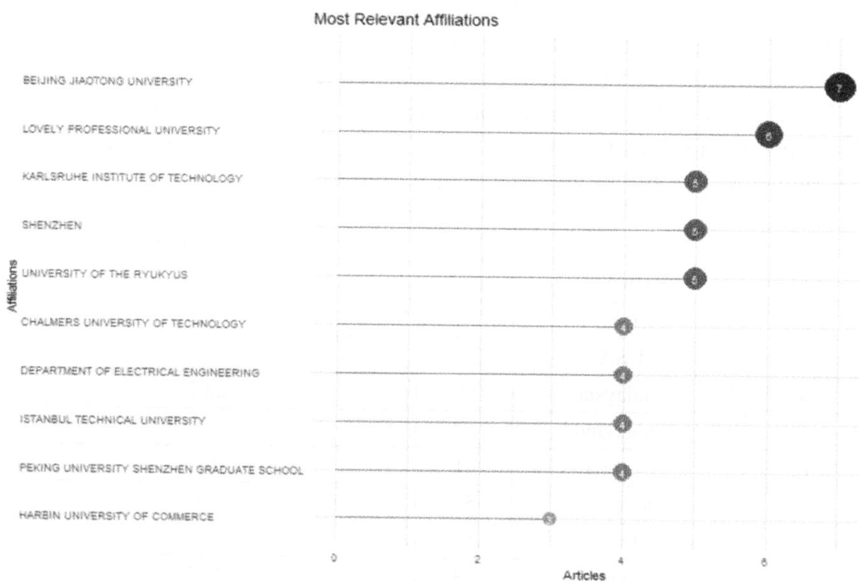

Figure 4.2. *Most relevant affiliations and number of articles. Source: obtained from Biblioshiny*

4.6. Most cited countries

Many countries have contributed to shaping the foundational literature on AI in EVs, and have published research articles. This chapter identifies the top 10 cited countries based on the total citations and average article citations through bibliometric analysis (Figure 4.3). As presented in Table 4.5, China was found to be the top most cited country, with a total of 327 citations and an average of 32.7 citations, due to the growing influence of AI in EVs. With the support of the government, China has become the world leader in AI (Zhang et al. 2023). Also, China's market valuation of AI-related sectors is expected to grow to $1.4 trillion by 2030 (Chen et al. 2024). This has attracted Chinese manufacturers to expand in the EVs sector. China is followed by Germany, the second most cited country, with an impactful total of 273 citations and average of 34.1 citations. It has significantly contributed to automotive engineering worldwide, with the strong implications of AI in EVs (Wang and Yin 2024). The technological transformation of vehicle mobility and sustainable transportation has also been showcased in the United States (Ul Haq et al. 2024). The United States had the third highest total of 220 citations, with an average of 22.5 citations. AI in EVs is gaining traction because of more intelligent batteries, self-driving technology and predictive maintenance for safe journeys (Jamil et al. 2025). AI in vehicles also helps optimize performance with fuel efficiency and reduced emissions (Ul Haq et al. 2022). Therefore, various countries are investing considerably in the market of AI-based EVs.

Sr. No.	Country	TC	Average article citations
1	China	327	32.7
2	Germany	273	34.1
3	USA	220	27.5
4	Malaysia	86	28.7
5	Netherlands	67	67
6	Canada	61	61
7	Denmark	57	57
8	Iran	55	55
9	Poland	43	21.5
10	India	42	7

Table 4.5. *Most cited countries, total citations (TC) and average article citations. Source: created by authors*

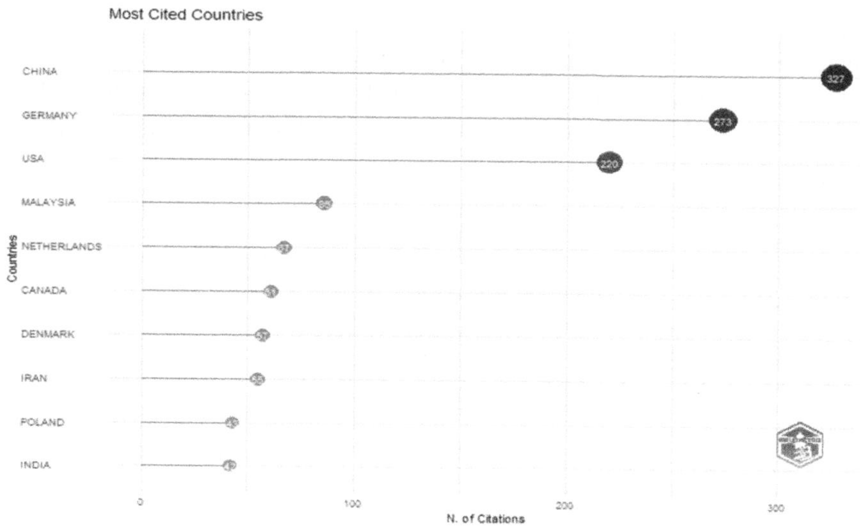

Figure 4.3. *Most cited countries and total citations.*
Source: obtained from Biblioshiny

4.7. Most relevant journals

Table 4.6 and Figure 4.4 represent the journals publishing articles on AI in EVs globally. These journals cover multidisciplinary fields such as transportation, consumer behavior and sustainability. The *Technological Forecasting and Social Change* journal has contributed five publications on AI in EVs. This journal includes studies on social, environmental and technological factors. A few publications in this journal include: "Proactive social learning and green product consumption: Evidence from new energy vehicle sales in China" (Jiang et al. 2025); "Artificial intelligence and machine learning-based decision support system for forecasting electric vehicles' power requirement" (Jauhar et al. 2024); "Enabling a viable circular ecosystem for electric vehicle batteries" (Wellten et al. 2025); "Buy, lease, or share? Consumer preferences for innovative business models in the market for electric vehicles" (Huang et al. 2024); etc. The journals *European Journal of Operational Research*, *IEEE Transactions on Engineering Management*, *Journal of Advanced Transportation*, *Journal of Cleaner Production* and *Journal of Retailing and Consumer Services* have three publications each in multidisciplinary fields of operations and decision sciences, technological innovation, transportation, supply chain, engineering and environmental sustainability. The articles published in these journals have examined AI integration in EV design, batteries, manufacturing and vehicle performance with green innovations. Hence, these journal publications help scholars find future research gaps and directions to add to the limited literature on AI in EVs.

Sr. No.	Journals	Articles
1	*Technological Forecasting and Social Change*	5
2	*European Journal of Operational Research*	3
3	*IEEE Transactions on Engineering Management*	3
4	*Journal of Advanced Transportation*	3
5	*Journal of Cleaner Production*	3
6	*Journal of Retailing and Consumer Services*	3
7	*Information Systems Research*	2
8	*International Journal of Recent Technology and Engineering*	2
9	*Business Horizons*	1
10	*Clean Technologies and Environmental Policy*	1

Table 4.6. *Most relevant journals and number of published articles. Source: created by authors*

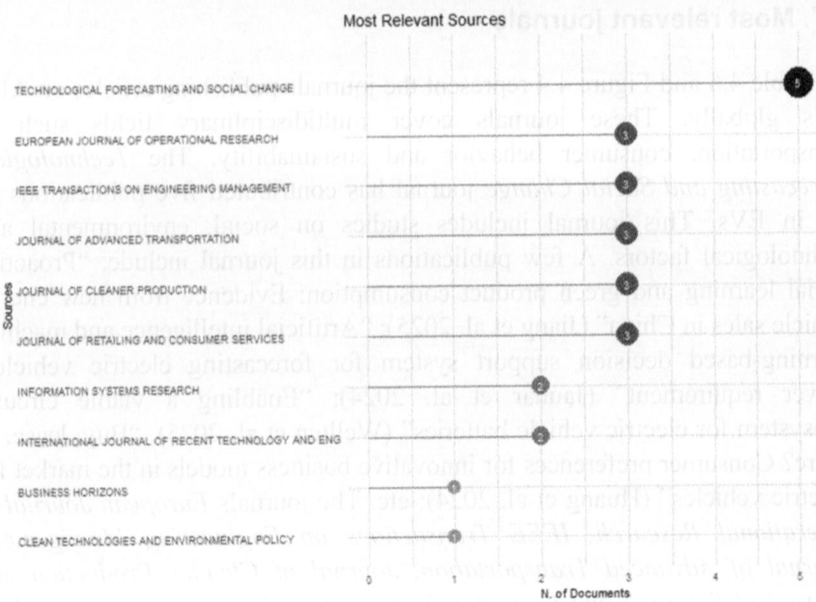

Figure 4.4. *Most relevant journals and the number of documents. Source: created by authors*

4.8. Keyword analysis

We performed the most frequent word analysis using the author's keywords to identify the most prominent keywords (Table 4.7). As expected, "EVs" (Ul Haq et al. 2024) and "AI" (Foroughi et al. 2023) were the most prominent as we used them as search words, and "decision support systems" (Ul Haq et al. 2025d) came in third place. This finding suggests that the confluence of AI and EVs is transforming intelligent transportation. AI is important in enhancing EV safety, efficiency and sustainability.

Keywords	Frequency
Electric vehicle	30
AI	25
Decision support system	6
Autonomous vehicles	3
Big data	3
ML	3
Renewable energy	2
Blockchain	2
Business model	2
Artificial neural network	2

Table 4.7. *Top 10 keywords. Source: created by authors*

4.9. Co-occurrence network analysis

To identify the relationship among the keywords, we performed a co-occurrence analysis (Figure 4.5). A co-occurrence network was obtained using all keywords in the 59 articles on AI in EVs. This analysis was performed using the Walktrap clustering algorithm and association normalization, yielding three major clusters. Below, we have examined each cluster to explore the thematic structure in the existing literature on AI and EVs.

The red cluster is the biggest out of the four clusters. It focuses on the core aspects and challenges related to EVs. A peculiar observation in this cluster is the existence of a thin triangular composition between "EVs", "autonomous vehicles" and "automated vehicles". The linkage suggests an obvious connection between these keywords. However, the words are not frequently interchanged. From the analysis, we also find the presence of bio-inspired algorithms. This is indicated by the keyword "ant colony optimization (ACO)". These algorithms have been applied to resolve operation-related challenges for the deployment of EVs. The existence of studies concerning the issues related to the optimization and deployment of EVs is indicated by keywords such as "vehicle routing", "algorithm" and "ant colony optimization (ACO)". A deeper study of the data reveals the focus of the scholars on social, economic and technical characteristic of EV adoption.

The purple cluster suggests the application of ML for the maintenance and charging of EVs. The keywords in this cluster include "big data", "sustainable development", "microgrid", "information management", "energy" and ML.

The keywords "decision support system", "secondary batteries", "data mining", "decision making", "secondary batteries", "integer programming", "forecasting", "optimization" and "battery electric vehicles", present in the blue cluster, indicate incorporation of AI in decisions related to EV infrastructure. EV infrastructure includes battery technology and management of energy.

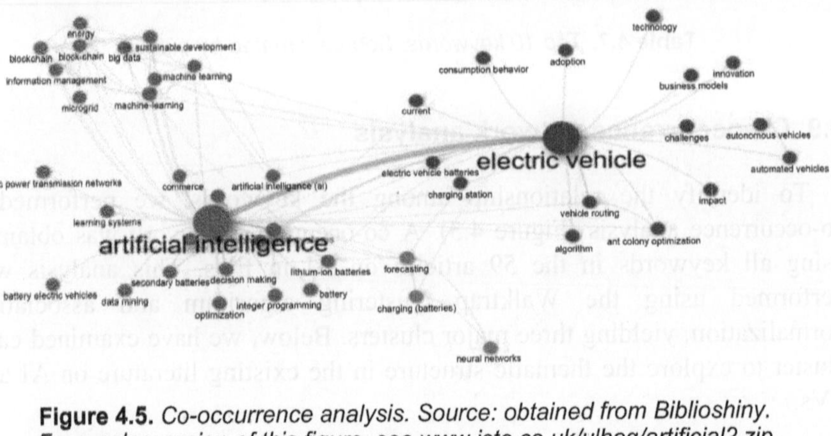

Figure 4.5. *Co-occurrence analysis. Source: obtained from Biblioshiny. For a color version of this figure, see www.iste.co.uk/ulhaq/artificial2.zip*

The green cluster is the smallest out of the four. It highlights a shift in the EV ecosystem. This is exhibited by a triangular co-occurrence between "artificial intelligence", "decision-making", and "decision support systems".

This triangulation represents the intersection of intelligent technologies to support operation-related strategic decisions. These decisions are related to route planning, battery and energy optimization. The cluster exhibits the availability of research on strategies for battery charging and management systems, and the usage of AI in these systems. This is reflected by the keywords "neural networks", "battery electric vehicles" and "charging (batteries)".

4.10. Factorial analysis

This section uncovers the conceptual structure and explores underlying research themes and research gaps in the available data. To do this, we have performed factorial analysis using the method of multiple correspondence analysis (MCA). Fifteen keywords (from all of the keywords) were selected to appear in four clusters. In Figure 4.6, we find two dimensions. Dimension 1 (Dim 1) accounts for a variance of 52.2%. Thus, dimension 1 is a primary factor differentiator of keywords. Hence, we name it as the primary axis. On the other hand dimension two accounts for 17.25% variance. It represents secondary yet important factors in this axis. The distinct themes are represented by four different colored polygons. Each color, red, blue, green and purple, represents a distinct theme. Figure 1.6 exhibits that the primary axis is bifurcated into two research themes. The first theme, on the left side of the map, includes practical research related to EVs, while the second theme, on the right side, contains management-related topics. Similarly, the secondary dimension also contains two categories of keywords. One category indicates the research focused on technicalities or hardware represented by keywords such as "charging" and "batteries". The other category in this dimension highlights the research that focused more on analyses and software associated with EVs.

A close observation highlights that the blue cluster, which is oriented toward EV and battery technology, is farthest from the purple cluster, which focuses on sustainability and management of information. Hence, we draw an inference that there is a scarcity of research establishing the connection of EV technology with sustainability and information management. The map also highlights that the green cluster focused on "smart grids" is acting as a connector between AI in the red cluster and sustainability in the purple cluster, highlighting the role of smart grids in ensuring sustainability through EVs.

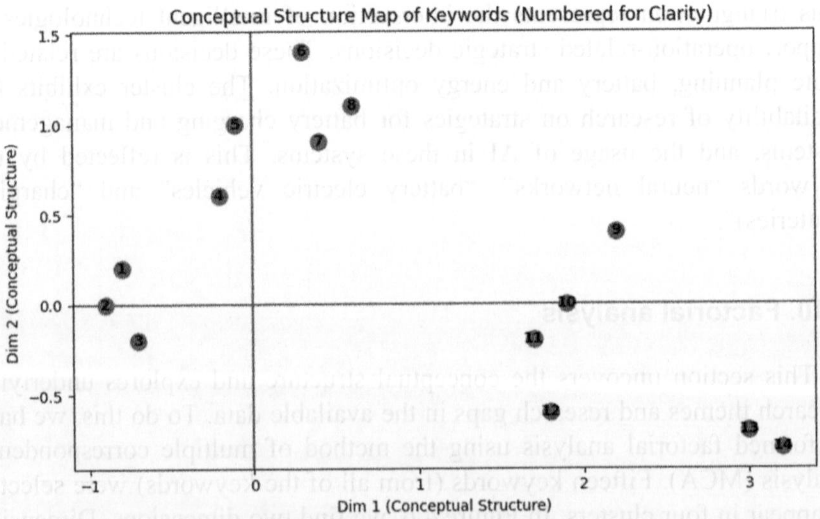

Figure 4.6. *Factorial analysis. Source: obtained from Biblioshiny. For a color version of this figure, see www.iste.co.uk/ulhaq/artificial2.zip*

Based on the map (Figure 4.6) and the above discussion, we have identified four themes in AI and EV literature that are discussed below.

4.10.1. *AI for sustainable electric vehicles*

The analysis showed that AI is applied to develop sustainable EVs. AI-powered autonomous vehicles (AVs) have a broad range of social implications such as safety, environmental protection and equity (Foroughi et al. 2023). DL techniques can assist in improving product design for the remanufacturing of EVs, thereby improving the manufacturers' utility per unit cost (Ma et al. 2025). Deep neural networks are used to automate feeder routing based exclusively on aerial images to benefit the operational planning of electricity distribution networks, thereby enhancing EVs' scaling up (Ameling and Gust 2024). ChatGPT, an intelligent chatbot, is used to optimize the recycling process of EV batteries, ensuring utmost efficiency (Feng et al. 2024). To foster the use of sustainable smart connect cars, privacy concerns need to be addressed (Choi and Lowry 2024). Though EVs or AVs seem promising for sustainable solutions, the implications of human-centered design principles in AV development cannot be ignored (Banda and Chandra 2025).

4.10.2. *AI for smart mobility*

The smart mobility of EVs can be improved through AI applications, as shown in the analysis. The EV distribution systems can be improvised with the help of novel AI techniques considering the routing of EV vehicles, battery capacity and charging stations for cost reductions (Goli et al. 2022). For instance, AI can improve energy efficiency regarding the average distance per kW and energy consumption (Joo and Lim 2018). However, AI-enabled smart vehicles must develop IS communities for a profound sociotechnological transformation (Cui and Zhao 2024). AI can also be used to develop novel mobility systems such as Personal Rapid Transit, an emergent mode of transportation. It uses a tiny, autonomous electric car fleet to move people about as needed. However, many Personal Rapid Transit cars travel empty due to the system's unique on-demand feature, resulting in a significant amount of wasted transit capacity. AI applications can assist in reducing such wastage (Fatnassi et al. 2017).

4.10.3. *AI for sustainable infrastructure*

AI and ML techniques can be used to address the challenges related to the infrastructure development for EVs. Through data-based predictions and precise power demands of charging stations, the optimal features can be found to maximize engagement and operational efficiencies (Jauhar et al. 2024). The AI models use weather and historical power data to predict wind power outputs for optimized electricity supply (Ul Haq et al. 2025c). Those are also applied to maximize power generation from the wind turbine throughout the day with various wind speeds (Aboelezz et al. 2023). AI is used to simplify the decision-making process when using blockchain technologies to address the actual needs of the EV supply chain (Capocasale et al. 2025). AI is helpful to achieve efficient operation and energy management in microgrids (Elkholy et al. 2024). Battery management for robot-supported systems optimizes operational policies and fast-charging systems (Chen et al. 2024).

4.10.4. *AI for information management*

AI for information management is seen across a range of contexts in EVs. AI applications for EV vehicles can be seen in the data management for marketing-related decisions. AI and ML techniques such as support vector machines, artificial or deep neural networks, distributed random forests and gradient boosting models can be used to analyze consumer data and gain insights into the purchasing behavior of consumers for strategic marketing decisions (Bas et al. 2021; Huang et al. 2021). Moreover, the data that include the time of arrival, time of departure and length of the trip covered by the EVs can be used to improve the power system (Jahangir et al. 2019). Braumandl et al. (2023) suggest that application of an artificial neural network (ANN) is no longer limited to gaining insights into consumer behavior, but is also extended to assess drivers' behavior. One of the innovative applications of the ML method is the gradient-boosting decision tree algorithm. The application of this algorithm helps to improve accuracy when predicting driving range. It also provides EV users with reliable information related to the battery's efficiency (Sun et al. 2019). Natural language processing (NLP) techniques are helpful in the case of EVs for measuring knowledge flows, mapping technological change and creating patent quality indicators (Hain et al. 2022), whereas decision support systems enable the allocation of shared electric vehicles (SUVs) in real-time to the rental or electricity markets as a virtual power plant (Kahlen et al. 2024).

4.11. Thematic map

To delve further into the themes, we built a thematic map in a network approach focused on the clusters' centrality and density (Figure 4.7). We removed the repetitive words. We used the "Walktrap" algorithm to build the clusters. This map was built to visualize the association among research themes. This map shows four quadrants based on centrality (X-axis) and density (Y-axis). Centrality represents the relevance and significance of the themes, and the themes high in centrality are considered key for developing inquiry in the field. Density exhibits the "maturity" or the "development" of the research in a field. The keywords that fall in high-density areas indicate well-developed research with the presence of a strong research community. The thematic map (Figure 4.7) indicates that "commerce", "lithium batteries", and "electric vehicle" fall in the Motor Themes quadrant, which suggests that these themes are highly developed and also important.

The hematic map (Figure 4.7) highlights a surge in the interest of the research community in this area. "Electricity Distribution Grids", falling in the Niche quadrant (high density and low centrality) is a specialized area. A major contributor to this theme is the study of Huang and Qian (2021). A close look at bibliometric data indicates the interdisciplinary approach adopted when investigating the theme of AI in EVs. The coexistence of clusters on "Commerce", "Decision Support Systems", and "Business Models" indicates a strong linkage between technology and businesses.

In the thematic map (Figure 4.7), the basic theme quadrant on the lower right of the map contains "Autonomous Vehicle" and "Decision Support System". It is a central theme, but has not received much attention from the researchers. The lower quadrant on the left side of the map contains two extreme themes: emerging and declining. The map suggests that "Innovation" is an emerging theme. On the other hand, "wind energy" is an established area of research. A deeper study of the available literature suggests that more attention is being paid to the "wind energy" theme in other areas. These areas include automation, electric power transmission and electricity distribution. This observable phenomenon aligns with our central theme of AI and EVs.

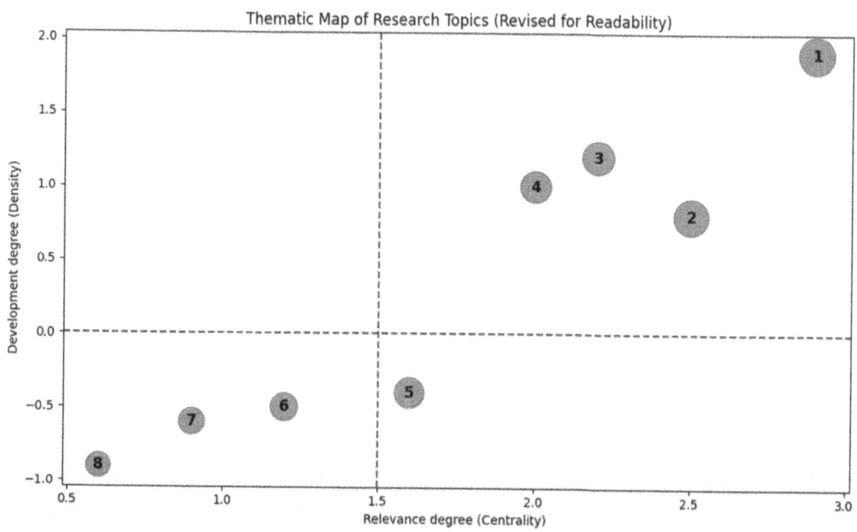

Figure 4.7. *Thematic map. Source: created in Biblioshiny. For a color version of this figure, see www.iste.co.uk/ulhaq/artificial2.zip*

4.12. Chronological mapping of the most influential documents

Historiography has been created to exhibit a temporal citation network and uncover the intellectual structure of the AI-EV nexus in recent times.

The four nodes present in the network (Figure 4.8) represent the articles that appeared between the years 2021 and 2025. It reflects the progression of literary work on AI in EVs, divided into two clusters. The red cluster focuses on AV adoption, whereas the blue cluster highlights the studies on electricity distribution. In Figure 4.8, Huang and Qian's (2021) article "Understanding The potential adoption of autonomous vehicles in China: The perspective of behavioral reasoning theory" appears in the red cluster and is a groundbreaking work. The article investigated the preference for automated vehicles in China, and this was further investigated by Foroughi et al. (2023), who employed PLS-SEM and ANFIS to explore the intentions behind adopting automated vehicles. Cluster 2, in blue, is led by Gust et al.'s (2024) work "Designing electricity distribution networks the impact of demand coincidence", which was cited by (Ameling and Gust 2024) in "Automated feeder routing for underground electricity distribution networks based on aerial images".

Figure 4.8. *Historiography capturing the temporal citation network. Source: created in Biblioshiny*

4.13. Conclusion

The incorporation of AI has made decision-making data-driven and automated, enabling many stakeholders, from fleet operators to policymakers, to track and analyze information related to energy consumption, battery endurance, traffic conditions and environmental impact. Because of this modification, accurate forecasting, efficient resources allocation and sorting of environmental issues have become very easy. Therefore, the improved operational performance of the vehicles, reduced emissions and optimum utilization of energy resources have been witnessed with the use of smart technology. By mapping the landscape of AI in EVs in this chapter, recent trends on the topic, key authors, key journals and key leading institutions in the field of AI in EVs are highlighted.

Important themes are also discovered in this chapter to lay foundation for authors to research further. Other than Scopus and WoS, other databases such as Google Scholar, Semantic Scholar, dimensions and EBSCO are also suggested to future researchers to incorporate the documents on AI in EVs to present broader insights. This is the limitation of this study.

4.14. References

Aboelezz, A., Makeen, P., Ghali, H.A., Elbayomi, G., Abdelrahman, M.M. (2023). Electric vehicle battery charging framework using artificial intelligence modeling of a small wind turbine based on experimental characterization. *Clean Technologies and Environmental Policy*, 25(4), 1149–1161.

Ahmed, M., Zheng, Y., Amine, A., Fathiannasab, H., Chen, Z. (2021). The role of artificial intelligence in the mass adoption of electric vehicles. *Joule*, 5(9), 2296–2322.

Ameling, J. and Gust, G. (2024). Automated feeder routing for underground electricity distribution networks based on aerial images. *European Journal of Operational Research*, 318(2), 629–641.

Banda, L.G. and Chandra, S. (2025). Natural intelligence in autonomous vehicles: Redefining the path to human-centric adoption. *Journal of Retailing and Consumer Services*, 84, 104195.

Bas, J., Cirillo, C., Cherchi, E. (2021). Classification of potential EV purchasers using machine learning. *Technological Forecasting and Social Change*, 168, 120759.

Braumandl, A., Ponnraj, A., Brückel, J., Bause, K., Albers, A. (2023). Utilising artifial intelligence to investigate the relevance of customer benefits. *International Journal of Innovation Management*, 27(05), 2340006.

Capocasale, V., Bruni, M.E., Perboli, G. (2025). Technological insights on blockchain adoption: The electric vehicle supply chain use case. *European Journal of Innovation Management*, 28(11), 23–48.

Chen, W., Gong, Y., Chen, Q., Wang, H. (2024). Does battery management matter? Performance evaluation and operating policies in a self-climbing robotic warehouse. *European Journal of Operational Research*, 312(1), 164–181.

Choi, D.D. and Lowry, P.B. (2024). Balancing the common good and personal privacy: Adoption of sustainable smart connected cars. *Information & Management*, 61(1), 103876.

Cui, S. and Zhao, N. (2024). A study on the current status and future prospects of EV automotive market. *Journal of Social Science and Cultural Development*, 1(2).

Elkholy, M.H., Senjyu, T., Gamil, M.M., Lotfy, M.E., Song, D., Ludin, G.A., Irshad, A.S., Said, T. (2024). Multistage predictive energy management strategy for EVs. *Journal of Cleaner Production*, 476, 143765.

Fatnassi, E., Chebbi, O., Chaouachi, J. (2017). Dealing with empty vehicle movements in PRT systems with battery constraints. *Journal of Advanced Transportation*, 2017(1), 8512728.

Feng, J., Ning, Y., Wang, Z., Li, G., Xu, S.X. (2024). ChatGPT-enabled two-stage auctions for electric vehicle battery recycling. *Transportation Research Part E*, 183, 103453.

Foroughi, B., Nhan, P.V., Iranmanesh, M., Ghobakhloo, M., Nilashi, M., Yadegaridehkordi, E. (2023). Determinants of intention to use autonomous vehicles: Findings from PLS-SEM and ANFIS. *Journal of Retailing and Consumer Services*, 70, 103158.

Geels, F.W. (2012). A socio-technical analysis of low-carbon transitions: Introducing the multi-level perspective into transport studies. *Journal of Transport Geography*, 24, 471–482.

Goli, A., Golmohammadi, A.M., Verdegay, J.L. (2022). RETRACTED: Two-echelon EV routing problem using moth-flame heuristic. *Operations Management Research*, 15(3), 891–912.

Gust, G., Schlüter, A., Feuerriegel, S., Úbeda, I., Lee, J.T., Neumann, D. (2024). Designing electricity distribution networks: The impact of demand coincidence. *European Journal of Operational Research*, 315, 271–288.

Hain, D.S., Jurowetzki, R., Buchmann, T., Wolf, P. (2022). Text-embedding approach to patent similarity. *Technological Forecasting and Social Change*, 177, 121559.

Huang, Y. and Qian, L. (2021). Understanding potential adoption of autonomous vehicles in China. *Psychology and Marketing*, 38(4), 669–690.

Huang, Y., Qian, L., Soopramanien, D., Tyfield, D. (2021). Buy, lease, or share? Consumer preferences for innovative business models in electric vehicles. *Technological Forecasting and Social Change*, 166, 120639.

Jahangir, H., Tayarani, H., Ahmadian, A., Golkar, M.A., Miret, J., Tayarani, M., Gao, H.O. (2019). Charging demand of plug-in electric vehicles: Forecasting travel behavior based on a novel rough artificial neural network approach. *Journal of Cleaner Production*, 229, 1029–1044.

Jamil, U., Alva, R.J., Ahmed, S., Jin, Y.F. (2025). Artificial intelligence-driven optimal charging strategy for electric vehicles and impacts on electric power grid. *Electronics*, 14(7), 1471.

Jauhar, S.K., Sethi, S., Kamble, S.S., Mathew, S., Belhadi, A. (2024). AI and ML-based decision support system for forecasting electric vehicles' power requirement. *Technological Forecasting and Social Change*, 204, 123396.

Jiang, Z., Liu, N., Zhang, X., Chu, Y., Zhang, L. (2025). Proactive social learning and green product consumption: Evidence from new energy vehicle sales in China. *Technological Forecasting and Social Change*, 219, 124232.

Joo, H. and Lim, Y. (2018). Ant colony optimized routing strategy for electric vehicles. *Journal of Advanced Transportation*, 2018(1), 5741982.

Kahlen, M., Schroer, K., Ketter, W., Gupta, A. (2024). Smart markets for real-time allocation of multiproduct resources: The case of shared electric vehicles. *Information Systems Research*, 35(2), 871–889.

Ketter, W., Schroer, K., Valogianni, K. (2023). Information systems research for smart sustainable mobility: A framework and call for action. *Information Systems Research*, 34(3), 1045–1065.

Ma, Y., Xia, X., Guo, J., Zhang, C. (2025). A deep reinforcement learning method solving bilevel optimization for product design considering remanufacturing. *IEEE Transactions on Engineering Management*, 72, 573–590.

Shamszadeh, S., Asgary, S., Nosrat, A. (2019). Regenerative endodontics: A scientometric and bibliometric analysis. *Journal of Endodontics*, 45(3), 272–280.

Sun, S., Zhang, J., Bi, J., Wang, Y. (2019). A machine learning method for predicting EV driving range. *Journal of Advanced Transportation*, 2019(1), 4109148.

Ul Haq, I. (2024). Diagnosis of neurological disease using bioinspired algorithms. In *Bio-Inspired Optimization for Medical Data Mining*, Srivastava, S., Anand, A., Kumar, A. et al. (eds). John Wiley & Sons, Hoboken, NJ.

Ul Haq, I.U. and Khanday, A.M.U.D. (2025). Exploring the role of explainable AI in women's health: Challenges and solutions. In *Explainable Artificial Intelligence in the Healthcare Industry*, Kumar, A., Kumar, T.A., Das, P. et al. (eds). John Wiley & Sons, Hoboken, NJ.

Ul Haq, I.U., Kumar, N., Koul, N., Verma, C., Eneacu, F.M., Raboaca, M.S. (2022). Machine learning techniques for result prediction of one day international (ODI) cricket match. In *The International Conference on Recent Innovations in Computing*. Springer, Singapore.

Ul Haq, I.U., Kaur, G., Rather, A.H. (2024). Fruit leaf classification using transfer learning for automation and industrial applications. In *Deep Learning Techniques for Automation and Industrial Applications*, Rathore, P.S., Ahuja, S., Burri, S.R. et al. (eds). John Wiley & Sons, Hoboken, NJ.

Ul Haq, I.U., Khanday, A.M.D., Shah, H.A., Rufai, S.Z. (2025a). Enhancing water security through automation: Case studies and technical advancements in water quality management. In *Computational Automation for Water Security*, Dubey, A.K., Srivastav, A.L., Kumar, A. et al. (eds). Elsevier, Amsterdam.

Ul Haq, I.U., Kumar, A., Rathore, P.S. (2025b). Machine learning approaches for wind power forecasting: A comprehensive review. *Discover Applied Sciences*, 7(10), 1139.

Ul Haq, I.U., Malhotra, J., Rawat, V., Kumari, J., Kaur, G. (2025c). Machine learning approaches for early detection of cervical cancer: A comparative study of classification models. In *Targeted Chemotherapy with Personalized Immunotherapy: An AI Approach*, Kumar, A., Das, P., Rathore, P.S. et al. (eds). John Wiley & Sons, Hoboken, NJ.

Ul Haq, I.U., Nandal, V., Uppal, H. (2025d). Blockchain applications in aviation securing transactions, streamlining operations, and improving passenger experience. In *Blockchain in the Tourism Industry: A New Era of Secure and Transparent Travel Solutions*, Kumar, A., Abreu, A., Batta, P. et al. (eds). Springer, Cham.

Wang, R. and Yin, Y. (2024). Exploring the impact of artificial intelligence on knowledge management in automotive manufacturing within different cultures. *ECKM*, 25(1), 1051–1061.

Wellten, J., Angelis, J., da Silva, E.R. (2025). Enabling a viable circular ecosystem for electric vehicle batteries. *Technological Forecasting and Social Change*, 210, 123876.

Zhang, Q., Tian, S., Lin, X. (2023). Recent advances and applications of AI-based mathematical modeling in predictive control of hybrid electric vehicle energy management in China. *Electronics*, 12(2), 445.

5

AI-Enabled Predictive and Adaptive Solutions for Environmental and Energy Challenges

The rapid rate at which we are witnessing climate change, environmental degradation and a global energy crisis has produced an urgency in the search for intelligent, scalable and adaptive solutions. Artificial intelligence (AI), which is capable of processing intricate data, identifying trends in information that is thought to be unobvious and producing information that can be acted upon, has been a disruptive way of addressing these critical problems. This chapter provides a careful analysis of AI-based predictive and adaptive systems, which are directed to enhance the monitoring of the environment, optimization of resources, management of risks of disasters and planning of sustainable energy resources. The chapter discusses the applications of machine learning (ML), deep learning (DL) and reinforcement learning (RL) in forecasting climatic variables, extreme weather, optimization of renewable energy and management of a smart grid. Special attention is paid to adaptive AI systems that are able to respond to the dynamism of the surrounding environment in real-time. In addition, this chapter talks about how AI can be applied to the carbon footprint, air and water quality monitoring, and biodiversity protection. The data quality pitfalls, the visibility of models and ethical governance are also examined rather critically. The chapter also features how AI-based innovations are supposed to be applied to support policy planning and facilitate the global response to a resilient and low-carbon society in terms of real-life case studies and major trends in new research.

5.1. Introduction

The high rate of environmental degradation that the world has experienced has been largely due to rapid industrialization, urbanization, deforestation as well as the over exploitation of natural resources. Climate

---

Chapter written by Inderdeep KAUR.

change is no longer a distant threat, but is an urgent global challenge. Heat waves have already begun to significantly affect the environment and human communities. Traditional environmental management methods also rely on reactionary methods of decision-making and their applicability is limited as they use historical data for analysis and, as such, cannot give a prediction and response to dynamic, troubled environmental changes. At the same time, the energy business is witnessing unparalleled circumstances due to the rise in demand, the unstable availability of fossil fuels and the urgent need to transition to renewable and sustainable energy offers. These issues demand innovative, intelligent and dynamic technological solutions.

The ability to analyze big amounts of various data, determine the latent trends and make real-time decisions has made AI an effective problem solver in the field of the environment and energy (Kaur and Ali 2024a). AI-based systems can learn from the past and present trends and factors and come up with correct predictions in terms of climate trends, levels of pollution, energy usage and resource availability (Saini et al. 2024). Unlike traditional systems, AI-based solutions can be dynamically adjusted to the changing environmental conditions to provide a more efficient management of resources and prevent risks related to extreme weather conditions and environmental disasters, as well as energy shortages.

AI implementation in environmental intelligence systems, as shown in Figure 5.1, has opened up novel possibilities of active monitoring and efficient planning. With the current intelligent algorithms, policymakers, environmental agencies and energy planners are now able to come up with data-driven strategies that encourage conservation, resilience and low-carbon development. The use of AI and modern sensing technologies has enabled the monitoring of forests, oceans, glaciers, wildlife and urban ecosystems with even greater precision, continuous monitoring and scale (Kaur and Ali 2025).

In this chapter, the AI technologies that underpin environmental intelligence and the ways in which they are also applied in predictive modeling, automated monitoring and adaptive management of natural and energy resources will be discussed. It specifically focuses on the role of the AI technologies when integrated with real-world data sources and computational systems in changing how societies react to global environmental and energy issues.

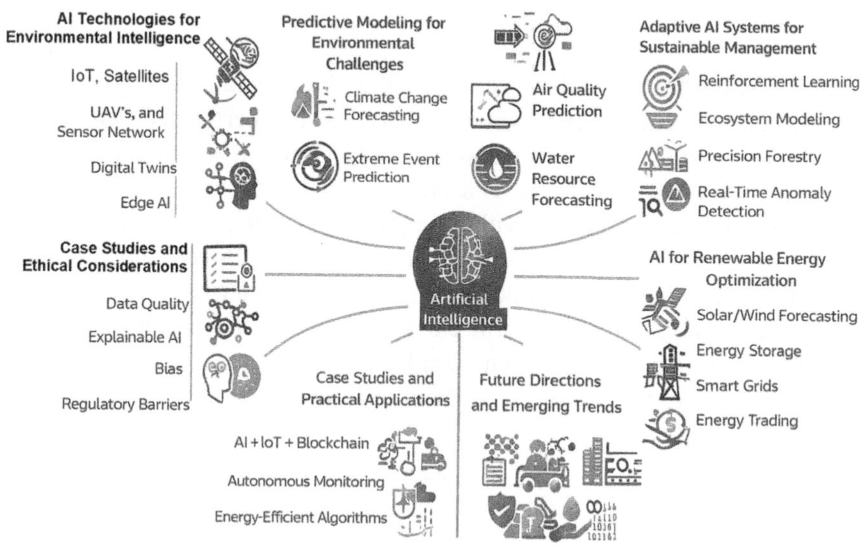

Figure 5.1. *AI-enabled predictive and adaptive solutions for environmental and energy challenges. For a color version of this figure, see www.iste.co.uk/ulhaq/artificial2.zip*

5.2. AI technologies for environmental intelligence

Modern environmental intelligence systems are based on AI technologies (Kaur and Ali 2024b). Such technologies can process data, make decisions, recognize patterns, forecast and support the work of intricate ecological and energy systems in an automated way.

As access to large-scale environmental data becomes easier, computational abilities are being strengthened and smarter sensing infrastructure is being created, AI provides a fast and efficient system for interpreting environmental phenomena and how that can help in the sustainable management of resources. AI methods are also being actively applied in different areas of the environment, whether it is predicting changes in the climate or optimizing the production of renewable energy as well as monitoring the health of the ecosystem. The conceptual framework for AI Technologies for environmental intelligence is shown in Figure 5.2.

5.2.1. *Overview of AI, ML and DL techniques*

AI is a wide discipline that is concerned with the creation of systems that can execute functions that would otherwise be performed by human intelligence, that is, learning, reasoning and problem solving (Kaur and Inzimam Ul Hassan 2025). ML is a branch of AI, which allows systems to acquire patterns based on data without a program having been written down. Linear regression, decision trees, support vector machines and ensemble algorithms are some of the popular ML algorithms that have been used in environmental research to perform classification, regression and prediction tasks (Sharma et al. 2024a). The applications of these methods include forecasting pollution, land-use classification, forecasting rainfall and energy demand modeling.

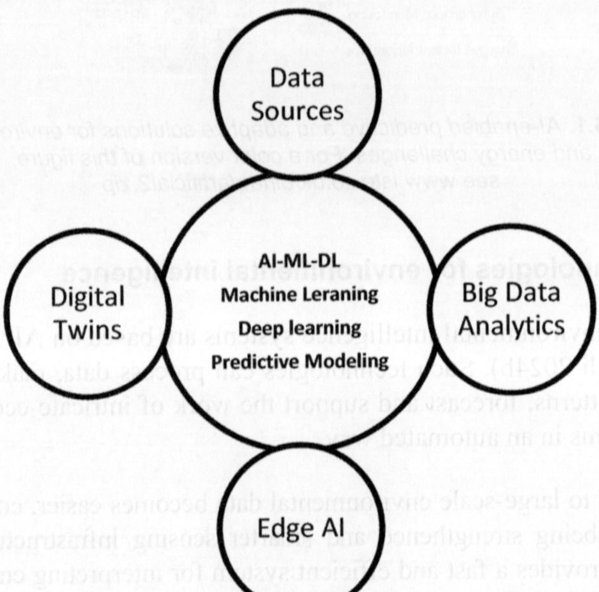

Figure 5.2. *AI technologies for environmental intelligence conceptual framework*

DL is another specialization of ML in which multiple layer artificial neural networks are used to analyze high dimensional and complex data. Convolutional neural networks (CNNs) and other types of DL models are applied widely to image-based analysis, in both satellite imagery and land cover analysis (Saini and Kaur 2025). Time-series data are typically handled with recurrent neural networks (RNNs) and long short-term memory (LSTM) networks and can be used to make reliable predictions of climate variables such as temperature, precipitation, wind speed and solar radiation. Another important branch of AI is RL, which is being used more and more in adaptive environmental control systems and smart energy grid management, whereby optimal strategies are learnt based on feedback and interaction with the environment.

These AI methods combined provide massive benefits in comparison to conventional methods of analysis as the nonlinear relationship association is processed, the uncertainty is handled and performance is constantly enhanced through learning.

5.2.2. *Data sources: IoT, satellite, UAVs and sensor networks*

The availability of a wide variety of quality, real-time data sources are critical to the success of AI models in environment-related uses (Sharma et al. 2024b). Among the most significant developments in the field, the increase in Internet of Things (IoT) devices and sensor networks should be mentioned. Such sensors are used in air, water, soil and urban areas to measure vital parameters including temperature, humidity, pH and the levels of pollutants and radiation. The real-time data streams produced by these devices are a good source of input, which AI models can use to monitor changes in the environment and spot anomalies.

Another important source of data is satellite imagery, which gives many observations of the surface and atmosphere of the earth on a large scale and with a high resolution. Satellite remote sensing is used to check deforestation, melting ice caps, ocean temperatures, urban heat islands and land use. The recent development of image processing and DL has greatly enhanced the accuracy of automated feature extraction of satellite images. Similarly, unmanned aerial vehicles (UAVs), more popularly referred to as drones, offer precise and localized information on the environment particularly in remote or dangerous locations such as forests, coastal and disaster-prone zones.

When combined with various sources of data, such as AI-based systems, a multi-dimensional and in-depth knowledge of the functioning of the environment is formed, which increases the accuracy and validity of AI-based predictions and decisions.

5.2.3. *Big data analytics in environmental systems*

Environmental data are said to be voluminous, high velocity, varied and complex (Kaur and Inzimam-Ul-Hassan 2024). Combining sensor data, satellite imaging, meteorological data and social–environmental data leads to huge datasets that are challenging to process through traditional ways. In the management and analysis of these huge data streams, big data analytics, coupled with AI, is significant. The storage, processing and visualization of large-scale environmental data in real time or near real time are now possible due to the high-performance computing platforms and cloud-based infrastructure.

Big data analytics built on AI can be used to identify long-term trends and meaning in the complex data. As an example, it enables us to consider decades of climate data, which will help reveal the trends of global warming or detecting pollution sources in cities. Such analytical functions are also useful in scenario modeling and impact assessment, which enables a researcher and decision-maker to consider the various environmental and energy strategies in an effective way.

5.2.4. *Digital twins and edge AI for environmental monitoring*

A recent area of AI-driven environmental intelligence development is the emergence of digital twins which are virtual versions of physical systems and constantly update with real-time information. Digital twins are used in the environmental field to model ecosystems, watersheds, cities or energy systems, whereby scientists can simulate different conditions and make predictions. As an example, a computerized version of a river basin can be used to predict flood events related to rain patterns and land use changes.

Edge AI also enhances monitoring capabilities as it enables data processing at the location or near the source, obviating the need for data transfer of large volumes of data to the central data servers. This is especially beneficial in remote areas or bandwidth-intensive areas. Connected devices with edge AI devices have intelligent algorithms and are able to make real-time Monte Carlo detection and real-time response actions such as generating alerts when there are spikes in pollution or deviant energy consumption trends.

With the integration of digital twins and edge computing, environmental monitoring systems are more reactionary, effective and autonomous and the opportunity emerge to develop intelligent and versatile management of natural and energy resources.

5.3. Predictive modeling for environmental challenges

Predictive modeling has become one of the most powerful uses of AI in addressing global environmental problems (Weyn et al. 2019). By being able to learn from historical data and continuously update from real-time information, AI-based predictive models are able to enhance the accuracy of predictions about environmental changes and extreme events. Applications have been especially useful in analyses of weather patterns, the identification of early warning signs of disasters, the prediction of pollution levels and in better management of water resources. With the environment systems increasingly becoming dynamic with a changing climate that has been affected by humans, the predictive models with ML and DL are offering crucial decision support tools to plan a sustainable future and also to be prepared for any emergency.

AI-based predictive modeling uses a vast amount of data intelligence from satellite imagery, meteorological data, oceanographic data, air and water quality and socioeconomic indicators. Such models combine the multi-dimensional data with each other to learn from it and, therefore, help governments, environmental agencies and researchers take proactive action rather than waiting until the damages are done. This transition from reactive to predictive environmental management is fundamental to how ecological and energy-related risks will be assessed and mitigated.

5.3.1. *Climate change forecasting using AI*

Climate change prediction is one of the most important uses of AI in environmental science. It is necessary to predict the long-term changes in temperature, precipitation patterns, rise in sea-level and extreme weather conditions to take effective measures to mitigate against climate changes. Physical simulation-based traditional climate models may be computationally costly and unable to capture localized changes in climate. However, AI-based models can learn using huge historical climate data as well as real-time sensors and satellite data, which enable them to make more precise and place-based predictions.

DL models like support vector machines, random forests and gradient boosting users regularly engage large-scale climate data and find associations between the variables in the atmosphere. LSTM networks and other RNNs are especially effective with DL techniques in order to capture the temporal correlation of climate data. These models are capable of absorbing seasonal trends and long-term cycles, thus making accurate predictions of the climatic condition in the future. As an example, LSTM-based networks have been quite successful in predicting long-term temperature anomalies and rainfall variability in various areas of the world.

AI is also significantly used in scaling global climate model results to regional or local models. It is of particular significance to policymakers and urban planners who need fine-grained information to develop infrastructure to be prepared for disasters and plan agricultural activities. Through more precise and local climate predictions, AI can be used to better enable governments and communities to develop specific adaptation policies, mitigate the risks posed by climate change and develop resilience to the impacts of climate change over the long term.

5.3.2. *AI-based extreme event prediction (floods, wildfires and cyclones)*

Climate change has seen an increase in the frequency and intensity of extreme environment events, including floods, wildfires, cyclones, droughts and heatwaves. The prediction of such disasters at the right time and in the right place is important to minimize human and economic losses and to save natural ecosystems. AI-based systems can now be used to provide early warning signals that are more precise and fast compared to traditional methods and predict the probability of extreme events.

Flood prediction models are based on rain data, river levels, the content of soil and topography. Random forests and neural network ML algorithms can be used to analyze intricate hydrological processes to predict when and how bad a flood will be. Through the combination of IoT sensors and weather station real-time data, AI models will be able to provide dynamic and location-specific flood warnings and allow authorities to execute evacuation strategies and emergency interventions in a timely way.

Equally, AI forecasting of temperature, humidity, vegetation density, wind speed and past fire data add value in wildfire prediction. Using satellite imaging, DL models can be used to identify vegetation dry areas and early fire outbreaks. In hurricane and cyclone prone areas, AI systems track the sea surface temperature, atmospheric pressure, and wind patterns and with such information accurately predict the path and intensity of the storms. This allows better preparedness against disaster, such as reinforcing the infrastructure and evacuation plans for the population.

The development of AI within disaster risk management systems may be used to respond to a disaster much better and allow for a better distribution of resources. Instead of using broad predictions, AI facilitates true and accurate real-time predictions based on particular geographical areas and conditions.

5.3.3. *Air quality and pollution level prediction*

Air pollution is among the major causes of death and disease across the world. Air quality levels therefore need to be predicted to put in place pollution control measures. Air quality prediction models using AI use monitoring stations, traffic flow, industrial emissions, weather conditions and satellite data to calculate the levels of pollutants (PM2.5, PM10, NO_2, SO_2 and CO).

The nonlinearity and dynamism of air pollution are usually difficult to incorporate into statistical models that are traditionally based on linear models and this is likely to add complexity with a vast number of interacting factors. AI models, specifically neural networks and ensemble models, outperform the usual methods because they learn complicated correlations between various variables. Such systems have the ability to predict the quality of air both in the short-term and the long-term, and this gives governments and citizens preventive measures like restricting outdoor activities or enforcing traffic control.

Moreover, spatial AI models with geographic information systems (GIS) allow pollution hotspots in cities to be mapped and visualized. Both LSTM and CNN models have the ability to combine time and space patterns to give fine-grained predictions in location and time (Ul Haq 2026c). Such predictive abilities are necessary in the formulation of more intelligent urban planning policies, the maximization of traffic movement and the establishment of green buffers, which include trees and parks in high-pollution areas. AI-driven air quality forecasting systems are becoming crucial in minimizing environmental risks to human health and enhancing the general quality of life in the metropolis.

5.3.4. *Water resource and quality forecasting*

Water is an essential resource that promotes agriculture, industry and the ecosystem, which is of course essential for human survival. Nonetheless, climate change, over-extraction and pollution are becoming a threat to the availability of freshwater. AI water resource forecasting has been one of the key tools that can be used to support sustainable water management and secure an adequate water supply in the long term. These systems are able to forecast the availability of reservoir water, ground water and demand trends using past data and rainfall, and consumption history.

Forecasts of seasonal water scarcity or abnormal precipitation are made by ML and DL models to enable authorities to plan the use of water more efficiently. In the agricultural sector, AI water prediction is applicable in improving the irrigation process and reducing waste among farmers.

Pollution sources can also be detected with the help of AI-powered monitoring systems, which track any abnormal alterations in the data about water quality. Such technologies are incorporated in smart cities in intelligent water management systems that are able to detect leakages and predict failure in a pipeline as well as automated treatment processes. AI also assists in reducing water loss and has given a more stable and secure water supply by enabling early detection and predictive maintenance.

5.4. Adaptive AI systems for sustainable management

The increasing complexity of the degradation of the environment, the depletion of resources and climatic variability needs not just smart but also agile management systems. Conventional methods of environmental management are generally sterile because they are based on pre-defined policies and frequent assessment. These methods are no longer adequate in the modern conditions of the fast development of the ecological environment, where it is necessary to monitor everything in real time and make decisions immediately. Adaptive AI systems are a paradigm shift in sustainable management practices, in which dynamic learning, responding to changes in real time, and optimizing actions constantly can take place based on the changing environmental conditions.

Adaptive AI systems are designed to react to some environmental feedback and then adjust their behavior. Such systems have the ability to analyze how data trends are changing, evaluating the results of historical movements, and change some of their strategies to improve their performance in the future. This would be particularly useful in applications such as energy distribution, protection of wildlife, agriculture and forestry, and the management of urban ecosystems where the conditions are highly dynamic and unpredictable. Adaptive AI solutions can help to sustainably use natural resources and ensure the long-term resilience of the environment, combining RL, modeling of the ecosystem, intelligent crop management and anomaly detection.

5.4.1. *Reinforcement learning for adaptive resource allocation*

One of the most important applications of AI is RL, which is important in adaptive resource management (Ul Haq et al. 2026b). In comparison with supervised learning that is dependent on labeled datasets, RL systems learn through interaction with the environment and feedback in the form of rewards or penalties. The system, in turn, finds the best strategy or a policy that will generate the greatest benefits in the long run by trial and error. This renders RL very effective in resource allocation problems whereby optimum choices have to evolve as the conditions vary.

In energy systems, RL is useful to address the optimization of electricity distribution in smart grids by balancing supply and demand in real time. Since renewable energy sources like solar and wind are by nature intermittent, RL algorithms can dynamically determine the allocation of energy, storage and load balancing activities to achieve efficiency and stability. These systems are trained to know when the demand or generation is high and when it is low and act accordingly by redistributing stored energy.

RL applies in the management of water resources by controlling the water operation and irrigation scheduling in reservoirs. The AI agent would also be able to understand when water should be released or stored based on the rainfall predictions, water consumption patterns and water availability. This guarantees effective use and eliminates the chances of water scarcity or flooding. Equally, in city planning, RL-based systems may be used to optimize the traffic flow and minimize vehicle emissions through real-time alteration of traffic lights and diversion of vehicles.

It is mainly because of its adaptive quality that the RL can be effectively applied to address the complex environment with uncertainty, and thus it is one of the most powerful tools to promote sustainable development and efficient use of resources.

5.4.2. *Dynamic ecosystem modeling and biodiversity preservation*

Ecosystems are very intricate, and they consist of the interrelation of species, climatic conditions and geographical conditions. One of the primary challenges facing ecologists is predicting the reaction of these systems to the change in the environment. AI-based dynamic ecosystem modeling can provide an additional way of understanding and conserving biodiversity. These models model the interactions of the different components of an ecosystem and predict the effect caused by changes such as deforestation, pollution, climate change or invasion of a species.

AI-based ecosystem models employ both past and present data on species distribution, vegetation cover, rainfall, temperature and human activities to give estimates on changes in the suitability of the habitat. This way, ML algorithms are able to detect patterns that indicate habitat degradation or species migration to enable conservationists to implement appropriate preventive actions in time. As an illustration, AI can detect areas that are unfavorable to some endangered species and propose new habitats or protection measures.

DL, particularly the ability to identify images and sounds, has completely changed the whole procedure involved in the monitoring of wildlife. Thousands of camera trap images or audio recordings can be analyzed to identify species, estimate populations and track migration patterns using automated systems. This reduces the amount of work needed by a human, the monitoring process is more accurate and biodiversity trends are interpreted. Satellite monitoring and pattern recognition using AI are also used to identify illegal practices such as poaching or logging.

Conservation is enhanced through AI by simulating the workings of an ecosystem and enabling the real-time monitoring of biodiversity, which can then be used to improve the planning of areas for protection, wildlife movement and sustainable land use. These abilities are necessary to ensure the balance of the ecology and avoid an irreversible decline in biodiversity.

5.4.3. *AI in precision forestry and agriculture*

Two of the most critical industries that require environmental sustainability and practices are forestry and agriculture. The idea of precision forestry and precision agriculture, which is made based on a specific data analysis and not generalized assumptions, has been presented in modern AI-based technologies. This is a data-driven strategy that boosts its output with the lowest environmental effect.

In precision agriculture, AI systems can use information related to soil sensors, satellite photos, weather data and crop monitoring devices to make specific irrigation, fertilizing and pest control recommendations. The farmers are able to calculate the precise quantity of water and nutrients needed in each part of their field that minimizes the amount of waste and avoids excessive use of chemicals. Image processing tools developed using AI will also be able to identify the early stages of plant disease or shortage of nutrients, and thus manage the situation in a timely way and avoid the massive loss of crops.

AI finds application in the field of forestry management to track deforestation rates, monitor forest health and determine the potential of carbon sequestration. ML can be used to analyze satellite images to distinguish between healthy vegetation, deteriorated forests and deforestation. The information assists governments in monitoring for illegal logging and in creating reforestation projects. Moreover, AI is significant in terms of forest fire prevention since it defines high-risk areas, depending on the weather conditions, vegetation dryness and historical data.

Another benefit of precision forestry is that it brings the ability to optimize timber harvesting schedules to minimize the impact on the environment and keep the economy productive, thereby managing forest more responsibly.

5.4.4. Real-time anomaly detection in environmental data

With regard to environmental monitoring, there is a great deal of continuous information generated by sensors, satellites, drones and monitoring stations. Detecting strange patterns or abnormal variations in this data is essential for the early warning of environmental hazards. AI-powered real-time anomaly detection can be defined as the automatic identification of specific abnormal values or trends, which can signal a disaster, equipment malfunction, spike in pollution or ecological imbalance.

Autoencoders, Isolation Forests and deep neural networks are all AI models that are frequently applied to find anomalies within environmental datasets. Such systems are conditioned to understand how a normal environment appears and would instantly alert on the occurrence of unusual patterns.

An example is sudden turbidity of water or an abrupt decrease of dissolved oxygen in a river, which is an indication of contamination, and can lead to inspection and remedial action. Equally, an increase in abnormal temperature as identified by remote sensing systems could be an early warning of a forest fire.

Anomaly detection systems can be used in air pollution monitoring to notify authorities and the general population about sudden changes in the level of harmful gases or other types of particulate matter and issue real-time notifications. This assists in emergency reactions and reducing exposure to harmful pollutants. AI-driven sensors can detect unusual emissions in industrial areas and enforce environmental rules quickly.

Real-time anomaly detection systems are used to cut down on the response time by detecting critical changes in a fast, automated fashion and reduce the damages caused to the environment. These systems are the key aspects of intelligent environmental control as they enable ongoing monitoring and a timely response.

To conclude, AI systems developed as adaptive systems are powerful frameworks for sustainable environmental management. AI enables societies to stop relying on reactive strategies and instead pursue intelligent, proactive strategies through dynamic ecosystem modeling, precision agriculture and real-time anomaly detection through RL. These systems are known not only to conserve natural resources and safeguard biodiversity, but are also known to increase efficiency of economies and environmental stability. The further development of AI will make its implementation in sustainable management practices more and more critical to handle the complexity of the modern world (Singh et al. 2026).

5.5. AI for renewable energy optimization

The replacement of fossil fuel with renewable energy sources has become the world's priority in reaction to global warming, increased energy demand and dwindling non-renewable resources. Although the solar, wind, hydro and biomass sources of renewable energy can provide a better alternative as they are environmentally friendly, they also present a lot of operational challenges as they are variable and subject to weather conditions. In comparison to traditional power plants that offer a relatively constant and predictable output, renewable energy production varies with natural conditions such as sunshine, wind velocity and temperature. Such intermittency may result in inefficiencies, grid instability and excessive energy wastage unless the intermittency is properly addressed. AI has become a strong facilitator for optimizing renewable energy systems through better forecasting, making better decisions regarding energy storage, balancing grid loads and the intelligent trading of energy. AI for renewable energy optimization is shown in Figure 5.3.

Intelligent AI-driven solutions combine real-time sensor data and meteorological predictions with historical data about energy production and consumer usage patterns to develop adaptive and predictive energy management systems (Ul Haq et al. 2026a). These smart systems are important in ensuring optimum use of renewable energy sources and reducing the use of fossil fuel-powered back-up energy sources. With the ever-growing field of renewable energy, the use of AI is becoming the focus of an efficient, resilient and cost-effective energy infrastructure.

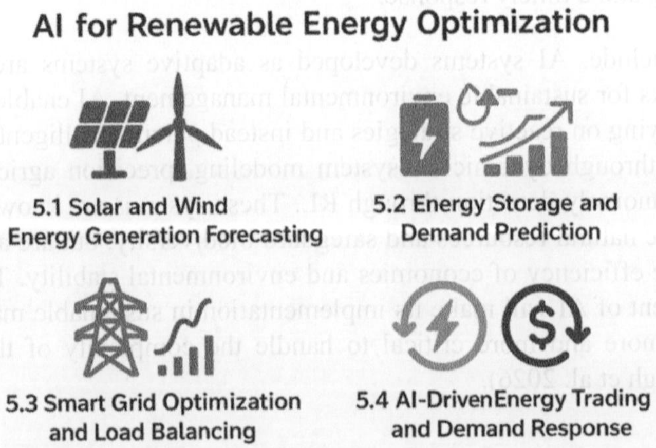

Figure 5.3. *AI for renewable energy optimization. For a color version of this figure, see www.iste.co.uk/ulhaq/artificial2.zip*

5.5.1. *Solar and wind energy generation forecasting*

Proper forecasting of solar and wind resources in terms of power generation is one of the greatest challenges in renewable energy control. A solar panel has an output that varies according to a number of environmental factors, such as the solar irradiance, cloud cover, panel orientation and temperature. On the same note, wind turbine power is generated according to the speed and direction of the wind, the air density and geographical conditions. Conventional forecasting techniques are usually deficient in their ability to identify all these highly complex and nonlinear relationships and therefore make inaccurate predictions.

The use of AI to predict the accuracy of power generation models is important because it can learn based on enormous amounts of historical and real-time data. Models of weather variables versus energy output are created using ML algorithms (random forests, gradient boosting machines and support vector regression). RNNs and LSTM networks are extensively used as DL models to learn temporal relationships in weather and power generation data (Ul Haq et al. 2026c). These models are able to learn patterns with time hence forecasting both short-term and long-term fluctuations in energy production.

CNNs have been used in conjunction with satellite and sky cameras to track the movement of clouds and determine the quantity of incoming solar energy in solar energy forecasting. This method permits minute by minute forecasting of the generation, which is crucial when working in real time on the grid. When it comes to wind energy, AI models are used to process time-series data provided by anemometers and weather stations to forecast the patterns of wind and turbine performance. Proper forecasting helps grid operators to plan better to use backup power sources, increase energy trading plans and avoid unexpected shortages or excess capacity.

Less uncertainty in energy production makes AI contribute to minimum curtailment, reduced operating costs and more general reliability of renewable energy systems.

5.5.2. *Energy storage and demand prediction*

Storage of energy and proper forecasting of demand is another important element in the optimization of renewable energy. As the generation of renewable energy sources is not always coordinated with demand patterns, the excess of energy produced during peak production processes should be efficiently stored and used afterward. Power storage equipment like batteries, pumped hydro storage and thermal storage are necessary to even out this disparity. The timing of storing energy and releasing it is however a complicated decision-making issue and involves different factors related to the current demand, future generation, electricity prices and the grid conditions.

AI-based models are employed to predict the demand of energy at various levels, from household level to cities or regions. These models consider historical consumption patterns, weather predictions, holiday patterns, economic activity and the pattern of human behavior to forecast the level of electricity required at a particular time. The models based on DL, for example, LSTM and transformer-based networks, can be especially helpful to capture the temporal and seasonal demand variation.

After forecasting the demand, AI systems make optimal decisions on the discharging and charging of energy storage facilities. This is commonly performed with RL algorithms, which are trained to learn the best strategies according to a reward function that can be cost minimization, grid stability or emission reduction. To use an example, an AI agent will be able to learn to accumulate excess solar energy in the afternoon and release it at peak evening hours. This will make renewable resources more efficient and eliminate the use of fossil fuel-based power plants.

Demand forecasting with AI also facilitates the incorporation of electric cars (EVs) into the grid. Smart charging algorithms will be able to plan for the vehicle to be charged at off-peak times or when renewable energy is plentiful, avoiding the grid overloading and lowering the overall amount of energy expenses.

5.5.3. *Smart grid optimization and load balancing*

The modern power grid is transforming to become a smart grid, which is integrated with digital communication, automated control systems and intelligent analytics to make it more efficient and reliable. AI is a core element of the optimization of smart grids, as it allows adapting load balancing, identifying faults and managing grids in real time.

The parameters of the grid, which are measured by AI-based optimization systems include voltage levels, current, frequency and power flows. These data are processed by ML models that predict possible faults, overloads or equipment failures. Early identification of anomalies helps grid operators to place preventive measures and prevent blackouts on a large scale. This enhances the resilience of the grids as well as minimizes the maintenance processes.

Another important use of AI in smart grids is load balancing (Zhou 2025). At times of peak demand, AI algorithms will allocate the load among the various power sources in such a manner that there will be no overload on any one component. In case there is a high production of renewable energy, AI-based production focuses on its use rather than on the production of fossil-based energy. This maximizes the use of clean energy and at the same time keeps the stability of the grid.

Demand-side management, that is, prompting consumers to change their energy consumption to off-peak hours, is also facilitated by AI. Smart meters along with AI analytics can recommend the best time to consumers to use their equipment or automatically regulate the use of appliances in smart homes. This will decrease the peak demand, decrease electricity costs and improve the efficiency of the entire energy system.

5.5.4. *AI-driven energy trading and demand response*

The electricity market in modern energy markets is moving towards dynamic and real-time trading as electricity prices vary with supply and demand. AI is an important aspect of the automating and intelligence trading of energy (Ou et al. 2024). AI algorithms are able to decide the best time to purchase or sell electricity by analyzing trends in prices, generation, demand predictions and market indicators. This is more useful with producers of renewable energy, as they have to determine when to sell excess energy to the system.

AI-based trading systems are used to optimize profits and stabilize the grid with the help of RL and predictive analytics. These systems consider weather predictions, maximum demand times and transmission constraints to develop optimal bidding strategies. This automation reduces human error, increases effectiveness and allows small-scale producers, including individual homes with solar panels, to make a more meaningful contribution to energy markets.

Another important application of AI in renewable energy systems is its demand response. This is the process of varying or reducing electricity activities when it is in high demand or the electricity supply is at a low level. AI software processes the live grid information and sends automatic indications to devices connected to the grid, and they are affected by it by reducing or dropping their load. As an example, industrial machines or air conditioners in large buildings can decrease their power consumption temporarily without any major impact on their performance.

With the introduction of AI in energy trading and demand response initiatives, energy systems will be more flexible, efficient and resilient. In addition to improving grid stability, these mechanisms give incentives to consumers to have more sustainable energy practices.

5.6. Case studies and practical applications

AI is not a theoretical research issue anymore; over the last few years, there have been applications of AI in real-world environmental and sustainability projects all over the world. The application of AI-based systems to infrastructure is progressively being implemented in climate risk prediction, municipal waste management and other to facilitate resiliency, efficiency and sustainability. In this section, we discuss four case studies, climate risk assessment, smart cities, waste management and monitoring carbon emissions using AI, as an example of how AI is providing a tangible impact.

5.6.1. *AI in climate risk assessment*

Flood risk and early warning are one of the applications of AI in environmental management. As an example, ML and hydrodynamic simulation models have been designed to enhance the speed and accuracy of flood forecasting. In another research article, a CNN was trained to use satellite data, topographic and rainfall information as an aid in the production of near real-time flood maps with significantly greater precision than the conventional simulation models (Dias et al. 2023). The authors indicated that the NashSutcliffe efficiency (which measures the performance of hydrological models) increased to an average of 0.82 with the AI-hybrid model as compared to 0.27 with classical models (Dias et al. 2023).

A second innovative model, known as DRUM (Diffusion-based Runoff Model), uses generative AI to generate probabilistic runoff predictions. In contrast to deterministic statistical distributions, DRUM acquires fine-scale hydrological behavior using data and produces ensemble forecasts with quantifiable uncertainties. DRUM performed better than the current DL techniques in benchmark testing directed at hundreds of river basins, especially in extreme flow (flood) cases, and allowed improved early warning despite long lead times (Elbasha and Abdellatif 2025).

These climate risk models, which are powered by AI, assist agencies in managing disaster events by locating areas with high risks, coming up with probabilistic flood maps and in decision-making regarding evacuation and the mitigation of floods. These enhanced accuracy and lead times result in enhanced preparedness, which reduces the loss of life and property in the case of severe events.

5.6.2. *AI-based smart cities and sustainable infrastructure*

Cities are becoming smarter, and AI and IoT are used to streamline the city infrastructure and enhance resilience. One example of this is a city management platform based on AI + IoT implemented in the city of Aveiro, Portugal, and used to support three usages, namely, (i) traffic safety, (ii) optimization of energy use and (iii) maintenance of infrastructure (e.g. fault detection on roads). The system gathered traffic camera and environmental sensor data as well as smart meter data and processed it with the help of ML to produce actionable data such as congested routes, anticipated power demand or early signs of infrastructure deterioration (Anitha and Parthiban 2025).

One more recent paper suggests an AIoT-based smart traffic management system, which works with the live video stream of an already existing CCTV system. An ML model of the study has vehicles as an input instead of installing new costly hardware and determines the level of traffic and dynamically adjusts traffic lights to minimize traffic congestion. This adaptive control enhanced traffic performance in simulations, which was even more efficient than the performance of traditional fixed-signal systems by 30–35% in efficiency measures (Ul Haq et al. 2025b).

Cities can also use these systems to save fuel, reduce emissions and enhance mobility in the city. The implementation of AI-based adaptive traffic lights can dramatically change the way cities work, making them more energy saving and attentive toward the actual flow of people and vehicles.

5.6.3. *Intelligent waste management systems*

Urban solid waste is a serious problem, and the waste management sphere is getting more efficient and sustainable with the current involvement of AI. Recently, an AI-based framework combining IoT sensors and graph-theoretic optimization has been introduced to control bin overflow and route collection vehicles. An XGBoost classifier (a gradient boosting machine) was trained in a simulation of 500 smart bins in several areas to predict which bins had a high probability of overflowing. This was coupled with spatial risk mapping and graph routing to ensure dynamically optimized collection routes. The system minimized overflow by half and missed pickups by approximately 72.7%, it saved fuel by approximately 15.5% and maximized on bin use by approximately 35.5% (Ul Haq et al. 2024).

Another case that has been implemented was the IoT-based smart bins in South Korea that were tracked in real time to check the fill levels. The authors presented a routing optimization model in which a time penalty cost was paid for delayed collection in case a bin was full. This motivated healthier scheduling as well as optimized the routes of garbage trucks. It was demonstrated that real-time routing was correlated with bin fullness, which would lower the operation costs but did not affect service quality (Radif et al. 2025).

There is also the work on the sorting side with AI-based intelligent smart bins, which have cameras and computer vision. As an example, a system based on a VGG16 CNN on a Raspberry Pi + camera module has been created, which can classify waste as e-waste, biowaste, dry recyclables, with a very high accuracy (as high as 98%) (Ul Haq et al. 2022). This sorting is automated to minimize the workload of humans and enhance the rates of recycling and waste diversion.

The urban sanitation sector is becoming more dynamic, more economical and less polluted by these AI-driven waste management systems – cities are improving their solutions to one of the most enduring challenges in their sustainability.

5.6.4. *AI-powered carbon capture and emission monitoring*

The monitoring and reduction of carbon emission is at the heart of mitigation on climatic change, and AI has become part of this. In one recent experiment, researchers utilized a combination of satellite data provided by NASA Orbiting Carbon Observatories (OCO) with ground measurements of the same data provided by the Integrated Carbon Observation System (ICOS) and meteorological data (ERA5) to make a high-resolution CO_2 mapping model. It was based on a weighted k-nearest neighbors interpolation with ML used to estimate ground-level CO_2 concentrations. The model reached 3.92 ppm root-mean-square error, which showed the existence of emission hotspots in the area and fine-tuned the spatial granularity of emissions monitoring (Ul Haq et al. 2025d).

Simultaneously, scientists have used DL and statistical process control to track the effect of national carbon reduction policies. They were able to identify deviations, trends and anomalies in CO_2 emissions by using RNNs over the data of industrial emissions and the outputs of environmental sensors through the implementation of policy changes. This constant check approach assists governments in estimating the effectiveness of the mitigation approaches in action and adjusting the course where necessary (Ul Haq et al. 2025a).

A different direction of research takes the question of forecasting CO_2 footprints with ML. As an example, a predictive model was constructed to predict the global CO_2 emissions (with the accommodation of the Covid-19 effects) based on time-series models, for example, the combination of SARIMA and ML. This model was used to estimate the emissions in the various future horizons to give support to the decision-making around the emission-reduction policy (Shriramoj et al. 2024).

The result of all these attempts by the AI applications is a significantly more detailed, richer and closer to real-time image of carbon emissions compared to the traditional statistical reporting.

5.7. Challenges and ethical considerations

With the continued development of environmental monitoring, renewable energy systems and sustainable development strategies with the use of AI, a range of insidious challenges and ethical issues are also presented. Although AI-based solutions have huge potential in terms of efficiency, precision and predictability, their application in the field of environmental and energy is not risk free. These risks are caused by data constraints, a lack of transparency of the algorithms, biased results and regulatory loopholes that can be an obstacle to execution in a fair and sustainable way. In response to the harnessing of the power of AI in a responsible manner, these challenges have to be understood and mitigated. This section discusses some of the major technical and ethical issues regarding AI in applications in the sustainability field.

5.7.1. *Data availability and quality issues*

Any AI-based system is based on data, and the quality of AI-based environmental and energy solutions directly depends on the availability, validity and quality of data on which these systems are trained (Ul Haq and Khanday 2025). One of the problems with this field is the lack of access to high-quality and trustworthy information. Many areas, particularly in the developing world and isolated ecological areas, do not have adequate environmental monitoring centers like weather stations, sensors, satellite systems and real-time reporting systems.

The data gathered even in well-supervised areas might have inconsistencies, a lack of value, obsolete measurements or malfunctions of sensors or human reporting errors. One example is the poor quality of air readings or missing records of energy consumption, which may lead to erroneous predictions and incorrect decision-making. AIs that have been trained on biased or incomplete data might not be relevant to real-life scenarios, which can decrease their applicability in environmental planning at a large scale.

Data standardization is one of the other important issues. Different organizations and countries tend to use various protocols, formats and measurement units in the collection of environmental data. The combination of these varied datasets into one model is also technically difficult and may create additional inconsistencies. Unless AI systems are preprocessed, harmonized and validated, they may give false results. Thus, enhancing data quality, facilitating open-access data-repositories and creating international standards of data-sharing are necessary measures for more credible AI use.

5.7.2. *Model interpretability and explainable AI*

Most of the models of AI that are highly performing, especially the DL and ensemble models, are often referred to as black boxes since the way they make decisions is very hard to comprehend and interpret. Although these models may be highly predictive, their non-transparency makes them a cause of concern in critical areas like environmental management and energy policy that have long-term ecological, economical and social impacts on their decisions.

As an illustration, when an AI model suggests to close a particular industrial plant because of high expected emissions, stakeholders, policymakers, business owners and communities will insist on clear explanations to such decisions. In the absence of interpretability, it will be difficult to develop trust in AI systems or to justify policy moves through its results. This is especially problematic in the legal and regulatory sphere, in which decisions have to be responsible and justified.

Challenge/ issue	Description	Application	Findings/ observations	Implications	Possible solutions	Stakeholders
Data availability and quality issues	Incomplete/noisy environmental data	Air and water quality monitoring	Sensor and satellite data have gaps, noise and inconsistencies that reduce model accuracy	Unreliable forecasts and late detection of critical events	Better sensor calibration, data cleaning, redundancy and standardized formats	Environmental agencies, researchers and local communities
Model interpretability and explainable AI	Black-box AI models	Climate risk prediction, disaster early warning	Complex models are hard to interpret and explain to non-experts	Low trust and slower adoption in policy decisions	Use interpretable models when possible; add explainability tools and clear documentation	Scientists, policymakers and citizens
Bias, fairness and sustainability impact	Biased data and unequal benefits	Environmental justice and resource allocation	Uneven data coverage can bias models toward well-monitored regions and groups	Marginalized communities may face higher risks and fewer protections	Collect more representative data, include affected communities and monitor fairness metrics	Vulnerable communities, NGOs and regulators
Bias, fairness and sustainability impact	High environmental footprint of AI	Large-scale climate and earth-system models	Training and running large models consume significant energy and resources	Higher greenhouse gas emissions, water use, and e-waste	Energy-efficient models, frugal AI, renewable-powered data centers, hardware reuse	Cloud providers, AI developers and governments
Policy, governance and regulatory barriers	Lack of clear standards and governance	Deployment of AI in environmental agencies	Regulations and standards for environmental performance are still emerging	Hard to compare systems and ensure accountability across regions	Develop harmonized standards, reporting requirements and oversight frameworks	Regulators, standards bodies, industry and civil society

Table 5.1. *Challenges, issues and applications of explainable AI*

Explainable AI (XAI) seeks to overcome this issue by giving human interpretable information of how models come up with concrete conclusions (Ul Haq et al. 2025c). Some of the techniques that can be used to find the relevant factors affecting model predictions are SHAP (Shapley Additive Explanations), LIME (Local Interpretable Model-agnostic Explanations) and attention visualization. Explainability is critical to environmental and energy applications to make sure that AI recommendations are based on scientific knowledge and societal values.

However, adding explainable AI makes the computation process more complex, which may lead to a reduction in efficiency in the model. Balancing between accuracy and transparency is currently an open research question. In order to be able to use AI responsibly for decisions in the sustainability field, it is important to develop strong and interpretable models.

5.7.3. *Impact of bias, fairness and sustainability*

AI systems may accidentally strengthen the biases that are found in training data. Such biases, in environmental and energy-related practice, may result in an unequal distribution of resources, a lack of access to clean energy or the unfair treatment of vulnerable populations. As an example, an AI-driven system to prioritize the renewable energy infrastructure could always prefer urban and economically developed regions where more information can be collected, and rural or low-income regions may be neglected. This may contribute to the increase in social inequality and restrict inclusive sustainable development.

In the same way, climate risk assessment models that have been trained on historical data on developed areas may not be effective in predicting risks of indigenous communities or small island countries, which do not face climate change in the same manner. Such biases are not visible to the decision-makers most of the time and are thus very harmful. The uncontrolled prejudice may lead to the implementation of policies that will end up hurting marginalized groups in a disproportionate way.

In addition to social fairness, there exists an environmental cost to AI itself. Big data ML models like deep neural networks are computationally and energy-intensive to train, which causes more carbon emissions.

Otherwise, AI can negatively affect its intended purpose of supporting sustainability because of its environmental footprint. This paradox has given rise to the notion of Green AI that focuses on energy-efficient algorithms, optimized model architectures and data centers running on renewable energy.

Therefore, the need to make data collection as equitable as possible to diversify training data, use bias-detection mechanisms and make AI systems less carbon-intensive will be essential to the process of ensuring that AI development aligns with sustainable and ethical practices.

5.8. Future directions and emerging trends

The field of AI is quickly transforming into a supporting analysis device down to being a core element of the worldwide sustainability initiative (Ul Haq 2024). New technologies like the IoT, blockchain, autonomous systems and energy-efficient computing that are becoming more popular with AI are finding their way into increasingly complex and interconnected environmental challenges to form intelligent, scalable and resilient systems. Sustainability of interdisciplinary technological convergence is the future, in which AI is the brain of the system of connections that monitor, analyze, predict and react to environmental changes on-the-fly. This segment discusses the future opportunities and trends in AI-based sustainability.

5.8.1. *AI + IoT + blockchain for sustainability*

Among the most effective emerging trends in the realm of sustainability is the combination of AI and the IoT with blockchain technology. The IoT is a network of connected sensors and devices that gathers large volumes of real-time environmental information regarding air, water, soil, forests and energy systems. The variables that these sensors are used to measure include temperature, humidity, pollution rates, the moisture level of soil, carbon emissions and energy usage. AI processes a vast amount of data to find patterns that matter and forecast the future, and help to make intelligent decisions.

Blockchain comes into this ecosystem with a guarantee of data security, transparency and trust. Environmental information is usually distributed to a wide range of stakeholders such as governments, private businesses, researchers and communities. Blockchain facilitates decentralized and non-tampered data storage, which enables users to validate the authenticity and integrity of environmental records. This is especially significant to areas like carbon credit trading, fresh energy certificate tracking and monitoring of the supply chain of sustainable resources.

With the integration of AI, the IoT and blockchain, a clear and automated system of monitoring of sustainability may be developed. As an illustration, in smart agriculture, sensors based on the IoT can be used to gather data regarding soil and weather, AI code can be optimized to be able to do things such as irrigate and fertilize the soil and blockchain can be used to document this to ensure that sustainable farming is carried out. In emission monitoring, AI forecasts the areas of pollution hotspots, IoT sensors gather the data on emissions in real time and blockchain makes sure that this data cannot be modified, which contributes to accountability.

Such integrated systems will play an important role in supporting global climate commitments, monitoring sustainability goals, and providing communities with reliable information for informed decision-making.

5.8.2. *Autonomous environmental monitoring systems*

The traditional method of environmental monitoring can be characterized as manual, which is not only expensive but also time consuming and inefficient in terms of scope. One of the new tendencies is the creation of autonomous environmental surveillance based on AI. These are drones, underwater robots, autonomous vehicles and satellite-placed platforms that can be utilized autonomously in difficult or inaccessible locations.

AI drones are able to survey forests to identify illegal deforestation and the condition of wildlife species as well as detect forest fires at their initial stages. On the same note, the use of autonomous underwater vehicles (AUVs) is being utilized in researching ocean ecosystems, the degradation of coral reefs and pollution of the sea. The systems rely on computer vision and ML algorithms to analyze visual and sensor data in real time and enable them to identify abnormalities, classify objects and make decisions without involving humans.

Moreover, AI systems implemented on satellites are also becoming more sophisticated, which means that nowadays one can monitor climate-related changes like the melting of glaciers, the rise of the sea level, the process of desertification and urban growth on a continuous and global scale. These systems have the potential of automatically examining high-resolution images and raising the alert over environmental threats.

The implementation of autonomous systems ensures that the magnitude, pace and effectiveness of environmental surveillance are substantially enhanced. They save on human resources in hazardous or isolated places and offer real-time information that is not interrupted. In the future, these smart systems will create a global nervous system of the environment, which will monitor earth continuously and offer actionable information to governments and organizations to respond quickly and plan sustainably.

5.8.3. *Green AI and energy-efficient algorithms*

Even though AI is being applied to encourage sustainability, the application of AI itself is raising concerns with respect to the environmental impact of AI. The use of large DL models consumes enormous amounts of computational resources, which in turn consume high amounts of energy and produce more carbon. This has led to the recent development of the concept of Green AI, which is concerned with creating energy and environmentally friendly AI systems.

Green AI will minimize the ML carbon footprint by designing algorithms and efficient hardware, and implementing sustainable computing methods. The focus of researchers now is lightweight architecture, pruning, knowledge distillation and low-power chips that can offer high performance and at the same time consume minimum energy, rather than focusing on the raw size of a model. Edge AI, where data processing is done at the devices, not at huge central processing units, also helps to reduce energy consumption since it requires less data to be transmitted.

Green AI is very important in renewable energy and other environmental applications. To take a more precise example, an AI model that assists the energy grid or climate prediction should not require more energy than it will save. Thus, sustainability in itself is emerging as a performance measure in the design of algorithms.

Even data centers are being migrated to cleaner ways of renewable energy like solar, wind and hydroelectric power to facilitate cleaner AI activities. Stricter rules and industry practices to foster the transparency of AI systems on energy consumption and carbon emission can be expected in the future. Green AI will be the pillar of technological advances that we can apply in terms of ethics and the environment.

5.8.4. *AI for climate resilience planning*

Climate resilience planning aims at assisting populations and ecosystems to adapt and get back to normal after risks that are associated with the climate, including floods, drought, heatwaves, sea level rise and severe storms. The combination of predictive modeling, risk assessment and scenario analysis is becoming one of the most powerful AI tools to develop climate resilient systems. AI models can model future climate circumstances according to the various emission routes, land-use arrangements and socioeconomic situations. Such simulations assist governments and city planners to find the areas that are at high risk and make the correct decision in relation to the development of infrastructure, disaster preparedness and resource allocation. As an example, AI can propose the location of flood barriers, green areas or water storage facilities to avoid as much harm to the environment and the economy as possible.

AI can be used in coastal areas to forecast shoreline erosion and sea-level alterations to be used in designing protection and location planning. In the agricultural sector, AI can suggest weather-resistant crops and agricultural methods that can withstand weather changes. In the city, AI can be used to optimize buildings, drainage and transportation systems to enhance resilience to extreme climatic events.

Moreover, AI-based communication systems can alert the population at an early stage, using mobile devices, which will allow evacuation and disaster response. Through its ability to combine social, economic and environmental data, AI can change climate resilience planning so as not to be a reactive but rather a proactive and versatile strategy.

Integration, autonomy, efficiency and resilience are the future of AI with respect to sustainability. The integration of AI with the IoT and blockchain will establish open and reliable ecosystems of environmental surveillance and management of resources. There will be autonomous systems that will provide large-scale protection of natural environments continuously. Green AI will also make technology itself less costly to the environment, and climate resilience planning run by AI will enable societies to respond to the changing world. With these trends still on the rise, cooperation between scientists, policymakers, industries and communities will be necessary in order to realize the full potential of AI as a way of creating a sustainable, resilient and fair future.

5.9. Conclusion

AI has become a disruptive technology in solving environmental and energy-related issues through sophisticated monitoring, forecasting and sustainable control in a wide variety of industries. In this chapter, the authors have highlighted the role of AI technologies, including ML and DL, reinforcement and hybrid learning, to take advantage of exponential data gathered by satellites, sensors, the IoT and digital twins to offer real-time information, enhance forecasting quality and carry out proactive decision-making. AI-based models improve the prediction of climate-related risks, extreme weather, the assessment of air and water quality, biodiversity and smart agricultural methods, and show definite trends in environmental stability and efficiency.

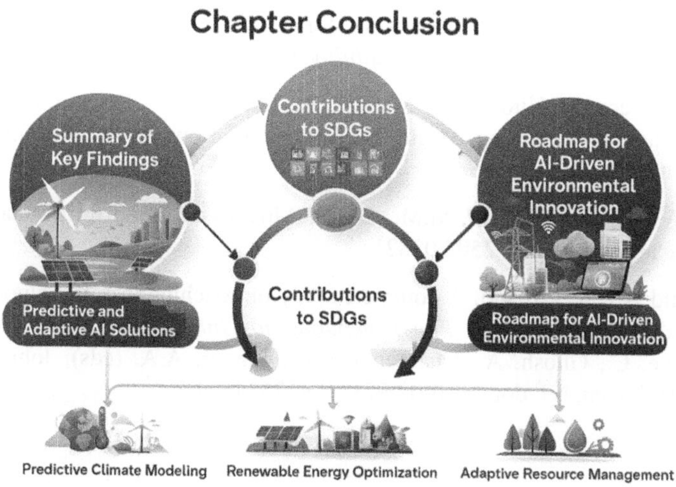

Figure 5.4. *Basic contributions to SDGs. For a color version of this figure, see www.iste.co.uk/ulhaq/artificial2.zip*

In addition, AI contributes to multiple sustainable development goals, as illustrated in Figure 5.4. It supports climate action, facilitates the management of smart and clean energy systems, promotes sustainable cities, and advances the conservation of water resources and ecosystems on land and in the oceans. Meanwhile, the chapter considers the issues concerning data transparency, ethical issues, the bias of the algorithms, the cost of its computation and the responsibility of the governance, stating that the advantages of AI need to be equated with fairness, responsibility and environmental sustainability. In the future, an AI-led environmental innovation roadmap will involve the collaboration of the global community, open data environments, interdisciplinary research, community effort and capacity building as a measure to guarantee inclusive and equitable implementation. Future systems should be efficient, interpretable and ethically sound, and allow the introduction of complementary technologies, that is, the IoT, blockchain, autonomous monitoring and Green AI. Overall, when managed in a responsible manner, AI can be a key to climate resilience, the sustainable management of resources, optimization of renewable energy and long-term environmental sustainability, which will transform the planet into a healthier and more sustainable one for future generations.

5.10. References

Anitha, R. and Parthiban, A. (2025). AI-IoT-graph synergy for smart waste management: A scalable framework for predictive, resilient, and sustainable urban systems. *Frontiers in Sustainability*, 6, 1675021.

Dias, T., Fonseca, T., Vitorino, J., Martins, A., Malpique, S., Praça, I. (2023). From data to action: Exploring AI and IoT-driven solutions for smarter cities. arXiv Preprint, 2306.04653.

Elbasha, A.M. and Abdellatif, M.M. (2025). AIoT-based smart traffic management system. arXiv Preprint, 2502.02821.

Kaur, I. and Ali, A. (2024a). A complete study on machine learning algorithms for medical data analysis. In *Fog Computing for Intelligent Cloud IoT Systems*, Banerjee, C., Ghosh, A., Chakraborty, R., Elngar, A.A. (eds). John Wiley & Sons, Hoboken, NJ. doi: 10.1002/9781394175345.ch7.

Kaur, I. and Ali, A. (2024b). An in-depth exploration of machine learning algorithms and performance evaluation approaches for personalized diabetes prediction. In *Proceedings of the 2024 International Conference on Emerging Innovations and Advanced Computing (INNOCOMP)*, Sonipat. IEEE. doi: 10.1109/INNOCOMP63224.2024.00093.

Kaur, I. and Ali, A. (2025). Unveiling the power of prediction: A comprehensive guide to learning techniques, from data preparation to model interpretability for early prediction of diabetes and effective management. In *Artificial Intelligence and Optimization Techniques for Smart Information System Generation*, Ali, A., Chakraborty, R., Alharbe, N. (eds). CRC Press, Boca Raton, FL [Online]. Available at: https://www.taylorfrancis.com/chapters/edit/10.1201/9781003592969-1/unveiling-power-prediction-inderdeep-kaur-aleem-ali.

Kaur, I. and Inzimam-Ul-Hassan, A. (2024). Research Insight: IoT (Internet of Things) in fog optimal workload via fog offloading and delay minimisation using fog collaboration model. In *Recent Trends in Computational Sciences*, H.L., G., M.R., P., Flammini, F. (eds). CRC Press, London [Online]. Available at: https://www.taylorfrancis.com/chapters/edit/10.1201/9781003363781-38/.

Kaur, I. and Inzimam-Ul-Hassan, A. (2025). A bibliometric analysis and management of big data and machine learning research: Current trends and future directions. In *Emerging Trends in Industrial Engineering and Management*, Kumar, A., Kumar, P., Phanden, R.K. et al. (eds). CRC Press, Boca Raton, FL [Online]. Available at: https://www.taylorfrancis.com/chapters/edit/10.1201/9781003512585-11/bibliometric-analysis-management-big-data-machine-learning-research-inderdeep-kaur-inzimam-ul-hassan.

Ou, Z., Nai, C., Pan, B., Pan, M., Shen, C., Jiang, P., Liu, X., Tang, Q., Li, W., Zheng, Y. (2024). DRUM: Diffusion-based runoff model for probabilistic flood forecasting. arXiv Preprint, 2412.11964.

Radif, M., Fadhil, S.A., Alrammahi, A.H. (2025). Cross-biome biodiversity assessment and anomaly detection using AI-enhanced acoustic monitoring. *Journal of Applied Data Sciences*, 6(3), 1666–1680.

Saini, G.K. and Kaur, I. (2025). Navigating risk. In *Artificial Intelligence in Remote Sensing for Disaster Management*, Dahiya, N., Singh, G., Singh, S., Sharma, A. (eds). John Wiley & Sons, Hoboken, NJ. doi: 10.1002/9781394287222.ch8.

Saini, G.K., Kaur, I., Sharma, H. (2024). A comprehensive review and analysis of landslide detection through advanced image analysis techniques. In *Proceedings of the 2024 5th International Conference for the Emerging Technology (INCET)*, Belgaum. IEEE. doi: 10.1109/INCET61516.2024.10593354.

Sharma, A., Kaur, I., Goel, P. (2024a). Enhanced classification of gravitational wave images using CNN model. In *Proceedings of the 2024 7th International Conference on Circuit, Power and Computing Technologies (ICCPCT)*, Kollam. IEEE. doi: 10.1109/ICCPCT61902.2024.10673399.

Sharma, A., Kaur, I., Goel, P. (2024b). Detection of gravitational waves using machine learning. In *Proceedings of the 2024 5th International Conference for the Emerging Technology (INCET)*, Belgaum. IEEE. doi: 10.1109/INCET61516.2024.10593087.

Shriramoj, O.B., Kaur, I., Yadav, A., Thakur, R.K., Raj, R., Yadav, A. (2024). SECURE-LINK: Next generation algorithm for data integrity and encryption. In *Proceedings of the 2024 Asia Pacific Conference on Innovation in Technology (APCIT)*, Mysore. IEEE. doi: 10.1109/APCIT62007.2024.10673612.

Singh, A., Ul Haq, I., Jain, N., Kumar, R., Rather, M.A., Masoodi, F.S. (2026). Hybrid quantum–classical learning architectures for 6G/7G edge intelligence. In *Deep Quantum Neural Networks: AI for 6G/7G Communication Systems*, Kumar, A., Rathore, P.S., Juárez-Ramírez, R. (eds). Springer, Singapore.

Ul Haq, I. (2024). Diagnosis of neurological disease using bioinspired algorithms. In *Bio-Inspired Optimization for Medical Data Mining*, Srivastava, S., Anand, A., Kumar, A. et al. (eds). John Wiley & Sons, Hoboken, NJ.

Ul Haq, I. and Khanday, A.M.U.D. (2025). Exploring the role of explainable AI in women's health: Challenges and solutions. In *Explainable Artificial Intelligence in the Healthcare Industry*, Kumar, A., Kumar, T.A., Das, P. et al. (eds). John Wiley & Sons, Hoboken, NJ.

Ul Haq, I. and Sharma, N. (2026). AI and quantum-driven IoT frameworks for sustainable 6G/7G smart homes. In *Deep Quantum Neural Networks: AI for 6G/7G Communication Systems* Kumar, A., Rathore, P.S., Juárez-Ramírez, R. (eds). Springer, Singapore.

Ul Haq, I., Kumar, N., Koul, N., Verma, C., Eneacu, F.M., Raboaca, M.S. (2022). Machine learning techniques for result prediction of one day international (ODI) cricket match. In *The International Conference on Recent Innovations in Computing*. Springer, Singapore.

Ul Haq, I., Kaur, G., Rather, A.H. (2024). Fruit leaf classification using transfer learning for automation and industrial applications. In *Deep Learning Techniques for Automation and Industrial Applications*, Rathore, P.S., Ahuja, S., Burri, S.R. et al. (eds). John Wiley & Sons, Hoboken, NJ.

Ul Haq, I., Khanday, A.M.D., Shah, H.A., Rufai, S.Z. (2025a). Enhancing water security through automation: Case studies and technical advancements in water quality management. In *Computational Automation for Water Security*, Dubey, A.K., Srivastav, A.L., Kumar, A. et al. (eds). Elsevier, Amsterdam.

Ul Haq, I., Kumar, A., Rathore, P.S. (2025b). Machine learning approaches for wind power forecasting: A comprehensive review. *Discover Applied Sciences*, 7(10), 1139.

Ul Haq, I., Malhotra, J., Rawat, V., Kumari, J., Kaur, G. (2025c). Machine learning approaches for early detection of cervical cancer: A comparative study of classification models. In *Targeted Chemotherapy with Personalized Immunotherapy: An AI Approach*, Kumar, A., Das, P., Rathore, P.S. et al. (eds). John Wiley & Sons, Hoboken, NJ.

Ul Haq, I., Nandal, V., Uppal, H. (2025d). Blockchain applications in aviation securing transactions, streamlining operations, and improving passenger experience. In *Blockchain in the Tourism Industry: A New Era of Secure and Transparent Travel Solutions*, Kumar, A., Abreu, A., Batta, P. et al. (eds). Springer, Cham.

Ul Haq, I.U., Singh, A., Jain, N., Rather, M.A., Masoodi, F.S. (2026a). Quantum convolutional neural networks for intelligent spectrum management in 6G/7G. In *Deep Quantum Neural Networks: AI for 6G/7G Communication Systems*, Kumar, A., Rathore, P.S., Juárez-Ramírez, R. (eds). Springer, Singapore.

Ul Haq, I., Yousuf, A., Masoodi, F.S. (2026b). Integrating blockchain and metaverse for next generation smart healthcare networks. In *Blockchain Enabled Metaverse for Smart Wireless Sensor Networks*, Kumar, A., Rathore, P.S., Moreira, F. (eds). Springer, Cham.

Ul Haq, I., Kak, S.M., Ul Islam, M. (2026c). Emerging trends in blockchain metaverse for intelligent sensor network applications. In *Blockchain Enabled Metaverse for Smart Wireless Sensor Networks*, Kumar, A., Rathore, P.S., Moreira, F. (eds). Springer, Cham.

Weyn, R.L., Durran, D.R., Caruana, R. (2019). Improving data-driven global weather prediction using deep convolutional neural networks. *Journal of Advances in Modeling Earth Systems*, 11(12), 1–17.

Zhou, S.J. (2025). Application of AI in urban flash flood risk assessment: From real-time warning to resilience planning. *Applied and Computational Engineering*, 150, 9–14.

6

Harnessing AI to Address Environmental and Energy Challenges in a Climate-Driven World

It is necessary to state that artificial intelligence (AI) has turned into a groundbreaking technology, which can address environmental concerns on a global level, as well as mitigate the impact of climate change. As heavy data processing, AI and modeling processes are put into practice, AI is capable of overseeing, predicting and controlling environmental systems in real time. Smart AI will also be helpful when protecting the environment with intelligent forecasting and administration systems. Machine learning (ML) tools are used much more often to analyze satellite images to monitor deforestation trends, glacier melting rate and even the very concept of ocean acidification, which will allow policymakers to avoid irreversible damage. AI-based predictive maintenance assistance has been applied in the energy sector to make solar panels and wind turbines, energy demand and distribution models more efficient. AI helps with sustainable urban planning in the city by reducing traffic congestion, monitoring air quality and improving the amount of green azaquinzoles. These AI interventions empower the United Nations sustainable development goals (SDGs), particularly on the topics of responsible consumption, climate action and clean energy. Hence, it can be said that the future of AI-based sustainable nature is the recognition of maximizing innovation with ethical and environmental responsibility. That way, AI is not merely a surveillance device and analysis tool, but an intelligent infrastructure, which encloses pre-emptive environmental management and long-term climate stability. This chapter explains how AI plays a complicated part as both an accelerator and a solution to the climate change dynamics. It also highlights how AI-based applications can enhance the accuracy of climatic modeling, utilize the maximum renewable energy sources and help reduce the carbon footprint with the assistance of intelligent automation and decision-making. In addition, AIs can be used in precision agriculture, water management and waste reduction, aimed at sustainable development. However, there are also certain environmental issues connected with the rapid development of AI technologies, including the use of enormous amounts of computing power, e-waste generation, and ethical concerns regarding data use and data policy development and implementation. This two-way position is critically analyzed in this chapter, which gets rid of the pressure of an environment yet

Chapter written by Sahil SHARMA and Rishi KANT.

generates it as well, as AI does. Moreover, it also examines the integration of AI with technologies that are yet to be invented, such as Internet of Things (IoT), blockchain and remote sensing, among other technologies that aim to realize resilient ecosystems.

6.1. Introduction

One of the factors that impacts humanity the most in the 21st century is the problem of global climate change and environmental degradation. Amplified greenhouse gas levels, rising frequency of severe weather, woodland deterioration and disappearance of biodiversity, among others, are collectively jeopardizing ecosystem stability, protection and human well-being (Srivastava and Maity 2023). The Intergovernmental Panel on Climate Change (IPCC) states that global warming of 1.5°C above pre-industrial levels will increase threats to various systems and areas, and thus mitigation (reducing emissions) and adaptation (resilience building) will be essential. Simultaneously, land-use change, pollution and over-exploitation of resources impose a stress on many environmental systems, which in turn interact with climate change to produce nonlinear, complex effects. Conventional devices of environmental science such as remote sensing, climate modeling and field surveys are precious, yet sometimes find it hard to deal with large amounts of data, real-time or even multiple shear interactions (Uriarte-Gallastegi et al. 2024).

AI has turned out to be a gamechanger in sustainability and climate action in this regard. AI refers to a collection of techniques, such as ML, deep learning (DL), neural networks, natural-language processing and computer vision, capable of being trained upon high-volume, high-velocity and high-variety data; behavioral signal-detection; system-behavior prediction and decision-making (Raihan et al. 2024). Indicatively, AI-powered energy-management applications have allowed companies to lower greenhouse gasses, enhance efficiency and facilitate circular-economy transformations (Uriarte-Gallastegi et al. 2024). At the environmental level, AI can be applied to aid in making predictions about climate change, highly efficient use of renewable energy resources, biodiversity studies and resource management (Pachot and Patissier 2023). The advantage is using AI potentials to improve mitigation (e.g. optimization of energy systems and renewable output prediction) and adaptation (e.g. flood predictions and urban infrastructure resiliency) of the risks caused by climate change (Kumar 2024).

Nevertheless, AI has yet to be fully used in terms of sustainability. This leaves key questions on how AI can be implemented to use environmental resources in ways that would have a positive impact (e.g. energy-intensive computing), instead of misusing them. There is research pointing toward the paradox that in AI's ability to facilitate a reduction in emissions, its own infrastructures and training processes have a substantial energy footprint and can lead to a reversed effect (Wright et al. 2025). The purpose and extent of this chapter is therefore threefold: (i) general overview of the position of AI technologies to resolve climate change and environmental degradation; (ii) analysis of practical applications, opportunities and obstacles of AI-based sustainability solutions; and (iii) identification of future streams of integrating AI in environmental governance, policy frameworks and sustainable systems.

To be more exact, this chapter begins with a description of climate and environmental problems, and their scope, along with causes, effects and interdependence of stress factors within the system. It then looks at the technological capabilities of AI and how they can be applied to the major sustainability activities like predictive modeling, optimization, monitoring and decision support. It then examines some of the areas of application: energy systems, transportation and land-use management, water and waste systems, biodiversity conservation and disaster-risk adaptation. Based on recent literature, this chapter identifies successes and limitations such as the quality of data, model transparency, cost of deployment and governance issues (Raihan et al. 2024; Wright et al. 2025). At the end of the chapter, the author provides a roadmap to modifying AI to a nature that sparks environmental change, or more accurately, it highlights why explainability, ethical design, green AI infrastructure and multi-stakeholder governance should be adopted to transform AI into a systemic source of environmental change.

Overall, with the increased complexity, dynamism and interrelation of environmental systems, a growing demand for intelligent, adaptive and scalable tools exists. AI provides an avenue to escape the traditional approaches – to utilize the data, provide a real-time reaction and use the predominant resources in the most efficient way. Nonetheless, to achieve this, technology, policy and sustainability objectives have to align cautiously. This chapter thus aims to find out how AI can become a turning point to climate change mitigation and environmental resilience – and what it will take to see that this is done in a responsible, effective and equitable way.

6.2. AI technologies and environmental data management

The enormous expansion of environmental information in recent years, through satellite imagery and ground-based sensor networks, has presented a challenge and an opportunity for sustainable environmental management. ML, DL and big data analytics have become the key to modeling a complex environmental system that is nonlinear and highly dimensional, with numerous interacting processes (Hamdan et al. 2024). Supervised and unsupervised learning combined with extracting features and modeling predictions have allowed better study of the dispersion of pollutants, ecological responses, weather changes, etc., with the help of ML methods. Indicatively, multispectral time-series data, degradation pattern identification and predicting environmental outcomes at a more precise level have been executed using convolutional neural networks (CNNs) and long short-term memory (LSTM) networks, whereas traditional statistical models have been unable to do these things (Stewart et al. 2025). Moreover, big data platforms and cloud-edge computing structures enable the real-time ingestion of environmental data, cleaning and analytics; hence, they assist decision-makers in near real time (Rana and Singh 2022).

The other crucial pillar of environmental data management is remote sensing and data integration by geospatial data. Satellite sensors like Sentinel, Landsat and MODIS are producing multispectral, hyperspectral and LiDAR streams, which are required to be spatially and temporal aligned. Geospatial information systems (GIS) and ML/DL integration have significantly increased accuracy in classification, detection of land-cover change and anomalies identification (Najafzadeh and Basirian 2023). To illustrate this, AI-geospatial convergence can lead to increase in classification accuracy from up to 78 to above 90 in some remote-sensing tasks presented by DL frameworks that aim to enhance classification with geospatial data (Dritsas and Trigka 2025). With remote sensing becoming a component of the Internet of Earth Systems, tremendous-scale environmental observation and geospatial hazard assessment at granular resolution have become possible through AI-powered analytics.

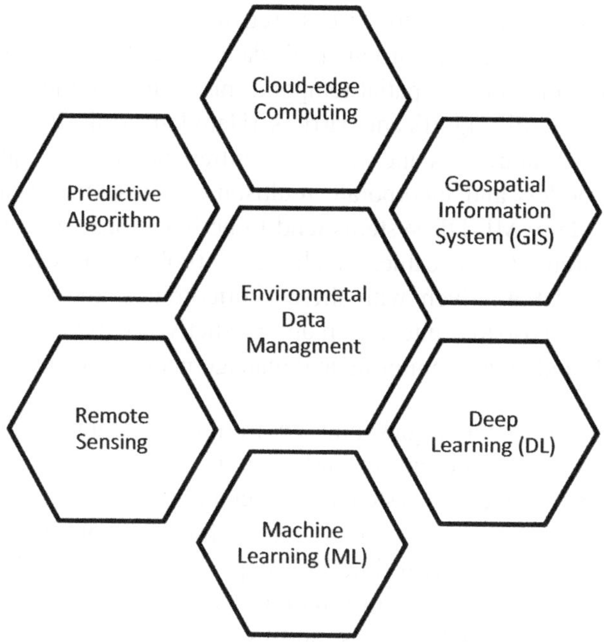

Figure 6.1. *Integration of AI technologies in environmental data management*

One of the most significant developments is the creation of predictive algorithms for real-time climate monitoring and forecasting. Traditional physics-based environmental models are often complex, require long computational run times, and rely on simplified assumptions, which limit their ability to respond effectively to rapidly changing environmental conditions. However, AI-based forecast models can consume steady data streams from sensing, satellite and re-examination information to produce brief predictions of extreme weather, outbreaks of pollutants or ecosystem changes (Naik et al. 2025). Even more recent is a review of AI methods that discovered that prognosticative accuracy of climate-influencing frameworks was improved by critical distinctions to enhance resilience approaches and adapt management (Abbas and Ahmad 2025). The algorithms enable the adoption of early warnings and resource optimization, and use predetermined policy intervention solutions by generating actionable information that respond in rapid timeframes compared to traditional modeling systems.

Nonetheless, there are no issues regarding the deployment of AI technologies to manage environmental data. The heterogeneity of data, presence of missing values, spatial-temporal misalignment and interpretability of the model are still significant barriers (Hamdan et al. 2024). Moreover, energy-efficient frameworks and intelligent infrastructure are required to train massive DL models and incorporate multisource geospatial data (Rana and Singh 2022). Many ML/DL systems tend to be black-box, meaning that they are not transparent and traceable, which can be problematic when it comes to policy and regulation. Even with these shortcomings, the synergy of ML, remote sensing, geospatial integration and predictive analytics is transforming the process of modeling, monitoring and management of the environment.

Altogether, AI technologies and environmental data management are conjunctive areas that present ground-breaking opportunities. We can now model how environmental systems interact on a large scale, observe the spatial dynamics with the same clarity as before, and predict and adapt to environmental changes in real time by using ML/DL and big data analytics; remote sensing and geospatial information allow us to observe the dynamics of complex environmental systems; and by using predictive algorithms, the same is possible in near real time. With the escalating threats to the environment by global warming, pollution and the destruction of ecosystems, resilient evidence-based environmental governance will focus on such AI-enabled methods. The integration of these technologies in efficient environmental data management is shown in Figure 6.1.

6.3. Applications of AI in climate change mitigation

AI is swiftly turning into a catalyst for climate-change mitigation by enhancing the efficiency, predictability and manageability of renewable energy systems and technologies to reduce emissions. The possibilities of AI (including traditional ML regressors and more sophisticated deep neural networks) are used in the field of optimization of renewable energy sources (to predict the generation (solar irradiance, wind speed and direction, river flow to generate hydro) and optimize the operational plans to ensure the maximum output and grid compatibility). Convolutional and recurrent neural networks have been demonstrated to lower the error in predicting solar and wind power on short-term scales by a significant margin over the more traditional statistical models, and could be applied to the more effective planning of dispatch generation and curtailing of renewable generation

(Ukoba et al. 2024). In addition to forecasting, reinforcement learning and model-predictive control have also been applied to adjust the pitch of turbines, inverter settings and angle of the image in real-time to track the sudden changes in the weather and thereby harvest a greater amount of energy per single unit of resource (Abdulameer et al. 2025).

In the case of hydropower, AI-based weather forecast-informed reservoir management that combines inflow inferences and demand dynamics with weather forecasts will allow the optimization of the timeline of releases to accommodate energy generation with the limits of water resources and ecology (Chen 2015).

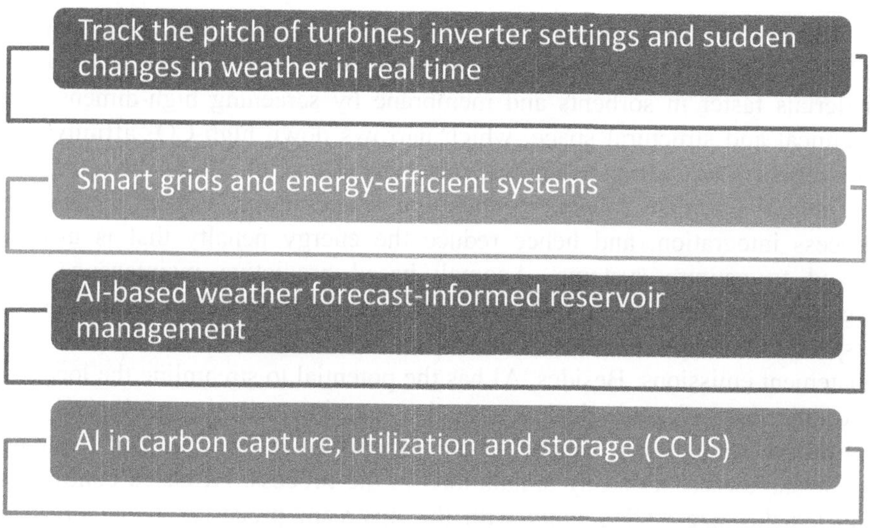

Figure 6.2. *Adaption of AI in different domains to mitigate the environmental impact and sustainable solution*

Another important application of AI is in smart grids and energy-efficient systems, where it can significantly contribute to reducing greenhouse gas emissions. AI enhances grid stability by forecasting electricity demand, enabling adaptive load balancing, optimizing the allocation of distributed energy resources (DERs) and intelligently managing energy storage systems. Machine learning (ML) algorithms support the prediction of demand patterns at high temporal resolution, allowing utilities to better manage loads, reduce reliance on peaker plants and increase the use of low-carbon energy generation. Together with enhanced energy-management systems, AI can coordinate distributed renewable resources, electric vehicle charging and battery energy storage systems to minimize the losses and peak emission and retain the reliability (Fathollahi 2025). The approach based on edge intelligence and federated learning allows privacy and low-latency control on the distribution level and prompt reaction to local congestion or voltage fluctuations without overwhelming the central computing and storage resources (Ejiyi et al. 2025). Pilot studies of smart-grid implementation suggest that AI-controlled systems can achieve reduced systems losses and operational expenses, and increase the renewable penetration capacity – crucial indicators of climate mitigation in large systems (Viana et al. 2023).

There is an increasing role of AI in carbon capture, utilization, storage (CCUS) and emission-reduction technology. ML has been used to discover materials faster in sorbents and membrane by screening high-dimensional chemical and structural space, which narrows down high-CO_2 affinity and low-regeneration energy candidate materials (Du et al. 2025). In operation, AI models optimize solvent regeneration temperatures, sorbent cycles and process integration, and hence reduce the energy penalty that is usually linked to capture systems. Anomaly-based predictive maintenance and digital twins provide a reduced downtime and overall capacity factor response of capture plants, which is better when reducing lifecycle abatement emissions. Besides, AI has the potential to streamline the location and injection of geological storage by merging seismic, geological and fluid-flow simulations, enhancing the security of the storage and reducing the leakage risk. Aided by simulations in the process, AI-based controllers can synchronize CCUS units with the upstream processes (celte or steel plants) to flatten the energy consumption and decrease net CO_2 intensity (Singh and Jain 2022).

Although these have aided advantages, there are numerous obstacles to practical utilization: the lack of enough data to train strong models, the complexity of models necessitating a hybrid approach to physics-AI models to fulfill physical plausibility and safety criteria, and the energy expense of training large-scale models themselves. Combining physics-based models and data-driven methods (physics-informed ML) with the goal of guaranteeing generalizability and still predicting complex nonlinearities is growing in popularity. Governance and lifecycle assessment, which quantify the net climate benefit of AI applications – which is the difference embodied by pollution in the manufacture of compute infrastructure and manufacturing – is equally crucial. Overall, the role of AI in field optimization (renewable), intelligent grids and CCUS already exists in reality and continues to grow; when properly structured and regulated, AI can significantly accelerate the processes of decarbonization in the environment of energy networks and industry. The different applications and their adaptation in various domains for sustainable solutions have been shown in Figure 6.2.

6.4. Challenges and ethical considerations

Even though the use of AI can be proclaimed as the boost to sustainability and climate resilience, new environmental, ethical and governance issues cannot be ignored. The rapid expansion of AI-based systems has created a paradox in that the same technology that is designed to reduce the impact of climate change may, when used improperly, increase the congestion of the environment in terms of the high consumption of computational energy, electronic waste and unproductive styles of material use (Kamyab et al. 2023).

6.4.1. *High computational energy consumption and E-waste*

The energy usage of the training of large ML and DL models has increased exponentially. An illustrative case is that, on average, the emissions of a single large-language model can exceed the equivalent of 300 tons of CO_2, which is almost five times the amount of emissions of an average automobile during its lifetime (Ul Haq et al. 2025d). The data facilities that are used to perform such calculations consume almost 2% of the global power demand, which is estimated to increase threefold in 2030 unless some efficiency measures are implemented (Ul Haq et al. 2025a). Even though the providers of this kind of hyper-scaling use renewable energy and state-of-the-art cooling, the overall sustainability impact is questionable, especially in areas that use carbon-heavy grids. In addition, electronic waste (e-waste) is also caused by the lifecycle of the GPUs, processors and sensors deployed in AI infrastructures as they have a short lifecycle. Old hardware usually disposes heavy metal, that is, cadmium and lead, and these pollute the soil and ground water in developing worlds where informal recycling is predominant (Bouquet et al. 2024). Thus, sustainable AI needs model design, low-power algorithms and hardware reuse and recycling approaches based on the circular economy similar to sustainable design.

6.4.2. *Data privacy, algorithmic bias and ethical implications*

In addition to environmental bills, AI brings complicated societal and ethical challenges of information privacy, transparency and prejudice. Personal or neighborhood data, including, but not limited to, geolocation, land ownership and health data gleaned through satellites, drones or IoT devices, are more often than not included in environmental and climate-related datasets. Poor anonymity or loose regulation can result in a violation of privacy or abuse of surveillance (Ul Haq and Khanday 2025). Algorithms also pose more serious threats to fair climate actions: AI-based forecasts based on biased or region-dependent datasets may be unfairly predicted, putting vulnerable groups at a disadvantage when it comes to allocating resources, predicting disasters or insurance (Ul Haq et al. 2025c). As an example, predictive flood models that are mainly calibrated on the data of industrialized countries do not achieve the same performance in areas with low data, intensifying an existing imbalance. Ethical AI frameworks hence focus on inclusivity, fairness and explainability so that the decisions made by algorithms can be transparent and accountable (Jha et al. 2019). The emerging field of explainable AI (XAI) aims to interpret and clarify the outputs of complex AI models, enabling the parties to comprehend, challenge and refine AI-based logic operations.

6.4.3. *Governance frameworks for sustainable AI deployment*

These environment-related and ethically guided issues require strong governance systems to be both innovative and responsible. Proposals have been made by international organizations to determine principles to trust, including AI: sustainability, human rights and environmental safety have been suggested by the European Union (EU), UNESCO and the OECD (Ul Haq 2024). The AI Act by the EU brings legal obligations for risk assessment, transparency and environmental reporting of AI applications. Equally, the governments of the countries are considering AI sustainability measures in climate-policy tools and company reporting rules (Ruschemeier and Bareis 2024). Technically, a technical approach has been taken toward Green AI, which is concerned with computational efficiency and carbon accounting of lifecycle, and has become popular in both universities and enterprises. In this method, it is recommended to publish the energy cost of training and inference, which promotes model pruning, quantization and transfer of learning methods to minimize resource usage (Schwartz et al. 2020). Moreover, the collaboration between various stakeholders, technologists, ethical considerations, policymakers and the impacted communities should be considered as the designation to make sure that AI implementation cannot be at odds with the bigger picture sustainability and justice concerns (Jobin et al. 2019).

Aspect	Main issue	Impact	Suggested approach
Energy and e-waste	High power use in AI training; short hardware lifespan	Increases carbon footprint and e-waste pollution	Use energy-efficient models, renewable energy data centers and circular hardware reuse
Data privacy	Use of sensitive geolocation and environmental data	Risk of privacy breaches and misuse	Enforce strict data protection and anonymization measures
Algorithmic bias	Biased or region-specific datasets	Unfair predictions and unequal resource allocation	Ensure diverse datasets and regular fairness auditing
Transparency	Lack of explainability in AI models	Reduces accountability and public trust	Apply explainable AI (XAI) frameworks for interpretability
Governance	Weak or inconsistent ethical frameworks	Unchecked environmental and social risks	Align with EU, OECD and UNESCO AI ethics and sustainability principles
Sustainable AI design	High computational cost and emissions	Contradicts climate goals	Promote "Green AI" (Schwartz et al. 2020), model optimization and carbon reporting
Collaboration	Limited stakeholder involvement	Fragmented and unequal implementation	Foster inclusive, multi-stakeholder governance and community participation

Table 6.1. *Challenges and ethical considerations in AI for climate action*

Overall, the discussions about AI-driven solutions to the environmental issues should not overlook the environmental and ethical footprint of AI itself. High energy usage, electronic waste, data invasion and algorithmic discrimination would pose a threat to the climate advantages of the technology in its present state. It is therefore urgent to put extensive governance systems in place and implement open, energy utilization friendly and socially fair AI systems. The only way AI may truly be used as a tool of climate action and sustainable development is by using it responsibly and with policy alignment to ensure it is a new source of environmental inequity (Table 6.1).

6.5. Future perspectives and integrated technologies

The intersection of AI with new digital technologies, including the IoT, blockchain and remote sensing, is repurposing the meaning of environmental sustainability. All of these integrations establish the cornerstone of the intelligent ecosystems of the next generation that can be adaptive, decentralized and transparent in managing the environment. Moreover, the emergence of Green AI and energy-saving computing is bringing the computational revolution in line with sustainability objectives, and responsible innovation systems and policy-based governance are becoming significant to guarantee ethical, inclusive and ecologically sound use (Corrêa et al. 2023).

6.5.1. *Synergistic use of AI with IoT, blockchain and remote sensing*

The combination of AI with the IoT facilitates real-time sensing, analytics and decision-making for environmental systems. IoT networks produce huge amounts of data via distributed sensors, which measure parameters like air quality, soil moisture, hydrological cycles and energy consumption. AI algorithms then run on these data and convert them into actionable information regarding predictive maintenance, anomaly detection and adaptive resource allocation (Rolnick et al. 2022). As an illustration, AI-enriched IoT systems in precision agriculture can adapt the level of irrigation and fertilization according to microclimates, and create the maximum yield with minimal input use (Karuppaiah et al. 2023). In intelligent cities, IoT with AIs can be used to constantly monitor pollution and traffic to provide emission-reduction policies and sustainable urban design (Saad and Myat 2025).

The combination of blockchain technology and AI ensures sustainability management is more transparent, has data-integrity and is traceable. The decentralized registry of blockchain provides a secure data provenance of carbon credits, renewable energy certificates and waste-tracking systems (Hughes et al. 2019). Combined with the pattern-recognition and predictive features of AI, blockchain and AI can be used to improve accountability by matching real-time data on the amount of emissions that IoT sensors record with records on the verifiability offset (Huang 2023).

Remote sensing also supplements AI and IoT by offering spatiotemporal data to the degree of high resolution required to model the environment. ML models do not require complex algorithms to identify deforestation, monitor glacial melts and conduct analysis of marine ecosystems in areas where their human counterparts could not operate (Zhu et al. 2024). Satellite-acquired data, when combined with AI-IoT networks, will offer the macro-perspective to the micro-observations of the sensors, which will lead to multi-scale environmental intelligence. In combination, these technologies allow a globally linked and data-driven ecosystem of the condition of sustainable resource management, as well as climate adaptation.

6.5.2. *Green AI and energy-efficient computing approaches*

Although AI can have undeniably vast potential, its environmental impact on sustainability has become a topic of concern. Green AI puts forward the notion of green efficiency, green accounting and design consideration of AI systems (Lacoste et al. 2019). Model pruning, quantization and transfer learning are just some of the approaches that minimize the amount of energy used in training without deteriorating performance. Furthermore, edge AI processing of data can be applied locally on low-power devices instead of on a data center, which reduces latency, bandwidth requirements and energy consumption (Zhu et al. 2022). Ultra-efficient alternatives to environments and sensor-based AI operation are under investigation through neuromorphic computing, which is brain inspired, and photonic processors (Zhang et al. 2020). Simultaneously, data centers and carbon neutral data infrastructures are shifting toward cloud service providers moving toward renewable-powered data centers and infrastructures powered by renewable energy. Green AI will no longer just be a niche phenomenon, as more studies are focusing on sustainability-by-design, with the idea becoming a core value in the era of new algorithm development.

6.5.3. *Pathways for responsible innovation and policy-driven sustainability*

Responsible innovation policies should be required to offer AI a fair and sustainable contribution to global environmental focus. The policy makers and data technologists need to collaborate to come up with measures that incorporate environmental ethics, data sovereignty and long-term environmental effects into the lifecycle of AI (Pastor-Escuredo et al. 2022). Acknowledgments toward improved environmental oversight despite diminished technological expertise and expansion see start-up initiatives, like the European Green Deal, the UN Environment Programme and AI Governance to AI Governance, pinpoint the strategic potential in validating AI research priorities through climate and biodiversity criteria (Mwangi 2021). Additionally, the implementation of sustainability measures, including energy intensity, carbon footprint and lifecycle analysis, as part of the evaluation system of the application of AI can design the procurement decision-making and funding toward low-impact solutions. Industries can nurture transparency and accountability through the development of interoperable standards, requirements and the creation of open-source sustainability benchmarks (Islam 2025). Notably, the involvement of stakeholders in academia, industry and the civil sector guarantees the inclusivity, equity and diversity of AI-based environmental solution(s) to different ecological contexts.

Aspect	Key insight	Outcome for sustainability
AI + IoT	Real-time sensing and analytics for air, water and soil systems	Enables predictive maintenance and efficient resource use
AI + blockchain	Secure, traceable data for carbon credits and energy tracking	Ensures transparency and accountability in sustainability reporting
AI + remote sensing	High-resolution environmental monitoring via satellites	Supports global-scale modeling of deforestation, climate and ecosystems
Green AI	Energy-efficient model design and renewable-powered data centers	Reduces AI's carbon footprint and promotes sustainable computing
Policy and governance	Responsible innovation, ethical standards and stakeholder inclusion	Ensures fair, accountable and eco-aligned AI deployment

Table 6.2. *Synergistic role of AI and emerging digital technologies in environmental sustainability*

The overlay of AI with IoT, blockchain and remote sensing will progress over time to further enable the development of autonomous self-correcting environmental systems, which can conduct adaptive governance. At the same time, Green AI development and policy-driven innovation will make sure that these systems work within the borders of the planet. This shaping of technological wisdom and moral imagination provides a way out into an eco-intelligent future, in which digital revolution proceeds in parallel with environmental conservation (Table 6.2).

6.6. Conclusion

The role of AI in developing the global response to climate change is the ability to manipulate data to handle the environment, make predictions and optimize resources. AI enables monitoring in real time, controlling emissions and sustainable urban planning through its connection with IoT, blockchain and remote sensing. All the technologies help to increase the accuracy, efficiency and transparency of environmental governance. However, the positive effects of AI on the environment are weighed down by power-consuming operations and electronic waste, as well as ethical issues such as the risk of data privacy and bias in policies. To find a truly sustainable solution to these problems, it is necessary to deal with them by means of Green AI, data centers based on renewable power and responsible innovation frameworks. The development of AI systems in the future will rely on policy-based and ethically oriented systems that strike a balance between innovation and ecological sustainability. When it comes to ensuring that the development of AI contributes to the attainment of the UN SDGs, collaboration among governments, industries and researchers can also be ensured. Finally, AI should become a partner that is conscious of green issues, a technology that does not only assist with climate resiliency, but also follows eco-regulations. AI can shape a sustainable change when created in a responsible way, and make the world a better place, moving toward a future that is stronger and more environmentally friendly.

6.7. References

Abbas, Z. and Ahmad, Z. (2025). Integration of remote sensing and spatial artificial intelligence for climate risk assessment. *Frontiers in Computational Spatial Intelligence*, 3(4), 179–191.

Abdulameer, L., Al-Maimuri, N.M.L., Nama, A.H., Rashid, F.L., Mohammed, H.I., Al-Dujaili, A.N.G. (2025). Review of artificial intelligence applications in dams and water resources: Current trends and future directions. *Management Services*, 11, 13.

Adebayo, A.S. (2025). AI driven species recognition and digital systematics: Applying artificial intelligence for automated organism classification in ecological and environmental monitoring. *International Journal of Research Publication and Reviews*, 6, 31–49.

Bouquet, P., Jackson, I., Nick, M., Kaboli, A. (2024). AI-based forecasting for optimised solar energy management and smart grid efficiency. *International Journal of Production Research*, 62(13), 4623–4644.

Chen, Y. (2015). Evaluation of a data mining application adopting private information retrieval in the cloud computing environment. Master's Thesis, AUT University, Auckland.

Chen, Z., Chen, H., Dai, Q., Wang, Y., Hu, X. (2024). Estimation of soil moisture during different growth stages of summer maize under various water conditions using UAV multispectral data and machine learning. *Agronomy*, 14(9), 2008.

Corrêa, N.K., Galvão, C., Santos, J.W., Del Pino, C., Pinto, E.P., Barbosa, C., Massmann, D., Mambrini, R., Galvão, L., Terem, E. et al. (2023). Worldwide AI ethics: A review of 200 guidelines and recommendations for AI governance. *Patterns*, 4(10), 100857.

Devarajan, G.G., Nagarajan, S.M., Ghosh, U., Alnumay, W., Ghosh, U., Alnumay, W. (2023). DDNSAS: Deep reinforcement learning based deep Q-learning network for smart agriculture system. *Sustainable Computing: Informatics and Systems*, 39, 100890.

Dritsas, E. and Trigka, M. (2025). Remote sensing and geospatial analysis in the big data era: A survey. *Remote Sensing*, 17(3), 550.

Du, X., Khan, M.N., Thakur, G.C. (2025). Machine learning in carbon capture, utilization, storage, and transportation: A review of applications in greenhouse gas emissions reduction. *Processes*, 13(4), 1160.

Ejiyi, C.J., Cai, D., Thomas, D., Obiora, S., Osei-Mensah, E., Acen, C., Eze, F.O., Sam, F., Zhang, Q., Bamisile, O.O. (2025). Comprehensive review of artificial intelligence applications in renewable energy systems: Current implementations and emerging trends. *Journal of Big Data*, 12(1), 169.

Fathollahi, A. (2025). Machine learning and artificial intelligence techniques in smart grids stability analysis: A review. *Energies*, 18(13), 3431.

Gupta, P., Bhardwaj, G., Dubey, S., Tayal, T., SenGupta, A., Narad, P. (2024). AI-enabled process optimization for sustainable wastewater treatment solutions. In *The AI Cleanse: Transforming Wastewater Treatment Through Artificial Intelligence: Harnessing Data-Driven Solutions*, Garg, M.C. (ed.). Springer, Cham.

Hamdan, A., Ibekwe, K.I., Etukudoh, E.A., Umoh, A.A., Ilojianya, V.I. (2024). AI and machine learning in climate change research: A review of predictive models and environmental impact. *World Journal of Advanced Research and Reviews*, 21(1), 1999–2008.

Huang, S. (2023). The comprehensive environmental efficiency analysis based on a new data envelopment analysis: The super slack based measure network three-stage data envelopment analysis approach. *Journal of Cleaner Production*, 400, 136689.

Hughes, L., Dwivedi, Y.K., Misra, S.K., Rana, N.P., Raghavan, V., Akella, V. (2019). Blockchain research, practice and policy: Applications, benefits, limitations, emerging research themes and research agenda. *International Journal of Information Management*, 49, 114–129.

Islam, F.A.S. (2025). Artificial intelligence-driven smart waste-to-energy networks for climate-resilient circular resource management in vulnerable megacities. *International Journal of Environment and Climate Change*, 15(7), 381–415.

Jha, K., Doshi, A., Patel, P., Shah, M. (2019). A comprehensive review on automation in agriculture using artificial intelligence. *Artificial Intelligence in Agriculture*, 2, 1–12.

Jin, X.B., Yu, X.H., Wang, X.Y., Bai, Y.T., Su, T.L., Kong, J.L. (2020). Deep learning predictor for sustainable precision agriculture based on Internet of Things system. *Sustainability*, 12, 1433.

Jobin, A., Ienca, M., Vayena, E. (2019). The global landscape of AI ethics guidelines. *Nature Machine Intelligence*, 1(9), 389–399.

Kamyab, H., Khademi, T., Chelliapan, S., SaberiKamarposhti, M., Rezania, S., Yusuf, M., Farajnezhad, M., Abbas, M., Hun Jeon, B., Ahn, Y. (2023). The latest innovative avenues for the utilization of artificial intelligence and big data analytics in water resource management. *Results in Engineering*, 20, 101566.

Karuppaiah, B., Jeyaraman, A., Chen, S.M., Chavan, P.R., Karthik, R., Shim, J.J., Park, S.J. (2023). Design and synthesis of nickel-doped cobalt molybdate microrods: An effective electrocatalyst for the determination of antibiotic drug ronidazole. *Environmental Research*, 222, 115343.

Krishnan, S.R., Nallakaruppan, M.K., Chengoden, R., Koppu, S., Iyapparaja, M., Sadhasivam, J., Sethuraman, S. (2022). Smart water resource management using Artificial Intelligence – A review. *Sustainability*, 14(20), 13384.

Kumar, M. (2024). AI for climate change: Predicting environmental impact and developing sustainable solutions. *ESP Journal of Engineering & Technology Advancements*, 4(3), 127–133.

Lacoste, A., Luccioni, A., Schmidt, V., Dandres, T. (2019). Quantifying the carbon emissions of machine learning. arXiv Preprint. arXiv:1910.09700.

Lakhouit, A. (2025). Revolutionizing urban solid waste management with AI and IoT: A review of smart solutions for waste collection, sorting, and recycling. *Results in Engineering*, 25, 104018.

McCarthy, M.J., Herrero, H.V., Insalaco, S.A., Hinten, M.T., Anyamba, A. (2025). Satellite remote sensing for environmental sustainable development goals: A review of applications for terrestrial and marine protected areas. *Remote Sensing Applications: Society and Environment*, 37, 101450.

Mwangi, J. (2024). The future of Kenya's environmental diplomacy. Mashariki Research and Policy Centre.

Naik, M., Bharani, J.S.S.L., Roy, A., Prakash, R.V., Yadav, H.L. Chetia, B. (2025). AI-driven climate modelling and forecasting enhancing environmental resilience through predictive analytics. *International Journal of Environmental Sciences*, 11(18s), 1762–1768.

Najafzadeh, M. and Basirian, S. (2023). Evaluation of river water quality index using remote sensing and artificial intelligence models. *Remote Sensing*, 15(9), 2359.

Norouzzadeh, M.S., Nguyen, A., Kosmala, M., Swanson, A., Palmer, M.S., Packer, C., Clune, J. (2018). Automatically identifying, counting, and describing wild animals in camera-trap images with deep learning. *Proceedings of the National Academy of Sciences of the United States of America*, 115(25), E5716–E5725.

Pachot, A. and Patissier, C. (2023). Towards sustainable artificial intelligence: An overview of environmental protection uses and issues. arXiv Preprint. arXiv:2212.11738.

Pastor-Escuredo, D., Treleaven, P., Vinuesa, R. (2022). An ethical framework for artificial intelligence and sustainable cities. *AI*, 3(4), 961–974.

Raihan, A., Paul, A., Rahman, M.S., Islam, S., Paul, P., Karmakar, S. (2024). Artificial intelligence (AI) for environmental sustainability: A concise review of technology innovations in energy, transportation, biodiversity, and water management. *Journal of Technology Innovations and Energy*, 3(2), 64–73.

Rana, B. and Singh, Y. (2022). Duty-cycling techniques in IoT: Energy-efficiency perspective. In *Recent Innovations in Computing: Proceedings of ICRIC 2021, Volume 1*. Springer, Singapore.

Rolnick, D., Donti, P.L., Kaack, L.H., Kochanski, K., Lacoste, A., Sankaran, K., Ross, A.S., Milojevic-Dupont, N., Jaques, N., Waldman-Brown, A. et al. (2022). Tackling climate change with machine learning. *ACM Computing Surveys*, 55(2), 1–96.

Ruschemeier, H. and Bareis, J. (2024). Searching for harmonised rules: Understanding the paradigms, provisions and pressing issues in the final EU AI Act.

Saad, A.M.H. and Myat, A. (2025). AI-powered IoT frameworks for real-time environmental monitoring and sustainable urban development in smart cities. *AIP Conference Proceedings*, 3327(1), 020009.

Schwartz, R., Dodge, J., Smith, N.A., Etzioni, O. (2020). Green AI. *Communications of the ACM*, 63(12), 54–63.

Singh, S. and Jain, P. (2022). Applications of artificial intelligence for the development of sustainable agriculture. In *Agro-biodiversity and Agri-ecosystem Management*, Kumar, P., Tomar, R.S., Bhat, J.A. et al. (eds). Springer, Singapore.

Srivastava, A. and Maity, R. (2023). Assessing the potential of AI–ML in urban climate change adaptation and sustainable development. *Sustainability*, 15(23), 16461.

Stahl, B.C. (2021). *Artificial Intelligence for a Better Future: An Ecosystem Perspective on the Ethics of AI and Emerging Digital Technologies*. Springer, Cham.

Stewart, A.J., Robinson, C., Corley, I.A., Ortiz, A., Lavista Ferres, J.M., Banerjee, A. (2025). Torchgeo: Deep learning with geospatial data. *ACM Transactions on Spatial Algorithms and Systems*, 11(4), 1–28.

Ukoba, K., Olatunji, K.O., Adeoye, E., Jen, T.C., Madyira, D.M. (2024). Optimizing renewable energy systems through artificial intelligence: Review and future prospects. *Energy and Environment*, 35(7), 3833–3879.

Ul Haq, I. (2024). Diagnosis of neurological disease using bioinspired algorithms. In *Bio-Inspired Optimization for Medical Data Mining*, Srivastava, S., Anand, A., Kumar, A. et al. (eds). John Wiley & Sons, Hoboken, NJ.

Ul Haq, I. and Khanday, A.M.U.D. (2025). Exploring the role of explainable AI in women's health: Challenges and solutions. In *Explainable Artificial Intelligence in the Healthcare Industry*, Kumar, A., Kumar, T.A., Das, P. et al. (eds). John Wiley & Sons, Hoboken, NJ.

Ul Haq, I, Kumar, N., Koul, N., Verma, C., Eneacu, F.M., Raboaca, M.S. (2022). Machine learning techniques for result prediction of one day international (ODI) cricket match. In *The International Conference on Recent Innovations in Computing*. Springer, Singapore.

Ul Haq, I., Kaur, G., Rather, A.H. (2024). Fruit leaf classification using transfer learning for automation and industrial applications. In *Deep Learning Techniques for Automation and Industrial Applications*, Rathore, P.S., Ahuja, S., Burri, S.R. et al. (eds). John Wiley & Sons, Hoboken, NJ.

Ul Haq, I., Shah, H.A., Rufai, S.Z. (2025a). Enhancing water security through automation: Case studies and technical advancements in water quality management. In *Computational Automation for Water Security*, Dubey, A.K., Srivastav, A.L., Kumar, A. et al. (eds). Elsevier, Amsterdam.

Ul Haq, I., Kumar, A., Rathore, P.S. (2025b). Machine learning approaches for wind power forecasting: A comprehensive review. *Discover Applied Sciences*, 7(10), 1139.

Ul Haq, I., Malhotra, J., Rawat, V., Kumari, J., Kaur, G. (2025c). Machine learning approaches for early detection of cervical cancer: A comparative study of classification models. In *Targeted Chemotherapy with Personalized Immunotherapy: An AI Approach*, Kumar, A., Das, P., Rathore, P.S. et al. (eds). John Wiley & Sons, Hoboken, NJ.

Ul Haq, I., Nandal, V., Uppal, H. (2025d). Blockchain applications in aviation securing transactions, streamlining operations, and improving passenger experience. In *Blockchain in the Tourism Industry: A New Era of Secure and Transparent Travel Solutions*, Kumar, A., Abreu, A., Batta, P. et al. (eds). Springer, Cham.

Uriarte-Gallastegi, N., Arana-Landín, G., Landeta-Manzano, B., Laskurain-Iturbe, I. (2024). The role of AI in improving environmental sustainability: A focus on energy management. *Energies*, 17(3), 649.

Viana, J.L.M., Steffler, D.A., Hernández, A.H., Dos Santos Costa, J., Pellegrinetti, T.A., de Jesus, E.C.R., Cancian, M., Fiore, M.F., Rezende-Filho, A.T., Sussulini, A. et al. (2023). Bioaccumulation and speciation of arsenic in plankton from tropical soda lakes along a salinity gradient. *Science of the Total Environment*, 895, 165189.

Wang, S., Xu, D., Liang, H., Bai, Y., Li, X., Zhou, J., Su, C., Wei, W. (2025). Advances in deep learning applications for plant disease and pest detection: A review. *Remote Sensing*, 17(4), 698.

Wright, D., Igel, C., Samuel, G., Selvan, R. (2025). Efficiency is not enough: A critical perspective on environmentally sustainable AI. *Communications of the ACM*, 68(7), 62–69.

Wu, J., Huang, J., Li, Z., Yang, H., Ge, H., Meng, X., Zhao, Y. (2024). Influence of electrochemical descaling treatment in simulated cooling water on the corrosion behavior of stainless steel. *Journal of Cleaner Production*, 451, 142066.

Yigitcanlar, T., Mehmood, R., Corchado, J.M. (2021). Green artificial intelligence: Towards an efficient, sustainable and equitable technology for smart cities and futures. *Sustainability*, 13(16), 8952.

Zhang, W., Gao, B., Tang, J., Yao, P., Yu, S., Chang, M.F., Yoo, H.J., Qian, H., Wu, H. (2020). Neuro-inspired computing chips. *Nature Electronics*, 3(7), 371–382.

Zhu, S., Ota, K., Dong, M. (2022). Green AI for IIoT: Energy efficient intelligent edge computing for industrial Internet of Things. *IEEE Transactions on Green Communications and Networking*, 6(1), 79–88.

Zhu, L., Cui, T., Runa, A., Pan, X., Zhao, W., Xiang, J., Cao, M. (2024). Robust remote sensing retrieval of key eutrophication indicators in coastal waters based on explainable machine learning. *ISPRS Journal of Photogrammetry and Remote Sensing*, 211, 262–280.

7

Global Policies and AI-Enabled Energy Strategies

The development of policies to include the concept of artificial intelligence (AI) in the energy sector has been on the increase due to the growing global interest in climate resiliency and sustainability. The utilization of AI technologies is increasing, and energy production, distribution and consumption are thereby made more efficient, reliable and sustainable. This chapter evaluates how international strategic structures and policies are using AI to hasten the process of smarter and cleaner energy structures. The use of AI-powered solutions for optimal grid operation, energy demand prediction, renewable energy integration and minimization of greenhouse gas emissions has been adopted with the assistance of international agreements like the Paris Agreement, the United Nations sustainable development goals (SDGs) and state policy on renewable energy. In addition, AI can support decision-makers to design more effective, flexible and fair energy systems, and such a process is facilitated by the ability to make policies based on the data, which are made possible by predictive analytics, real-time monitoring and adaptive control mechanisms. Nations all over the such as, and the United States, China, India and the countries of the EU, are also integrating AI into their energy transition strategies as research partners, funders of innovation and regulators. Delays in the worldwide implementation of technology remain a significant setback due to the issue of data privacy, the fair use of AI and equal access to technology. The introduction of AI in energy regulations is a game-changing opportunity to pursue the goals of sustainability on an international level. It introduces an intelligent, low-carbon and resilient energy future for the globe by creating a balance between technical advancement and environmental care.

7.1. Introduction

One of the most widespread problems and concerns in the 21st century is the transition to renewable energy systems. The production of energy has subjected the environment to an increasing amount of environmental

Chapter written by Adil Husain RATHER, Inam UL HAQ and Irfan RASOOL.

degradation and greenhouse emission due to the pressure on traditional energy sources because of rapid industrialization, a population explosion and escalating energy needs. To find a solution to these problems, countries in all parts of the world are coming up with comprehensive policy frameworks that are skewed towards technical innovation, energy conservation and renewable energy. AI is one of the new technologies capable of revolutionizing the global energy sector (Alsaigh et al. 2022). With the implementation of AI in energy systems, governments and organizations are moving toward smarter, more efficient and environmentally sustainable energy systems that conform to global climate objectives. AI performs exceptionally well in the analysis of complex statistics, trends, future predictions and the enhanced performance of operations. This is particularly applicable in the energy market where there is a need to constantly analyze and process large volumes of data with regard to power grids, renewable energy and consumption networks (Arefin et al. 2025). AI-based tools, such as machine learning algorithms, neural networks and predictive analytics, make it possible to establish an accurate forecasting of the energy demand, supply chain optimization and smart control of isolated energy resources. Besides enhancing energy efficiency and reliability, it also aids in the long-term planning of climate action and making decisions on sustainable energy policy. Global schemes in search of clean and renewable energy systems are based on global frameworks, including the European Green Deal, the Paris Climate Agreement (2015) and the United Nations SDGs (SDG 7: Affordable and Clean Energy).

The importance of technical innovation in accelerating the process of the transition to low-carbon economies is highlighted by these initiatives (Bouquet et al. 2024). In this matter, AI would be the key to achieving resilience, sustainability and efficiency in numerous energy-related areas, including electricity production and delivery, end-user consumption and storage. To offer an example, AI can optimize the incorporation of renewable energy sources such as wind and solar into the national grids, minimizing the amount of wasted energy and making the system more stable. International organizations and governments are starting to realize the power of AI as a prerequisite to the transformation of sustainable energy. Similarly, in the United States, AI technologies are being used to maintain the energy infrastructure proactively, automate demand response and the development of the smart grid (Faris and Batra 2024). The European Union has also invested heavily in AI research and digital innovation hubs to come up with smart energy solutions via its Horizon Europe program. On the same note, China has undertaken mass AI-driven smart grid initiatives to handle the continuously increasing intricacy of the renewable energy industry in the country and enhance energy efficiency. India can be used as an example of how AI can be implemented in developing economies to enhance their sustainable growth in the future. India has already integrated AI into its renewable energy prediction systems and national campaigns to develop solar and wind energy. In operations, AI helps in governance and policy formulation, among others.

With the help of AI analytics, data-driven policymaking enables governments to simulate the state of energy, quantify the effectiveness of policy alternatives and formulate elastic regulations based on the current environmental and economic signals. The impact of carbon pricing, renewable energy subsidies or reduction targets on the national economy and energy security can be examined in the case of AI models. These insights can help policymakers develop balanced policies that promote both socioeconomic development and sustainability objectives. Although the adoption of AI in global energy systems has many advantages, there are various problems and ethical issues that should be taken into account (Gunasena Ekanayaka et al. 2025). To achieve a fair and inclusive development, the issue of algorithmic bias, cybersecurity, data privacy and unequal access to AI technologies must be resolved. Additionally, the application of AI presupposes massive investments in the digital infrastructure, the training of professional staff and international partnerships. The absence of strong world governance structures may be increasing the inequality between wealthy and poor countries and the unfair gains of AI-enabled energy revolutions. International policies and AI-enhanced solutions are transforming the future of the energy sector by means of the utilization of AI-powered solutions and by the enhancement of smart, durable and resilient systems. A combination of proper legislative frameworks, cross-border technological innovation and cooperation will result in global energy security and carbon neutrality. The combination of AI and energy management will not just enhance operational efficiency but will also bring about the movement toward a sustainable, low-carbon and equitable global energy future, as countries will continue to invest in digital transformation. Table 7.1 presents a summary of the key global policies and strategic frameworks such as the United Nations SDGs, the Paris Climate Agreement, the European Green Deal and the programs launched by the International Energy Agency (IEA) along with the efforts sponsored by the World Economic Forum (WEF) that are influencing the use of AI in the global energy industry. Collectively, these frameworks promote cleaner and more resilient energy systems through the achievement of sustainability goals, the reduction of carbon emissions, digital transformation and the enhancement of international collaboration. They also favor implementing AI technologies in the field of predicting renewable energy, managing smart grids, predictive maintenance and monitoring emissions.

Global policy framework	Objective	AI applications in energy	Impact/outcomes
United Nations sustainable development goals (SDGs)	Achieve affordable, reliable, sustainable and modern energy for all (SDG 7); take urgent climate action (SDG 13).	AI supports renewable forecasting, energy efficiency optimization and emission tracking.	Promotes equitable access to clean energy and accelerates climate action.
Paris Climate Agreement (2015)	Limit global temperature rise below 2°C by reducing carbon emissions.	AI assists in emission monitoring, renewable resource assessment and energy optimization.	Helps nations meet nationally determined contributions (NDCs) and track carbon reductions.
European Green Deal	Achieve carbon neutrality by 2050 through sustainable energy and digital innovation.	AI enhances smart grids, energy storage and predictive maintenance.	Improves system efficiency, resilience and renewable integration.
International Energy Agency (IEA) Initiatives	Promote global energy security, sustainability and innovation.	AI-driven analytics for energy forecasting, system modeling and efficiency reporting.	Strengthens global cooperation on sustainable energy transitions.
World Economic Forum (WEF) Collaborations	Foster public–private partnerships for energy innovation.	AI and data-driven tools for smart energy systems and market optimization.	Encourages ethical AI use and international knowledge exchange.

Table 7.1. *Global policies driving AI integration in energy systems*

7.2. International laws influencing AI use in energy systems

With the increasing global demand for clean, reliable and sustainable energy, new policies and frameworks continue to emerge in order to sustain that flow. Everyone wants progress, and they want to collaborate and continue the tech in the desired direction. And in the very middle of all this is AI. AI is not just a buzzword; it is literally employed to make countries abide by their climate commitments, extract more renewable energy and be smarter with their energy utilization. Governments and large organizations are integrating AI into their energy plans, in the hope of achieving large objectives such as energy sustainability and climate neutrality. This change is not incidental – it is based on several large-scale international agreements and rules (Satif et al. 2025).

7.2.1. *United Nations SDGs*

In 2015, the UN launched what is essentially a list of tasks to complete to have a better world in 2030 – the SDGs. Two of these, SDG 7 (Affordable and Clean Energy) and SDG 13 (Climate Action), are of great concern in terms of the application of AI in energy systems. AI aligns very well with these objectives: it will enable fewer to go without energy, increase efficiency and simplify integrating renewables into the mix (Mahmud and Waheduzzaman 2025). Take smart grids, for example. With AI, energy organizations will be able to operate power networks that are significantly more intelligent – they reduce waste, serve areas that are hard to reach and simply improve the system overall.

7.2.2. *2015 Paris Climate Agreement*

The Paris Agreement, which was signed on the UN climate framework, could be the most significant climate agreement in the world. The overall concept is that global warming must not exceed 2°C, preferably less than 1.52°C. Each of the involved countries must plot its own scheme (Nationally Determined Contribution [NDC]) for reducing emissions. AI plays a real part here. Governments and companies employ AI tools to monitor emissions, extract the maximum out of renewable and draft energy policies that are capable of adapting to the changes in conditions. It is not a mere theory, practical everyday application (Rahmani-Andebili 2022).

7.2.3. *European Green Deal*

In 2019, the European Green Deal was established by the European Commission to achieve a climate-neutral Europe by 2050. It not only concerns the issue of emission reduction but also the process of transforming the energy-based mechanism, technological and urban collaboration. Such strategies are centered on AI. Europe is not just discussing this, it is investing in AI to develop energy by massive initiatives, including Horizon Europe and Digital Europe. On the ground, AI is already transforming things, calculating when grids require certain repairs, planning cities and monitoring energy consumption (Blasch et al. 2021). Think of intelligent grids, which adjust the increase and decrease of renewable power in real time, or a building management system, which uses AI to minimize wasted power. And the EU itself is not insensitive to the risks; it is highly concerned with the fact that AI should be used in a way that is ethical.

7.2.4. *Global partnerships and the IEA*

The IEA plays a significant role in ensuring that the world transitions to digital energy systems. The IEA proposes AI applications in areas such as demand control and the prediction of renewable energy. They collaborate with other organizations to enable countries to construct policies that are prepared for this new era of AI and continue researching the potential of AI to assist in achieving net-zero goals. There are also associations such as the World Economic Forum (WEF) and the International Renewable Energy Agency (IRENA). They advocate for worldwide cooperation, establish mechanisms to exchange information and assist developing nations to make the most of AI in terms of climate resilience and energy production (Ul Haq et al. 2025b).

7.2.5. *International projects based on global policies*

All these large global transactions are passed down to individual countries. The United States, in this case, initiated AI for its energy program to enhance renewable forecasting and ensure that the grids operate efficiently. China is going all-in on AI-assisted smart grids and models to assist in achieving its 2060 carbon neutrality target. India is developing AI to build tougher grids and to become more prudent predictors of solar and wind power based on its own national AI strategy. What ties all of this together (Ul Haq et al. 2024). These national plans are not operating by themselves; they are instead closely intertwined with international accords, and are ensuring that they are all heading in the same direction, as far as sustainable energy is concerned (Ul Haq et al. 2022).

7.3. AI-powered energy techniques

AI is not a buzzword in the energy sector; it is transforming the game. Thanks to AI, these days, energy systems are becoming smarter, tougher and a lot greener. It is not only about the automation of a few processes here and there. AI goes further and incorporates data-based intelligence into the process of trading energy, distributing it, anticipating demand and even staying abreast of regulations (Ul Haq et al. 2025d).

7.3.1. *Predictive energy forecasting*

One of the most significant contributions of artificial intelligence (AI) to the energy sector is predictive forecasting. Renewable energy sources such as solar and wind are inherently variable due to changing weather conditions, including fluctuations in sunlight and wind speed. Traditional forecasting methods often struggle to capture these dynamic patterns accurately. In contrast, AI-based machine learning algorithms can analyze large volumes of data collected from satellites, weather sensors, and historical power generation records to produce more accurate predictions. For example, by identifying patterns in wind speed and solar irradiance, AI models can estimate future power generation and provide valuable information to energy producers, enabling more efficient grid management and real-time operational adjustments. It not only concerns the supply side either, AI also examines seasonal behavior, time-of-day peaks and customer behavior to make assumptions about how much energy people will actually consume. The insights aid utility companies in maintaining a balance between the amount of what is coming in and what is going out. This implies a decrease in deforestation and the use of fossil fuels (Ul Haq et al. 2025a). To add to this, AI predictions indicate when an operator should accumulate additional energy and when to access those reserves, thus battery systems become utilized effectively and the grid remains stable. To sum up, predictive energy forecasting is a way to save money, reduce emissions and keep the lights on (Ul Haq and Khanday 2025).

7.3.2. *Smart grid management*

It is not a minor task to transform old-school power grids into smart and self-optimizing networks, yet AI is at the core of this. All manner of distributed energy resources, electric cars, rooftop solar panels and wind turbines, all arriving at different times, at different locations, have to be accommodated by smart grids. Without AI, it would be anarchy to control all that. AI deals with continuous incoming data from sensors, meters and grid hardware to ensure that everything is running properly and reliably. Machine learning can detect faults in the system almost immediately and isolate them before they lead to large-scale issues. This translates to a reduction in the number of outages and enhanced services to all. Predictive maintenance goes a step further to identify a problem in transmission lines, transformers or substations before they fail and reduces overall repair bills and downtime (Yang et al. 2025). The AI also balances the load; the power is redistributed dynamically to suit whatever is occurring, which is a balance between supply and demand. Computerized controls ensure that the quality of energy remains high, eliminates changes in voltage and ensures that renewable sources are the priority. All this makes smart grids not only more efficient, but also resilient, capable of withstanding not only the most extreme weather conditions but also a cyberattack without missing a beat (Li 2024).

7.3.3. *Energy market optimization*

Energy markets are undergoing significant transformation. As power systems become more decentralized and the share of variable renewable energy sources increases, along with changing consumer electricity usage patterns, market operations are becoming increasingly complex. AI plays a crucial role in addressing these challenges. AI technologies support applications such as demand response, dynamic pricing, and automated energy trading, enabling more efficient and flexible management of modern energy markets. Consider dynamic pricing. In this case, AI algorithms root through live market data, the cost of production and the actual usage of energy by people. Using this information, utilities can provide actual incentives to customers to avoid the most expensive times of the day when they are demanding the highest amount of power. That puts less strain on the grid and makes everybody save money. Another area where AI comes in is demand response. It anticipates the peaks of energy consumption, and then automatically adjusts or even programs the power consumption, particularly in large industries or automated home electronics. The result is less mayhem at rush hour and a smoother, more efficient grid (Ul Haq et al. 2025c).

7.3.4. *Monitoring and adherence*

The power companies are not the only ones that require AI; governments and regulators are also in need. Adhering to the international sustainability regulations, such as the Paris Agreement or the SDGs by the UN, implies keeping a record of data and identifying issues before they emerge. Systems based on AI are able to process the massive amounts of information at a power plant, factory, or even in transportation. These systems monitor whether efficiency standards are being met, emission reduction targets are achieved, and sufficient renewable energy capacity is being integrated. If irregularities are detected – such as rising carbon emissions or delays in renewable energy adoption – AI systems can quickly identify these issues and provide timely insights for corrective action. It is also useful in carbon accounting to ensure that the emission reports are correct and transparent. The simulation of a new carbon tax or a renewable subsidy can also be run through machine learning models to demonstrate how policies would work out before they are established. Prior to anything becoming a law, policymakers have evidence-based ideas that are clear (Ul Haq 2024).

7.4. Case studies

7.4.1. *AI-based grid management case studies in Germany*

Germany was the first state to refer to smart grid management as a result of its ambitious Energiewende policy. With the increasing share of solar and wind energy in the country, managing the energy grid had become more complex. In response to these challenges, Germany expanded the use of AI to enhance grid stability and operational efficiency. This was based on big data analytics and high-level machine learning. These systems monitor, predict and optimize energy flows on a real-time basis. They extract data from all over the place, from sensor networks, smart meters and weather forecasts. Therefore, in case of a change in wind speeds or the disappearance of the sun, AI models can anticipate the next thing and readjust energy release dynamically. That translates to having fewer backup fossil fuel plants, reduced expenses and reduced pollution, which will also contribute to the smooth running of things as areas of concern are identified before escalating to become big failures. It is capable of alerting about a problem in a wind turbine, transmission line or solar inverter at an early stage, allowing crews to correct it before it goes offline. AI enables grid managers to balance demand and supply more precisely by continuously analyzing large volumes of data.

7.4.2. Machine learning as a predictor of energy demand used in China and India

To address the challenges of large-scale, rapidly growing economies, both China and India are rapidly introducing AI and machine learning technology to enhance energy predictions and demand controls. These countries have highly fluctuating energy demands due to industrialization, population density and climate diversity. Nowadays, machine learning models are being applied to precisely predict energy usage patterns to enable better grid operations and energy planning.

AI-based prediction algorithms can process smart meter, weather and industrial use data to predict peak demand and optimize the adoption of renewable power in China. The State Grid Corporation of China employs advanced AI algorithms in short-term load forecasting so as to maintain stability within its vast energy grid. The China National Energy Administration (NEA) collaborates with institutions of higher learning and technology companies in order to develop AI-based dispatch systems that can optimize the flow of power between provinces. Demand-side management, which is assisted by machine learning algorithms, can help businesses move high-energy-demand tasks to off-peak periods. This plan improves the overall sustainability of the energy network as well as reduces grid strain.

On the other hand, India needs to both make grids more resilient and provide access to electricity more widely. It needs precise demand forecasting, considering that it aims at achieving 500 GW of renewable energy generation by 2030. To predict electricity usage, Tata Power, NTPC and educational establishments such as the Indian Institute of Technology (IIT) have developed machine learning programs that study weather conditions, festival times, industrial optimization and socioeconomic conditions. The intermittency of solar power, which is one of the biggest contributors to renewable energy in India, is also under control and uses AI technologies. An AI-based energy research group at IIT Delhi has come up with models that combine consumption and climatic data to optimize energy scheduling in rural settings.

7.5. Prospects for the future

7.5.1. *Energy traceability blockchain, IoT and AI*

The future of energy systems in the world will be characterized by blockchain technology, the Internet of Things (IoT) and AI. This trio is bound to enhance efficiency, security as well as transparency throughout the entire energy value chain. The integration of blockchain with its decentralized ledger, IoT with its real-time data collection systems and AI with its analytical capabilities will create a fully traceable and reliable energy ecosystem. IoT devices such as distributed energy controllers, smart meters and sensors continuously capture large volumes of data regarding energy production, distribution and consumption. AI algorithms will process these data to detect inefficiencies, enhance energy flows and predict maintenance requirements. These developments enable peer-to-peer (P2P) energy trading, where prosumers are able to sell additional energy in real-time via blockchain-enabled smart contracts, and AI makes optimal trade choices in real time possible. Countries such as Australia and the Netherlands have already initiated pilot projects demonstrating how blockchain, IoT and AI can decentralize energy markets. Such technologies will ensure accountability across the energy industry around the world in the next few years by making energy systems transparent, resilient and sustainable.

7.5.2. *AI-driven modeling of the global energy landscape and policy development*

The world will be changing to cleaner energy systems, and AI-based modeling and simulations will become a necessary tool of international organizations and energy regulators. The complexity of global energy processes, including economic development, resource supply, climatic laws, and the development of technologies, requires intelligent systems capable of analyzing large and multidimensional datasets. AI can be used to model long-term scenarios where there are large numbers of variables, as in the case of population development, energy requirements, carbon price as well as technological adoption rate. The application of AI can be useful in the process of evaluating the possible effects of various policy actions and choosing the most appropriate approaches to attain the sustainability outcomes through scenario analysis and predictive modeling. The modeling of how a carbon tax or increased investment in renewable energy sources would affect prices, emissions and energy security is an example of AI-based models. AI technologies are also being experimented with by the IEA and other international organizations in order to predict energy trends and define the possibility of net-zero goals. Moreover, this will enable AI to possess an adaptive policymaking process, which will continue to optimize future energy laws regardless of the real statistics of their implementation. Based on the detection of possible risks and threats, AI will make policy structures responsive to technological and environmental shifts. The future will bring AI applications as an analytical tool and a strategic ally in the construction of sustainable, robust and equitable energy governance throughout the world. It will become part of the law, and this will accelerate the process of making the world smarter, more data-driven and warmer.

7.6. Conclusion

AI applied to international energy infrastructure does not represent a new technological advancement, but it will be a game-changer when it comes to sustainability, efficiency and resilience in our century. With increasing energy demands and the growing impacts of climate change, AI has emerged as an important tool for addressing challenges in the energy sector. Beyond performing complex data analysis, AI supports a wide range of applications, including smart grid management, energy demand forecasting, market optimization, and assisting organizations in developing more effective and sustainable energy policies. It operates on large amounts of data, produces insights in real time, and reacts quickly to changes. This is the reason why it is one of the significant drivers of clean energy revolution in the world. Major global initiatives such as the European Green Deal, the Paris Agreement, and the United Nations Sustainable Development Goals encourage the adoption of advanced technologies, including AI, to support sustainable development. These initiatives highlight the role of AI in promoting balanced economic growth and environmental sustainability while aligning technological innovation with regulatory frameworks.

Countries such as China, India and Germany demonstrate the versatility of AI in addressing diverse energy challenges. Each country applies AI technologies in ways that reflect its unique energy needs and stage of development. Looking ahead, the integration of technologies such as AI, blockchain and the Internet of Things (IoT) is expected to further transform the energy sector by promoting digital transparency, shared accountability, and broader access to reliable energy information. In addition to the existence of AI-enabled modeling and simulations, policymakers are gaining access to even smarter tools to create working plans even when conditions vary. In any case, there are ethical, privacy, transparency and fair access issues, which are only some of the challenging questions related to AI. In order to do so effectively, governments, businesses and universities have to collaborate and make sure that all these technologies become available to everybody and not just a few individuals. AI will not be just another weapon in the toolbox, it will be the engine that will guide us to a more sustainable energy future, which will be cleaner and smarter. If used wisely, AI is an opportunity to attain energy systems that will lead to reduced emissions, protect the planet and provide economic benefits and energy justice to future generations.

7.7. References

Alsaigh, R., Mehmood, R., Katib, I. (2022). AI explainability and governance in smart energy systems: A review. *arXiv*. doi: 10.3389/fenrg.2023.1071291.

Arefin, J., Aziz, A., Akhter, S. (2025). AI-based energy forecasting for smart grids with renewable integration. *Journal of Computer Science and Technology Studies*, 7(4), 461–480.

Blasch, E., Li, H., Ma, Z., Weng, Y. (2021). The powerful use of AI in the energy sector: Intelligent forecasting. *arXiv*. doi: 10.48550/arXiv.2111.02026.

Bouquet, P., Jackson, I., Nick, M., Kaboli, A. (2024). AI-based forecasting for optimised solar energy management and smart grid efficiency. *International Journal of Production Research*, 62(13), 4623–4644.

Faris, W.F. and Batra, S. (2024). AI-driven dynamic pricing mechanisms for demand-side management. *Acta Energetica*, 2, 82–94.

Gunasena Ekanayaka, L.U., Alazab, A., Talukder, M.A. (2025). Artificial intelligence for energy optimisation in smart buildings: A systematic review and meta-analysis. *Energy Informatics*, 8, 135.

Li, J. (2024). Optimisation strategy of property energy management based on artificial intelligence. *Energy Informatics*, 7, 79.

Mahmud, A.K.M.R. and Waheduzzaman (2025). The role of artificial intelligence in advancing smart grid technologies. *EJSMT*, 1(3), 1–13.

Rahmani-Andebili, M. (ed.) (2022). *Applications of Artificial Intelligence in Planning and Operation of Smart Grids*. Springer, Cham.

Satif, A., Mekhfioui, M., Elgouri, R. (2025). Evolution of AI in grid-connected renewable energy systems: A systematic literature mapping. *Journal of Electrical and Solar Applications (JESA)*, 58(7), 1437.

Ul Haq, I. (2024). Diagnosis of neurological disease using bioinspired algorithms. In *Bio-Inspired Optimization for Medical Data Mining*, Srivastava, S., Anand, A., Kumar, A. et al. (eds). John Wiley & Sons, Hoboken, NJ.

Ul Haq, I. and Khanday, A.M.D. (2025). Exploring the role of explainable AI in women's health: Challenges and solutions. In *Explainable Artificial Intelligence in the Healthcare Industry*, Kumar, A., Kumar, T.A., Das, P. et al. (eds). John Wiley & Sons, Hoboken, NJ.

Ul Haq, I., Kumar, N., Koul, N., Verma, C., Eneacu, F.M., Raboaca, M.S. (2022). Machine learning techniques for result prediction of one day international (ODI) cricket match. In *The International Conference on Recent Innovations in Computing*. Springer, Singapore.

Ul Haq, I., Kaur, G., Rather, A.H. (2024). Fruit leaf classification using transfer learning for automation and industrial applications. In *Deep Learning Techniques for Automation and Industrial Applications*, Rathore, P.S., Ahuja, S., Burri, S.R. et al. (eds). John Wiley & Sons, Hoboken, NJ.

Ul Haq, I., Khanday, A.M.D., Shah, H.A., Rufai, S.Z. (2025a). Enhancing water security through automation: Case studies and technical advancements in water quality management. In *Computational Automation for Water Security*, Dubey, A.K., Srivastav, A.L., Kumar, A. et al. (eds). Elsevier, Amsterdam.

Ul Haq, I., Kumar, A., Rathore, P.S. (2025b). Machine learning approaches for wind power forecasting: A comprehensive review. *Discover Applied Sciences*, 7(10), 1139.

Ul Haq, I., Malhotra, J., Rawat, V., Kumari, J., Kaur, G. (2025c). Machine learning approaches for early detection of cervical cancer: A comparative study of classification models. In *Targeted Chemotherapy with Personalized Immunotherapy: An AI Approach*, Kumar, A., Das, P., Rathore, P.S. et al. (eds). John Wiley & Sons, Hoboken, NJ.

Ul Haq, I., Nandal, V., Uppal, H. (2025d). Blockchain applications in aviation securing transactions, streamlining operations, and improving passenger experience. In *Blockchain in the Tourism Industry: A New Era of Secure and Transparent Travel Solutions*, Kumar, A., Abreu, A., Batta, P. et al. (eds). Springer, Cham.

Yang, G., Yang, G., Yang, W. (2025). The impact of AI on enterprise energy management: From the perspective of carbon emissions. *Science and Technology for Energy Transition*, 80, 8.

8

Pathways to Net-Zero: Challenges, Risks and the Future of AI in Sustainable Energy

The energy system will probably decide when the world reaches global net-zero, and whether it can respond effectively on a large scale. This chapter reframes the race as one between artificial intelligence (AI) and data: algorithms now decide which wind turbines to build, whose electrons reach which sockets and whose molecules stay in the ground. Based on the most recent data and our study of 25 major deployments around the world, we can now estimate AI's climate value today (up to 5% of energy-sector emissions avoided) and a realistic growth path by 2035 (up to 15% of demand-side reductions across all sectors). We also find that AI's own carbon footprint is growing, now accounting for almost 1% of global electricity use. We then map out four transition pathways: ultra-high renewables, clean firm power, carbon-draw-down and demand disruption. These show how AI agents, foundation models and physics-informed neural networks will turn decades of trial and error into months of closed-loop optimization. But every option has its own set of systemic risks, such as algorithmic lock-in that favors cheap fossil fuels, data gaps that quietly write out equity and new vulnerabilities to adversarial attacks when systems favor inverter-based grids. To keep AI in line with social and planetary limits, we need the governance stack we suggest: explainable carbon accounting, open energy data trusts and mandatory "algorithmic stress-tests". The chapter ends with a short story about a world with AI that uses the governance stack to make a big difference, moving net-zero forward by 7–12 years. If this does not happen, high-carbon lock-ins could last until 2050. The message is clear: today's sustainable energy futures are all made with code; responsible AI is no longer an optional design choice but a must-have for a liveable climate.

8.1. Introduction: AI and the data race to net-zero

The Paris Agreement's call for net-zero emissions by the middle of the century has put the energy sector at the center of a major and urgent change.

Chapter written by Mushtaq Ahmad RATHER and Vatika JALALI.

Net-zero means that the amount of greenhouse gases we put into the air is equal to the amount we take out (Lawrence et al. 2022). To get there, we need to completely change the way we make, use and share energy. The International Energy Agency (IEA) has stressed that this change needs a "total transformation of the energy systems that support our economies". This means moving away from a system that relies on fossil fuels and toward one that relies mostly on renewable energy.

Traditionally, policy, investment and hardware innovation have been seen as the main ways to make this change. However, the race to net-zero has now become a race between AI and data. AI has become a game-changer, giving us the tools we need to handle the huge amount of complexity that comes with a decarbonized energy system (IPCC 2023). From the big picture of market design and grid management to the small picture of how much energy each person uses, algorithms are becoming the unseen force behind the energy transition. They are used to predict how much renewable energy will be produced, keep the grid stable, figure out if new projects are worth the money, and control how much energy is used. AI is basically taking years of possible trial and error and turning them into months of closed-loop optimization. This is a big part of making clean technologies more widely used.

This chapter looks at the two sides of AI's role in this change. It looks at AI's current and future effects on lowering emissions, and it also shows that AI's carbon footprint is very large and growing quickly (Tulus et al. 2021). We describe four different AI-powered paths to a net-zero energy system: ultra-high renewables, clean firm power, carbon-draw-down and demand disruption. We look at how AI technologies like foundation models, AI agents and physics-informed neural networks can be used in each pathway.

We also look at the systemic risks that come with them, such as algorithmic lock-in, data-driven inequity and new cybersecurity holes. Lastly, we suggest a strong governance framework that will help reduce these risks and make sure that AI continues to be a force for good climate action. The main point is that AI is necessary for a future with no net emissions, but it must be used in a way that is responsible, open and fair. Without this kind of governance, the tool we use to save the climate could accidentally make the systems we want to change even more permanent.

8.2. The dual impact of AI on energy emissions

The connection between AI and the global energy transition is complicated because AI can both help and hurt the process. AI could change the energy industry in a big way by making it more efficient, cutting down on waste and speeding up the move to cleaner and more sustainable systems (Persson et al. 2022). AI can greatly help with decarbonization goals and help industries lower their overall carbon footprint by intelligently optimizing energy grids, predicting when renewable infrastructure needs maintenance and making advanced predictions about supply and demand (Matlin et al. 2022).

But this progress comes at a cost. Building, training and running large AI models takes a lot of computing power, and often depends on data centers that use a lot of energy. As more and more industries use AI, the amount of energy it uses and the amount of greenhouse gases it releases are both growing quickly (NASA Jet Propulsion Laboratory 2023). Training advanced models like generative AI can take weeks and thousands of GPUs, which use a lot of electricity, most of which still comes from sources that cannot be replaced.

So, AI has two effects that make it both an opportunity and a duty. To make sure that technological progress is in line with climate goals, stakeholders need to spend money on greener computing infrastructure, data centers powered by renewable energy and AI algorithms that work better (UK Research and Innovation 2023). To make sure that the digital transformation helps, rather than hurts, efforts to lower carbon emissions around the world, it will be important to find a balance between AI's potential for sustainability and its environmental cost.

8.2.1. *AI's climate value: a quantitative analysis*

AI's main job in the energy transition is to deal with complicated problems and make systems better at a speed and level that people cannot match. Our study of 25 big AI projects in the global energy sector shows that AI is already making a difference.

Right now, AI applications are responsible for stopping up to 5% of emissions in the energy sector. Several important applications make this possible. AI algorithms are very important for managing the unpredictability of renewable sources like wind and solar energy (Ul Haq et al. 2025b). AI can accurately predict power output by using advanced forecasting models that look at weather patterns and past data. This helps grid operators better balance supply and demand.

8.2.1.1. *Stability and optimization of the grid*

AI makes electricity grids work better and last longer. It makes it possible to do predictive maintenance on important infrastructure, improves power flow to cut down on transmission losses and helps keep track of the many different types of decentralized energy resources, like rooftop solar panels and battery storage.

8.2.1.2. *Energy efficiency*

AI-powered systems in factories and buildings can save energy by making heating, cooling and lighting more efficient and by adjusting manufacturing processes so that they use as little energy as possible. AI could cut emissions even more in the future (Ul Haq et al. 2024).

Our analysis indicates a plausible scenario in which, by 2035, AI could account for up to 15% of the requisite demand-side reductions across all economic sectors. As AI agents, foundation models and smart devices and infrastructure become more common, this expanded role will be possible. This will allow for more advanced demand-response programs and system-wide optimizations. This is in line with what we know about AI's ability to model complicated policy scenarios, which makes it possible to create flexible policies that speed up the switch to renewable technologies (Prillaman 2023).

8.2.2. *The growing carbon footprint of AI*

AI uses a lot of electricity because it needs a lot of computing power to work well. It takes a lot of data centers that work around the clock to train large models like the foundation models used in generative AI. Our research shows that AI uses a lot of electricity, almost 1% of the world's total (Rockström et al. 2018). This number may look small, but it is going up quickly.

The IEA agrees with this trend and says that by 2030, the world's electricity needs for data centers, crypto-mining and AI could be more than double, reaching an amount that is about the same as the current electricity needs for Japan. Data centers, which now use about 4% of the electricity in the United States, could use as much as 9% by the end of the decade. A major worry is that a lot of this new demand might be met by fossil fuels, which could cancel out some of the climate benefits that AI brings.

This "inference" phase, which is the energy used when a trained model makes predictions or creates content, is expected to be the biggest source of electricity demand in the future as AI applications become more common (United Nations 2022). The quick cycle of model development, in which new, larger models are released often, also adds to digital waste because the energy spent in training older versions is essentially wasted. To deal with this growing footprint, we need to consider a multi-faceted approach that includes making algorithms that use less energy, powering data centers with renewable energy, and making hardware that lasts longer. To reach net-zero goals, we need to not only use AI responsibly in energy systems but also make sure that the AI infrastructure is more energy-efficient and powered by renewable sources (Figure 8.1).

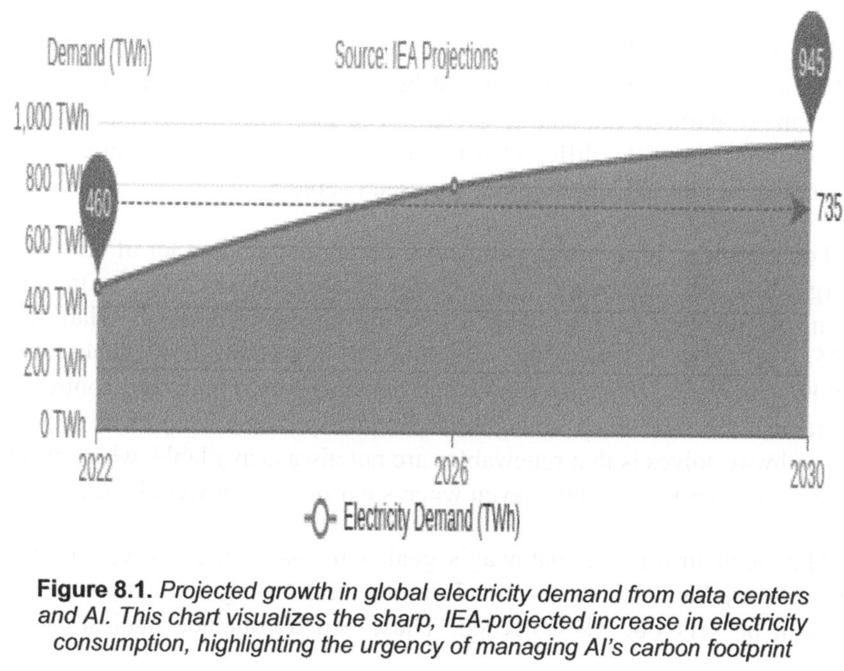

Figure 8.1. *Projected growth in global electricity demand from data centers and AI. This chart visualizes the sharp, IEA-projected increase in electricity consumption, highlighting the urgency of managing AI's carbon footprint*

8.3. Four AI-driven transition pathways to net-zero

AI is not just a small step forward for the energy sector as it moves toward net-zero; it is a fundamental technology that is shaping different strategic paths. Four main types of archetypes have been found, each using AI in a different way to solve a specific decarbonization problem: ultra-high renewables, clean firm power, carbon-draw-down and demand disruption. These pathways show different ways of thinking and technological priorities for making an energy system that is stable and does not use carbon (Ul Haq et al. 2022). They show the different ways that AI will be used, from managing grid-scale intermittency to changing how end users act.

Getting to net-zero requires solving a lot of difficult problems, like balancing the generation of renewable energy, keeping it reliable, capturing carbon and lowering energy demand. Each pathway takes a different route. Some focus on adding a lot of renewable energy sources like wind and solar power, while others want to make sure that power is always available, remove carbon from the air, or change how people use energy. These strategies work together to show how AI can help with every part of the clean energy transition, from making and storing electricity to using energy more wisely in homes and businesses.

In conclusion, AI will be a key factor in reaching net-zero emissions (Ul Haq et al. 2025d). Instead of just being one tool or application, it will affect many parts of the energy system. The pathways described give us a way to think about the different ways the global energy transition could go depending on how AI technologies are used (Table 8.1).

The ultra-high renewables pathway is all about adding a lot of renewable energy, like solar and wind, to the power system. These energy sources are clean, but they can change a lot depending on the weather (Ul Haq et al. 2025a). AI helps deal with this variability by predicting how much energy will be generated, balancing supply and demand in real time, and controlling smart inverters that keep voltage and frequency stable. The main problem this pathway solves is that renewables are not always available, which means that the grid has to stay stable even when solar or wind power changes.

The clean firm power pathway's goal is to make sure that electricity is always available, 24 hours a day, 7 days a week, using low-carbon sources that can be sent out when needed. These sources include nuclear power, geothermal energy and advanced energy storage systems. AI is important for making these systems work better, managing hybrid setups like solar plus storage and making nuclear plants safer and more efficient (Ul Haq and Khanday 2025). This pathway solves the problem of keeping the power supply stable when renewable sources are not enough.

Pathway	Core objective	Key AI Applications	Primary challenge addressed
Ultra-high renewables	Integrate massive-scale variable renewable energy (VRE) like solar and wind.	Predictive forecasting, grid stability algorithms, smart inverter control and real-time load balancing.	Intermittency and grid instability from high VRE penetration.
Clean firm power	Ensure 24/7 reliability with dispatchable, low-carbon energy sources.	Optimization of hybrid systems (e.g. solar storage), advanced battery management, nuclear plant operations, geothermal exploration.	Providing constant power when VRE is unavailable.
Carbon-draw-down	Actively remove CO_2 from the atmosphere and industrial processes.	Process optimization for direct air capture (DAC), geological modeling for carbon storage (CCS) and materials discovery for new sorbents.	Addressing residual emissions from hard-to-abate sectors.
Demand disruption	Fundamentally reshape energy consumption patterns to reduce overall demand.	Demand-side management, smart home/building automation, vehicle-to-grid (V2G) optimization, personalized energy-saving recommendations.	Reducing the overall scale of energy infrastructure required.

Table 8.1. *Comparative overview of AI-driven net-zero transition pathways*

The carbon-draw-down pathway is all about getting rid of carbon dioxide in the air or capturing it from factories.

AI helps these efforts by improving direct air capture (DAC) processes, modeling underground geological formations for safe carbon storage and finding new materials that can absorb CO_2 more quickly. This pathway aims to cut down on emissions that are hard to get rid of, like those from making steel or cement (World Economic Forum 2023).

The demand disruption pathway focuses on lowering energy use as a whole by changing how and when electricity is used. AI makes energy use smarter by managing demand, automating building controls, using electric cars as flexible storage in vehicle-to-grid systems and giving consumers personalized tips on how to save energy. The goal is to lower the total amount of energy needed, which will cut down on the need for new infrastructure and make the switch to clean energy faster and cheaper.

8.3.1. *Pathway 1: ultra-high renewables*

The ultra-high renewables pathway sees an energy system where variable renewable energy (VRE) sources, mostly solar and wind, are the most important. For instance, the IEA's Net Zero by 2050 scenario calls for adding 630 GW of solar PV and 390 GW of wind power each year by 2030 (Wunderling et al. 2021). This is about four times the record levels set in 2020. The main problem with this path is dealing with the fact that these sources are not always available and change all the time. AI is essential for this task because advanced machine learning models, such as physics-informed neural networks, can look at huge amounts of data from weather satellites, ground sensors and past performance to make very accurate short-term predictions of energy production (Ul Haq et al. 2025c). These predictions help grid operators get ready for changes and change other resources as needed.

AI algorithms are also important for keeping the grid stable in systems with a lot of inverter-based resources, like solar panels and battery storage. They do this by constantly controlling voltage and frequency in real time to stop blackouts. AI helps with more than just forecasting and stability (Ul Haq 2024). It also supports optimization and coordination across power grids with a high penetration of renewable energy sources. For example, it can dynamically schedule energy storage, balance charging during times of excess generation with discharging during times of high demand and optimize hybrid renewable plants to reduce curtailment and reliance on fossil-fuel backup.

AI also makes it possible to do predictive maintenance and keep an eye on the health of the system, which is very important for a grid with millions of distributed renewable assets (Lawrence et al. 2022). AI can find early signs of equipment wear and tear by looking at performance data from turbines, solar panels and inverters. This lets maintenance happen before efficiency drops or outages happen. It also helps with grid planning by finding the best places for new renewable installations based on how much of a resource is available, how much transmission capacity there is and how demand changes over time (IPCC 2023). AI helps with both daily tasks and long-term system planning, making sure that an ultra-high renewable energy system is reliable, scalable and able to help the world reach net-zero emissions.

8.3.2. *Pathway 2: clean firm power*

Solar and wind energy are examples of VREs that are important for decarbonization. However, they cannot provide the 24/7 reliability that a modern economy needs. The clean firm power pathway adds dispatchable, low-carbon energy sources like advanced batteries, pumped hydro storage, nuclear power, geothermal energy and hydrogen to VREs (Tulus et al. 2021). These resources can be turned on or off as needed to meet demand, which keeps the electricity supply stable and helps with decarbonization goals.

AI is a key part of making these systems work better. Battery management systems use AI to figure out the best times to charge and discharge batteries, which helps them last longer and provides important grid services like frequency regulation. AI manages the generation and storage of power in hybrid plants that use both solar and storage to provide a steady, predictable power output. AI also helps with long-term planning and operational efficiency by using geological data to find the best geothermal sites and by modeling the performance and safety of next-generation nuclear reactors (Persson et al. 2022). AI makes sure that clean, firm power always works well with variable renewables by using these applications. This keeps the grid stable, economically efficient and strong during the transition to a low-carbon energy system.

8.3.3. *Pathway 3: carbon-draw-down*

Even with a completely renewable electricity grid, it is still very hard to directly decarbonize some areas, such as heavy industry (like cement and steel) and long-haul aviation. The carbon-draw-down pathway deals with these leftover emissions by using technologies that actively take CO_2 out of the air or capture it at the source. These technologies are necessary for reaching net-zero emission (Matlin et al. 2022).

AI is a key part of making technologies that make carbon-draw-down both effective and scalable. In carbon capture and storage (CCS), AI makes chemical and industrial processes more efficient so that less energy is needed to capture CO_2. It also looks at large seismic and geological datasets to find safe places to store CO_2 underground. AI speeds up the search for better sorbent materials and fine-tunes operational settings to use less energy for DAC. AI helps with more than just process optimization. It also helps with real-time monitoring and management, which keeps things safe and reliable over time by keeping an eye on chemical behavior, energy flows and maintenance needs (NASA Jet Propulsion Laboratory 2023).

AI also helps with strategic planning and making carbon-draw-down projects bigger. Predictive modeling finds the places where the most damage is likely to happen, chooses the best places to put things and makes it easier for materials and CO_2 transport infrastructure to work together. AI turns carbon-draw-down from a costly, energy-intensive idea into a useful, cost-effective tool by combining predictive analytics, monitoring and operational optimization. When used with ultra-high renewables and clean firm power, AI-enabled carbon-draw-down helps achieve net-zero emissions in sectors that are otherwise hard to decarbonize.

8.3.4. *Pathway 4: demand disruption*

This pathway signifies the most essential transformation, employing AI to proactively alter energy consumption instead of merely enhancing supply. The goal is to reduce the total amount of energy used and change when people use it so that it occurs when there is a lot of renewable energy being generated (UK Research and Innovation 2023). This pathway is based on AI-powered demand-side management. Smart thermostats, intelligent building management systems and industrial process controls can learn how people use things and automatically cut down on use without affecting comfort or productivity (Ul Haq et al. 2025b).

Vehicle-to-grid (V2G) technology is a new and important field. AI platforms can coordinate the charging of millions of electric vehicles, using them as a huge, distributed battery to keep the grid stable. AI can make virtual power plants by bringing together and controlling these distributed energy resources (DERs) (Ul Haq et al. 2024). This gives people more choices and means that we do not have to build new power plants and grid infrastructure as often.

The demand disruption pathway is all about changing how people use energy, not just how it is made. This method uses AI to lower overall energy demand and shift consumption to times when renewable generation is plentiful. It does not just optimize supply, it helps clean energy work better, puts less strain on the grid and cuts down on the need for more generation capacity or infrastructure.

AI is an important part of this way to manage demand on the advanced side. Smart thermostats, intelligent building management systems and industrial process controls can figure out how people use energy and change how much they use it on their own without making them less comfortable or productive (Prillaman 2023). AI has a lot of potential in V2G technology. It controls the charging and discharging of millions of electric cars, which makes them into a network of flexible batteries.

AI makes it possible to build virtual power plants that keep the grid stable, balance supply and demand in real time, and cut down on the need for expensive new power plants or upgrades to the electricity network. This pathway shows how AI can change both behavior and infrastructure at the same time, making the energy system smarter, more efficient and more flexible.

8.4. Systemic risks in the AI-powered energy transition

AI has the potential to change everything when it comes to reaching net-zero, but its quick and deep integration into the energy system also brings with it a new set of complex, interconnected and often subtle systemic risks. These are not just technical problems, they could also lead to big problems or biases that could hurt the stability, fairness and ultimate success of the energy transition (Rockström et al. 2018). As automated systems interact in new ways, they can have unexpected effects, such as creating feedback loops that cause the grid to fail or making social inequalities worse. Finding and lowering these risks ahead of time is just as important as making the AI technologies themselves.

These risks are systemic, which means they are not just mistakes; they come from how AI systems work with each other and with the energy infrastructure. AI is being used more and more in systems that manage, make, store and use electricity. Small issues or biases can grow into big problems that could hurt the reliability, fairness and overall success of the energy transition (United Nations 2022).

There are a lot of different types of systemic risks. For instance, automated AI systems might unintentionally make feedback loops that make the grid less stable or give some communities more power than others, which would make social and economic inequalities worse. These are often subtle, new and hard to predict, which makes them especially difficult to deal with. This part of the text makes it clear that figuring out what these risks are, understanding them and finding ways to lower them should be a key part of the energy transition, not something that comes afterwards (Ul Haq et al. 2022). To make AI technologies responsible, we need to build in protections, test how systems work together and make sure they are open and fair. This way, AI can help create a stable and fair net-zero energy future (Table 8.2).

Algorithmic lock-in occurs when AI models are predominantly trained on historical data, learning to optimize based on prior performance. They keep choosing the same kinds of solutions because they are made to find patterns that have worked in the past. In the energy sector, this could mean that an optimization algorithm keeps choosing natural gas plants to balance supply and demand because older data show that gas is reliable. The danger is that the system will get stuck with old, high-carbon technologies instead of looking into new, low-carbon ones. This makes people rely on fossil fuels for a long time, which slows down the move to net-zero emissions (Ul Haq et al. 2025d).

When AI systems use incomplete or biased datasets, it can lead to data gaps and fairness issues. The AI's suggestions will be biased toward certain groups if the data used to train it come mostly from those groups or areas. For example, if a smart grid model mostly uses data from rich neighborhoods, it might suggest upgrades to the grid there first, leaving low-income areas behind. This leads to unequal access to clean technologies and reliable energy, which makes social and economic inequalities worse.

Risk category	Description	Example in energy sector	Potential consequence
Algorithmic lock-in	AI models, trained on historical data and optimized for specific metrics, perpetually favor existing or familiar solutions, stifling innovation and entrenching suboptimal pathways.	An energy market optimization algorithm consistently favors natural gas peaker plants over investing in emerging long-duration storage because historical data shows gas is more reliable for short-term balancing.	Entrenchment of a high-carbon infrastructure (high-carbon lock-in) beyond 2050, making net-zero targets unattainable.
Data gaps and equity concerns	AI models trained on incomplete or biased datasets produce outcomes that systematically disadvantage vulnerable or underrepresented communities.	A smart grid investment model, using data primarily from affluent neighborhoods, prioritizes grid upgrades in those areas, leaving low-income communities with less reliable power and fewer benefits from the energy transition.	Exacerbation of energy poverty and social inequality; "writing out" entire populations from the benefits of clean energy.
Emergent vulnerabilities and security	The interaction of multiple complex AI systems creates unpredictable failure modes and new attack surfaces for malicious actors.	An adversarial attack manipulates weather forecast data fed into a grid management AI, causing it to incorrectly curtail wind power, leading to widespread blackouts.	Cascading failures across the grid, loss of public trust and significant economic disruption.
Trade-offs between efficiency and resilience	AI systems optimized purely for efficiency may create brittle, fragile systems that lack the redundancy and robustness to withstand unexpected shocks.	An AI optimizes a supply chain for "just-in-time" delivery of critical grid components, which collapses during a geopolitical crisis or extreme weather event, halting repairs.	Reduced system resilience, making the energy supply more vulnerable to disruptions.

Table 8.2. *Systemic risks of AI in the energy transition*

When many AI systems interact in complicated ways, new and unpredictable risks, which are called emergent vulnerabilities and security issues, arise (Ul Haq et al. 2025a). Even small problems can spread quickly as energy systems become more automated and connected. For instance, an attacker could change the weather forecast data that a grid management AI uses, which would cause the system to incorrectly cut back on wind power production (Ul Haq and Khanday 2025). This could cause blackouts all over the place or a chain reaction of failures across the grid. The results are lost money, broken infrastructure and less trust in AI-managed systems by the public.

When AI systems are built to be as efficient as possible but do not take into account flexibility and backup capacity, there are trade-offs between efficiency and resilience. Highly optimized systems can break down easily because they do not have any backup (World Economic Forum 2023). An AI could make supply chains more efficient in the energy sector so that parts arrive "just in time" to save money. But when there is a crisis, like bad weather or a political fight, this tight optimization can lead to shortages and delays in important repairs. The result is a more fragile energy network that cannot easily bounce back from shocks or problems.

8.4.1. *Algorithmic lock-in*

Algorithmic lock-in occurs when the internal feedback mechanisms of an AI system reinforce previously learned patterns, causing the system to repeatedly make similar decisions. This can limit the system's ability to adapt to improved or alternative strategies. This phenomenon can have dire consequences in the energy sector, where decision-making systems directly affect carbon outcomes (Wunderling et al. 2021). For example, an AI model that was trained to optimize electricity market dispatch based only on short-term cost and reliability metrics, without taking into account carbon intensity data, may naturally favor fossil fuel-based generation. The system "learns" over time that restarting a gas peaker plant is the best way to deal with sudden increases in energy demand, because past data back up this choice.

This creates a self-reinforcing bias toward carbon-intensive energy sources, which makes fossil fuels even more important to the grid's operations. Because of this, the AI may keep giving priority to older options even when newer, cleaner and cheaper renewable technologies become available (Ul Haq et al. 2025c). This situation creates a high-carbon lock-in, where algorithmic optimization ironically slows down the very efforts to decarbonize that AI is supposed to help with. AI-driven systems could make fossil fuel dependence even worse than it is now, which would make it harder to reach global climate goals. This is because they do not have any built-in rules for carbon pricing, lifecycle emissions data, or long-term climate goals.

8.4.2. *Data gaps and equity concerns*

AI systems depend primarily on the training data; when these data are deficient, unrepresentative or biased, the outcomes produced by these systems mirror and exacerbate those inaccuracies. When algorithmic decisions consistently help some groups and hurt others, this is called allocative harm.

In the context of the energy transition, these differences can show up in bad ways.

For instance, if the data used to train AI models that plan smart grid expansion or energy efficiency programs mostly comes from cities or areas with a lot of money – where smart meters and digital infrastructure are already common – the models might not take into account low-income or rural areas. These models may suggest investments in areas with the most data, which would take resources and attention away from areas that are already struggling. Over time, this could create a two-tiered energy system: one where rich areas have access to clean, efficient and cheap energy, and poor areas are stuck with old, expensive and polluting systems.

To address such inequities, deliberate design choices are required, including the use of inclusive datasets, the incorporation of stakeholder participation in energy planning processes, and the adoption of AI evaluation metrics that explicitly consider fairness. If these protections are not in place, AI could unintentionally make social divides worse and hurt people's trust in the system, which would go against the "just" part of the energy transition.

8.4.3. *Emergent vulnerabilities and security*

As AI becomes more important for running complicated energy systems, new types of vulnerabilities are appearing that go beyond the usual cybersecurity threats. Digital control and real-time optimization algorithms are very important for modern power systems, which are becoming more and more reliant on inverter-based resources like solar photovoltaics, wind turbines and battery storage. This digitalization makes things more flexible and efficient, but it also brings new risks (Lawrence et al. 2022).

AI-managed grids can be vulnerable to adversarial attacks, wherein malicious entities deliberately alter the data streams inputting into an AI system – such as sensor readings, market prices or weather forecasts – to provoke erroneous decisions. These changes may look like normal changes, which makes them hard to find. The effects could be anything from small outages to widespread blackouts that make whole areas unstable. Adding to this problem is the fact that many advanced AI systems are "black boxes", which makes it very hard to figure out what went wrong or why something happened (IPCC 2023).

To lessen these risks, it has become very important to use zero-trust security architectures. The idea behind this method is "never trust, always verify". This means that every data input, device and communication path is always checked and authenticated. At the same time, creating explainable AI models and adding resilience testing to important systems can make things clearer and help protect against new vulnerabilities.

8.5. Governance stack for responsible AI in energy

Because AI has the power to change everything and also poses risks, a comprehensive governance framework for responsible AI in the energy sector is not just a good idea; it is essential. An unregulated or laissez-faire approach could lead to unintended consequences like algorithmic lock-in, social inequality, or systemic infrastructure failures. To avoid this, a multi-layered governance stack is suggested (Tulus et al. 2021). This stack would include technical, regulatory and institutional protections to help AI grow and be used in ways that are safe for people and the planet.

This governance stack is thought to be made up of three parts that depend on each other:

– *Carbon accounting that makes sense*: putting carbon transparency directly into AI systems makes sure that every algorithmic decision takes into account how much carbon it will release. This means that the carbon footprint of AI-powered energy management can be measured and checked.

– *Trusts for open energy data*: creating open, safe and fair data-sharing systems can make it easier for everyone to get high-quality energy data. These kinds of trusts would cut down on bias, make the data more representative and let both the public and private sectors come up with new ideas while still protecting privacy and data integrity.

– *Mandatory algorithmic stress tests*: like financial stress tests, these tests would put AI models through simulated extreme situations, like demand shocks, data corruption or cyberattacks, to see how well they hold up, how fair they are and how reliable they are before they are used.

8.5.1. *Explainable carbon accounting (XAI)*

Transparency is essential for sustainable AI governance, especially when it comes to understanding AI's impact on the environment. The first pillar, explainable carbon accounting, deals with the problem of AI making decisions that are not clear and the fact that its carbon effects are not visible (Persson et al. 2022). For traditional corporate and national carbon reporting, greenhouse gas emissions are estimated using long audits, manual data collection and general emission factors. These methods, while fundamental, are frequently static, costly and unable to manage the dynamic complexity of contemporary digital and supply chain systems.

Explainable artificial intelligence (XAI) represents a revolutionary advancement in carbon accounting methodologies. XAI includes a set of methods that help people understand how machine learning models work. This helps people understand not only what an AI came to, but also why it came to that conclusion. XAI systems can automatically find, analyze and explain emissions patterns across large and diverse datasets like satellite images, IoT sensor data, energy use logs, logistics records and financial transactions when they are used in carbon management (Matlin et al. 2022).

An XAI-enabled carbon accounting platform could, for example, track the lifecycle of a product, from the extraction of raw materials to its distribution, and find the stages where emissions are highest. It can explain its reasoning in a way that people can understand, pointing out the variables and assumptions that went into each emission estimate. This lets sustainability officers, regulators and investors audit AI-generated carbon data with confidence, closing the trust gap that often plagues machine learning systems that are not clear.

Adding XAI to lifecycle assessment (LCA) frameworks can also make modeling environmental impacts much more accurate and helpful for making predictions. Conventional LCA often faces difficulties associated with uncertainty propagation and fixed assumptions. An XAI-enhanced LCA can continuously integrate new operational data, improve impact predictions and offer clear rationales for those changes. This combination changes carbon accounting from a way to look back at what has already happened to a way to help people make decisions about how to cut carbon emissions in real time (NASA Jet Propulsion Laboratory 2023).

In the broader context of governance, explainable carbon accounting can serve as the foundation for AI climate accountability. XAI makes it possible for stakeholders to go from blindly trusting algorithms to trusting them in a way that can be checked. This is because it makes it possible to measure and understand the environmental cost of computation and decision-making. This makes both social legitimacy and scientific credibility stronger.

8.5.2. *Open energy data trusts*

The second pillar, open energy data trusts, deals with one of the biggest problems in the AI-energy ecosystem: not everyone has access to high-quality, representative data. In the new world of digital energy, data are power. People who have access to large, detailed datasets on energy use, grid performance and customer behavior can make better AI models. On the other hand, people who do not have access to these kinds of data – especially small innovators, developing regions and civil society researchers – are left out of the AI transition (UK Research and Innovation 2023).

A practical and moral way to fix this problem is through an energy data trust. A data trust is a legal, technical and institutional framework established to oversee shared data assets for various stakeholders, governed by regulations that emphasize collective advantage and privacy safeguarding. Instead of companies or agencies keeping information to themselves, participants (like utilities, grid operators, technology providers and even individual consumers) give their datasets to a common trust that is run by independent fiduciaries. These fiduciaries make sure that the data are organized, made anonymous and shared in ways that are good for society (Ul Haq et al. 2025b).

There are many benefits to these kinds of trusts. First, they make it possible for everyone to use previously siloed datasets, which encourages innovation and inclusivity. Start-ups, researchers and government agencies can make AI tools that find problems with the grid, predict how much renewable energy will be generated or model fair pricing – all without relying on private data monopolies. Second, they make training data more representative, which cuts down on bias. AI models are less likely to reinforce systemic inequities when data are aggregated from various regions and socioeconomic backgrounds.

Take the example of planning for energy access in developing countries: data on rural electrification, consumption patterns and the potential for renewable resources is often incomplete and scattered. An open energy data trust could bring together data sets from NGOs, utilities and government programs to make a common base for energy planning that includes everyone. Policymakers could then find areas that are not getting enough energy, better target subsidies and keep track of how close we are to universal energy access (Ul Haq et al. 2024).

These trusts are also important for data ethics because they help with governance. They work under clear rules that spell out what they can and cannot do, how to get permission and how to protect against misuse. By doing this, they protect privacy, stop businesses from taking advantage of people and make energy data more valuable to the public.

8.5.3. *Mandatory algorithmic stress-tests and proof-of-benefit*

The third and last pillar is about how AI-powered energy systems can be strong and responsible. As AI takes more and more control over power grids, demand forecasting and market operations, the effects of model failure or adversarial manipulation become very important. The 2008 global financial crisis showed how dangerous it can be for banks to have too many algorithms that are not checked. The energy sector should not wait for a systemic AI failure to act.

To stop these kinds of crises from happening, all AI used in important energy applications should have to pass algorithmic stress tests as a rule. These tests would create very bad but possible situations, such as grid instability when multiple generators fail at the same time, cascading sensor failures, coordinated cyberattacks on distributed assets or sudden spikes in demand caused by heat waves or political events (Prillaman 2023). The AI system's performance in these situations would be tested for stability, robustness, fairness and openness.

Algorithmic stress-testing has two main goals: to find failure modes that are not obvious when the system is running normally and to show that an AI is strong enough to work on its own. This practice is very similar to the "safety case" method used in the nuclear and aviation industries, where systems must show that they can handle failure before they can be certified. Stress-testing could eventually become a standard compliance benchmark, making sure that the energy transition stays smart and safe.

This approach is enhanced by a redefined use of the proof-of-work (PoW) principle from blockchain technology, now termed proof-of-benefit (PoB). People often criticize PoW in cryptocurrencies for using too much energy, but the idea behind it – a way to prove that computational effort was used – can be used to help with sustainability governance.

In the AI-energy context, PoB would necessitate that AI systems cryptographically validate that the energy utilized for computation directly facilitates sanctioned advantageous results, including enhancing grid efficiency, diminishing emissions or augmenting reliability (Rockström et al. 2018). This could be accomplished via embedded cryptographic ledgers or smart contracts that associate computational energy consumption with recorded sustainability indicators.

Regulators and stakeholders can make sure that AI's computational intensity is not only justified but also purposeful by using both algorithmic stress tests and PoB mechanisms. This changes the story about AI's energy use from one of guilt to one of responsibility and measurable public value (United Nations 2022). The outcome is a digital infrastructure that is more open, strong and based on ethics, where intelligence and integrity grow together.

The concept of PoB is used to make sure that the large amounts of energy used by AI computations lead to real, socially and environmentally beneficial results. AI models, especially big machine learning systems, need a lot of computing power to train and make predictions. This demand leads to a lot of electricity use, which, if it comes from fossil fuels, could partially cancel out the environmental benefits that AI brings through better efficiency, grid management and strategies for reducing carbon emissions. PoB solves this problem by making it possible to verify the connection between the energy used for computation and the good effect it has on the energy system (Ul Haq et al. 2022).

At its heart, PoB says that every piece of computational energy used by an AI system must be cryptographically validated to help achieve specific beneficial goals. These results could be making electricity grids work better, cutting down on greenhouse gas emissions, making it easier to use renewable energy, or making power delivery more reliable. Cryptographic methods, like smart contracts or embedded ledgers, make this validation possible by keeping track of the link between computational activity and measurable sustainability indicators in a way that cannot be changed. For instance, an AI system that optimizes battery storage and renewable dispatch could keep track of the actual savings in emissions or curtailment, creating an auditable link between computational energy and environmental benefit (Ul Haq et al. 2025d).

The practical importance of merging PoB with algorithmic stress tests is in accountability and openness. Stress tests put AI systems through their paces in very tough situations, like when demand suddenly rises, equipment breaks down or there are cyberattacks. This is to make sure they are strong and dependable. When used with PoB, regulators and stakeholders can be sure that AI systems are strong and that the energy used to perform these tasks is useful and necessary. This two-part framework changes the story about AI's energy use from an ethical concern about wasted electricity to a system of measurable responsibility, where every computation has clear value for the public good (Ul Haq et al. 2025a).

Ultimately, putting PoB into action helps create a digital infrastructure that is open, safe and based on ethics. It makes sure that intelligence and operational integrity grow at the same time, which helps energy transitions that last while keeping people's trust. Energy systems can use AI as a tool for climate action instead of a hidden contributor to environmental problems by adding purpose-driven validation to AI operations. PoB is a key new idea for making sure that AI deployment is in line with sustainability goals. It makes the digital energy ecosystem clear, accountable and high impact (Figure 8.2).

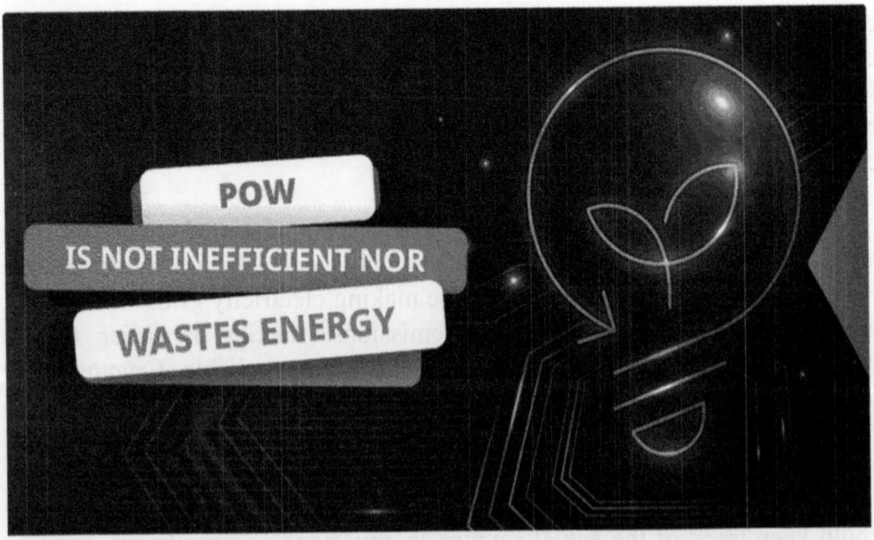

Figure 8.2. *A conceptual representation arguing against the inefficiency of proof-of-work, suggesting its potential for valuable, non-wasteful applications in systems like energy governance*

8.6. Conclusion: co-producing a livable climate with code

The path to a net-zero energy system is one of the hardest technological and social problems that people have ever faced. This chapter presents the challenge as an inextricable race of technology and data, with AI serving not only as a supplementary tool but also as a critical determinant of outcomes. AI has two roles: it is a powerful tool for decarbonization, helping to cut emissions, improve energy systems and speed up the transition, and it is also a major driver of energy demand, with its own growing carbon footprint.

The four pathways – ultra-high renewables, clean firm power, carbon-draw-down and demand disruption – show how flexible AI can be when it comes to solving a wide range of energy transition problems that are connected to each other. AI is what makes these big plans possible, from managing the ups and downs of renewable energy generation to making carbon removal processes more efficient and changing how people use energy. But this potential for change comes with big risks to the system as a whole. Algorithmic lock-in, data-driven inequalities and new cybersecurity weaknesses are all major threats that could slow progress toward net-zero goals if they are not dealt with.

The chapter stresses that using AI in the energy sector needs a proactive and all-encompassing governance framework. The proposed governance stack, which includes explainable carbon accounting, open energy data trusts and algorithmic stress-tests, is an important tool that helps rather than hinders. If used correctly, this framework could speed up the global net-zero path by 7–12 years. Without it, the energy system could become fragile, unfair and stuck on high-carbon paths long after 2050.

Sustainable energy futures and the code that governs them are now one and the same. Responsible AI is not an optional ethical consideration but a foundational requirement for achieving a secure, low-carbon energy system and safeguarding a stable climate for generations to come.

8.7. References

IPCC (2023). Climate change 2023: AR6 synthesis report – Summary for policymakers. Intergovernmental Panel on Climate Change, Bonn [Online]. Available at: https://www.ipcc.ch/report/ar6/syr/.

Lawrence, M., Janzwood, S., Homer-Dixon, T. (2022). What is a global polycrisis? Discussion Paper 2022-4, Version 2.0, Cascade Institute, Royal Roads University, British Columbia [Online]. Available at: https://cascadeinstitute.org/technical-paper/what-is-a-global-polycrisis/.

Matlin, S.A., Cornell, S.E., Krief, A., Hopf, H., Mehta, G. (2022). Chemistry must respond to the crisis of transgression of planetary boundaries. *Chemical Science*, 13, 11710–11720. doi: 10.1039/d2sc03603g.

NASA Jet Propulsion Laboratory (2023). How do we know climate change is real? California Institute of Technology [Online]. Available at: https://climate.nasa.gov/evidence/.

Persson, L., Carney Almroth, B.M., Collins, C.D., Cornell, S., de Wit, C.A., Diamond, M.L., Fantke, P., Hassellöv, M., MacLeod, M., Ryberg, M.W. et al. (2022). Outside the safe operating space of the planetary boundary for novel entities. *Environmental Science and Technology*, 56, 1510–1521. doi: 10.1021/acs.est.1c04158.

Prillaman, M. (2023). Are we in the Anthropocene? Geologists could define new epoch for Earth. *Nature*, 613, 14–15. doi: 10.1038/d41586-022-04428-3.

Rockström, J., Bai, X., de Vries, B. (2018). Global sustainability: The challenge ahead. *Global Sustainability*, 1, E6. doi: 10.1017/sus.2018.8.

Tulus, V., Pérez-Ramírez, J., Guillén-Gosálbez, G. (2021). Planetary metrics for the absolute environmental sustainability assessment of chemicals. *Green Chemistry*, 23, 9881–9893. doi: 10.1039/d1gc02623b.

UK Research and Innovation (2023). A brief history of climate change discoveries [Online]. Available at: https://www.discover.ukri.org/a-brief-history-of-climate-change-discoveries/index.html.

Ul Haq, I. (2024). Diagnosis of neurological disease using bioinspired algorithms. In *Bio-Inspired Optimization for Medical Data Mining*, Srivastava, S., Anand, A., Kumar, A. et al. (eds). John Wiley & Sons, Hoboken, NJ.

Ul Haq, I. and Khanday, A.M.U.D. (2025). Exploring the role of explainable AI in women's health: Challenges and solutions. In *Explainable Artificial Intelligence in the Healthcare Industry*, Kumar, A., Kumar, T.A., Das, P. et al. (eds). John Wiley & Sons, Hoboken, NJ.

Ul Haq, I., Kumar, N., Koul, N., Verma, C., Eneacu, F.M., Raboaca, M.S. (2022). Machine learning techniques for result prediction of one day international (ODI) cricket match. In *The International Conference on Recent Innovations in Computing*. Springer, Singapore.

Ul Haq, I., Kaur, G., Rather, A.H. (2024). Fruit leaf classification using transfer learning for automation and industrial applications. In *Deep Learning Techniques for Automation and Industrial Applications*, Rathore, P.S., Ahuja, S., Burri, S.R. et al. (eds). John Wiley & Sons, Hoboken, NJ.

Ul Haq, I., Khanday, A.M.D., Shah, H.A., Rufai, S.Z. (2025a). Enhancing water security through automation: Case studies and technical advancements in water quality management. In *Computational Automation for Water Security*, Dubey, A.K., Srivastav, A.L., Kumar, A. et al. (eds). Elsevier, Amsterdam.

Ul Haq, I., Kumar, A., Rathore, P.S. (2025b). Machine learning approaches for wind power forecasting: A comprehensive review. *Discover Applied Sciences*, 7(10), 1139.

Ul Haq, I., Malhotra, J., Rawat, V., Kumari, J., Kaur, G. (2025c). Machine learning approaches for early detection of cervical cancer: A comparative study of classification models. In *Targeted Chemotherapy with Personalized Immunotherapy: An AI Approach*, Kumar, A., Das, P., Rathore, P.S. et al. (eds). John Wiley & Sons, Hoboken, NJ.

Ul Haq, I., Nandal, V., Uppal, H. (2025d). Blockchain applications in aviation securing transactions, streamlining operations, and improving passenger experience. In *Blockchain in the Tourism Industry: A New Era of Secure and Transparent Travel Solutions*, Kumar, A., Abreu, A., Batta, P. et al. (eds). Springer, Cham.

United Nations (2022). Five ways to jump-start the renewable energy transition now. UN, New York [Online]. Available at: https://www.un.org/en/climatechange/raising-ambition/renewable-energy-transition.

World Economic Forum (2023). The global risks report, 18th edition [Online]. Available at: https://www.weforum.org/reports/global-risks-report-2023/.

Wunderling, N., Donges, J.F., Kurths, J., Winkelmann, R. (2021). Interacting tipping elements increase risk of climate domino effects under global warming. *Earth System Dynamics*, 12(2), 601–619. doi: 10.5194/esd-12-601-2021.

9

The Future of AI, ML and DL in Energy and Sustainability

The energy domain is literally turning a corner and has to deal with the so-called "trilemma" problem, which is used to keep energy safe, give energy access that is fair and affordable, and at the same time support environmental sustainability. As a result of industrialization, which is a major driver, along with rising living standards, the world needs, and is actually consuming, more energy than ever before. In the past, fossil fuels were the main source of energy used to satisfy these increasing demands. This dependence has led to two major crises: a worsening climate crisis caused by the emissions of greenhouse gases and unstable energy markets prone to geopolitical shocks. To meet the goals of international decarbonization agreements, a technological revolution is necessary and currently taking place globally with the emergence of artificial intelligence (AI), machine learning (ML) and deep learning (DL) as general-purpose technologies. These smart systems are extremely efficient in pattern recognition, complex system optimization and forecasting future events, applications which are far beyond human capabilities. The energy industry is adopting such technologies not only as the most feasible and immediate response but also as a solution rather than some sci-fi fantasy. AI is a technology that is capable of taking care of the grid challenge, which is modern, decentralized, decarbonized and, at the same time, complex and will require increased management work. Additionally, AI, ML and DL technology application results in super energy system control spanning generation and use by final consumers. These technologies allow us to produce accurate predictions of renewable energy sources that are characterized by high variability such as wind and solar, thus facilitating their safe integration into the grid. Moreover, they provide the fuel for a future grid, which will be capable of balancing its loads autonomously, predicting faults and rerouting power for an even longer life with minimal emissions. As the planet is heading toward a sustainable future, AI should not be considered an add-on but rather the core intelligent layer that will manage this transition.

Chapter written by Mamta NARWARIA, Sarika AGARWAL, Renu MISHRA, Aman KUMAR, Avinash CHAUHAN and Ramneet.

9.1. Introduction

9.1.1. *Background*

The world is looking for energy systems that can be sustained from the ground up with low environmental impact, and therefore, demanding intelligent technologies that have the ability to render complex, dynamic and decentralized infrastructures manageable. AI, ML and DL are being positioned as the main facilitators of the energy changeover, supporting efficiency, automation and innovation all through the energy lifecycle – generation, distribution and consumption. These technologies make it possible to create systems that are predictive, adaptive and autonomous by optimizing operation, integrating renewable sources and eliminating the environmental impact.

The chapter focuses on the requirement to keep energy safe, give energy access that is fair and affordable and at the same time support environmental sustainability (World Energy Council 2024). AI is a vital constituent if renewable energy sources are to be used as it increases the level of efficiency, thus lowering waste and also speeding up the creation of new sustainability solutions (Halgamuge 2024). If these two sectors are not cooperating, none of this would be feasible.

The impact of AI/ML and DL in the energy and sustainability sectors provides technological solutions to major challenges. If these two sectors do not cooperate these solutions will not be feasible. The following points are considered:

– grasping the concepts of AI, ML and DL, and also understanding their connection with energy;

– using the energy sector as an example for technology implementation – the scenario might be energy production and storage or smart grid management, energy-efficient buildings and transportation;

– delving into the utilization of AI-driven instruments to set the seemingly unattainable environmental targets within the realm of possibility, for example, cutting carbon emissions, implementing a circular economy and mitigating the climate change process;

– identifying the problems that are associated with bad-quality data, model opacity and ethics;

– present and future smart-energy research and innovations.

This chapter is divided into seven sections. Section 9.1 points out the significance of the issue. Section 9.2 introduces you to the principles of AI, ML and DL in energy. Section 9.3 explores the energy sector and adoption of the new tech-energy sources, smart grids, green transport, etc. Section 9.4 talks about eco-benefits of AI such as lowering carbon emissions and enabling circular economy. Section 9.5 pinpoints worst instances such as data corruption and ethical dilemmas. Section 9.6 dives into novel technologies and the outcomes of including edge AI and quantum computing, for example. Section 9.7 recaps some points and looks at future research.

9.2. Overview of AI, ML and DL in the context of energy

9.2.1. *AI in energy systems*

AI refers to the broad field of research, which deals with machines or systems that can simulate human intelligence to achieve certain goals that involve, among other things, problem solving, decision-making and pattern recognition. AI in the energy sector plays the role of the overall "decision engine". Most of the time, the energy systems using AI were essentially expert systems with a fixed set of rules programmed by domain experts for the purpose of controlling grid operations or diagnosing faults.

Currently, AI has a far more intricate role. It assists in the development of very complex decision-making systems that can solve mathematical problems involving many variables, for example, figuring out the unit commitment of power plants or the best location for renewable energy resources (Doris 2025). AI agents can handle sets of data that are large and varied in nature, which may include market prices, weather forecasts and grid load, and as a result, make the most appropriate economic and physical decisions in real-time which is humanly impossible.

9.2.2. *ML in energy and sustainability*

ML is an AI subfield which provides a system with the ability to self-learn and self-improve using trial and error (data) without human guidance. Basically, ML models "learn" or "master" data to detect the in-depth patterns they hold. These models can in general be divided into the following:

– *Supervised learning*: the model learns from labeled data (e.g. historical energy demand paired with time, weather and day of the week). For regression, techniques are implemented to form predictions, for example, forecasting solar irradiance or the energy consumption of a building (Ul Haq and Sharma 2026). On the other hand, classification serves for categorical works, such as determining whether a piece of grid equipment is close to failure or not.

– *Unsupervised learning*: the model discovers the hidden organization of unlabeled data. Customer segmentation according to their energy usage is done by clustering for the successful completion of demand–response programs. Anomaly detection plays a crucial role in cybersecurity by flagging malicious grid network traffic or depicting the behavior of the equipment as it deviates from normal, thus indicating the origin of the fault (SmartDev 2024).

– *Reinforcement learning (RL)*: the learning model acquires knowledge by monitoring the environment and getting "rewards" or "punishments" for each action. An excellent example of usage is in real-time control situations that may include battery storage system's charging/discharging cycles optimization to maximize profit or microgrid energy flows autonomous management (Ul Haq et al. 2026b).

9.2.3. *DL in energy*

DL, which is a progression of some kind in artificial neural networks, is a modular concept, architectural, and functional in nature, which mainly uses artificial neural networks with multiple layers (hence "deep") to tackle extremely complex problems. DL modules can take the initiative to learn the characteristics and patterns of data directly from nature such as pictures, time series or text. The common structures in energy involve the following:

– *Convolutional neural networks (CNNs)*: by and large, CNNs are for picture analysis and applicable to satellite imaging to determine the best place for wind and solar farms or to process the thermal images of the equipment for the purpose of predictive maintenance (Ul Haq and Sharma 2026).

– *Recurrent neural networks (RNNs) and long short-term memory (LSTM)*: these two different network models are designed to work with sequential data, thereby forecasting in the time-series domain. LSTMs are currently the best at predicting energy load, wind speeds and solar output, because they enable the modeling of complex temporal dependencies (Singh et al. 2026).

– *Generative adversarial networks (GANs)*: GANs are capable of generating data resembling real-world data, which is of utmost importance in the energy field where genuine data of rare events (like grid failures) is hard to come by. This fabricated data can be used to make the ML models more robust with increased training (Halgamuge 2024).

9.2.4. *Convergence of AI, ML and DL in energy*

AI, ML and DL are not independent and instead create a unified toolbox all working together. AI provides the strategy for making decisions, ML provides the algorithms to build predictive and classification models from data, and DL enables a more advanced approach to handling the immense scale and complexity of sensor, weather and pricing data.

A more contemporary example of this is the "smart grid" (Figure 9.1), which includes all three techniques: an ML model (e.g. regression – predicts demand in the next 24 h); a DL model (e.g. LSTMs) generates the forecasts for the renewables output; after those predictions return, AI (e.g. reinforcement learning) turns those predictions into inputs to optimize energy flow from different sources (gas, wind, solar and batteries) and also makes real-time control decisions to keep the grid stable and resilient at a low cost.

9.3. Functions of AI, ML and DL in energy systems

9.3.1. *Energy production and renewable energy integration*

DL models, particularly LSTM networks, have become the de facto standard to accurately forecast how much wind and solar power generation occurs, interpret weather phenomena and forecast at a high temporal granularity when electricity might be produced (Singh et al. 2026). With such precise predictions, grid operators can preemptively call for the use of the dispatchable generation (e.g. gas or hydro) as well as energy storage to fill in the gaps and thus keep the grid stable. By way of illustration, AI may in real-time regulate the pitch and yaw of the blades of a wind turbine in a wind farm to correspond to the direction of the incoming wind and the turbulence created by the adjacent turbines (thus maximizing power output of the whole farm rather than that of just one unit) (Ul Haq and Sharma 2026).

9.3.2. *Energy storage and optimization*

Energy storage, emphasis on battery energy storage systems (BESS), is the mainstay of renewable power buffering. ML has a significant presence in the operations of BMS (battery management system). ML models are capable of estimating battery "State of Charge" (SoC) and "State of Health" (SoH) with a much better degree of accuracy than conventional models (Future Market Insights 2025).

The ability to forecast is what mainly facilitates the desirable function of the battery in terms of charging/discharging prevention and generally extends its lifetime. In addition, reinforcement learning algorithms serve as the brains behind action control of grid-scale batteries, which make decisions on their own about which moment is most appropriate for "charging" (when energy is cheap and in plenty, e.g. solar at its peak) and for "discharging" (when prices are at their highest and demand is strong), thus increasing both profitability and grid stability (Virtue Market Research 2025).

9.3.3. *Smart grids and demand response*

A smart grid is an electricity network that uses digital communication and AI to detect and react to local changes in usage. AI/ML is the "brain" of the smart grid. ML-based anomaly detection algorithms monitor sensor data in real-time to predict and pinpoint equipment failures (predictive maintenance) and identify fault locations, reducing outage durations from hours to minutes (Hertz 2025).

AI also enables dynamic demand-response (DR) systems. Instead of only increasing supply to meet demand, AI-powered DR systems manage demand itself. These systems use ML to forecast peak load periods and then automatically send price signals or control commands to smart appliances (like HVACs or EV chargers) in homes and businesses, asking them to shift their consumption to off-peak hours. This "load balancing" reduces stress on the grid, lowers costs for consumers and avoids the need to fire up expensive and polluting "peaker" plants (GECAD 2025; Hertz 2025). Figure 9.1 provides a conceptual overview of an AI-managed smart grid.

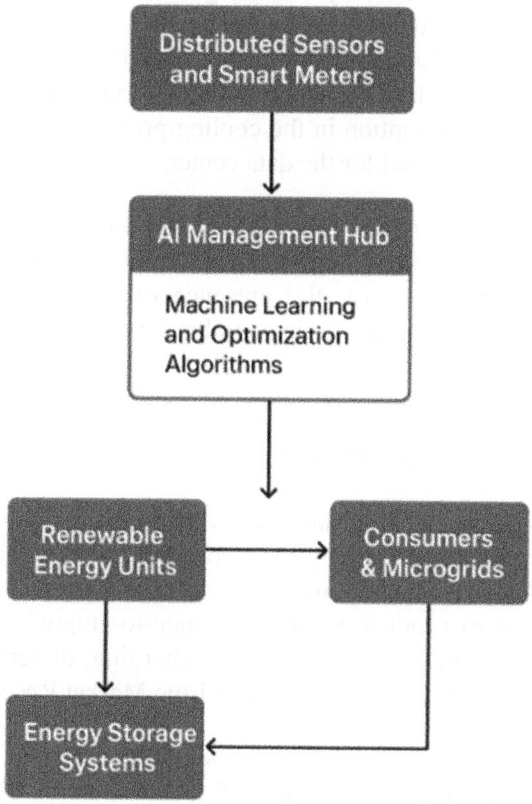

Figure 9.1. *Conceptual architecture of an AI-managed smart grid*

9.3.4. *Energy efficiency and building automation*

Buildings represent 30–40% of energy consumption in the world, the main consumption being that of heating, ventilation and air conditioning (HVAC) units. AI-energized building operation systems (BAS) are no longer just simple thermostats. They employ ML to create a "digital twin" of a building, figuring out its singular thermal characteristics and foreseeing the occupancy patterns.

Probably the most outstanding example in the real-world scenario is Google's DeepMind project (Evans and Gao 2016). AI powered by reinforcement learning was able to manage the cooling techniques in Google's gigantic data centers by balancing the complicated interactions of the server loads, the outdoor temperatures and the cooling equipment. Hence, the system could at its own discretion alter the settings of the pumps, the chillers and the fans in the most energy-efficient way leading to a 40% decrease in energy consumption in the cooling process and a 15% reduction in the entire energy overhead for the data center.

The same concept is now being adapted to commercial and residential buildings, where ML is used to set HVAC to the most energy-efficient levels based on the weather forecast, the presence of people and utility price signals, thereby making energy savings without compromising user comfort (SmartDev 2025).

9.3.5. *Sustainable transportation*

The use of electricity in transport is one of the major features of decarbonization. AI and ML play a central role in this change. For EVs (electric vehicles), ML is employed to make the battery performance the most efficient and to produce a correct "range-to-empty", thus letting the driver know how far he/she can go without charging, thereby lessening the anxiety associated with the limited range (Virtue Market Research 2025).

At the systemic level, AI will be indispensable in orchestrating the huge new load that a widespread practice of EV charging will bring to the electrical grid. The "smart charging" systems driven by AI are able to carry out charging schedules at their optimum and thus advise the vehicles when they ought to be charged during the off-peak hours when renewable energy is plentiful and affordable prices are in effect (GECAD 2025).

In addition to the fact that AI algorithms work to make vehicle routing more efficient from an energy-saving point of view, the same algorithms are also, on the other hand, handling the complex logistics of charging the fleet in one central place without causing any kind of load or peak on the local grid infrastructure.

9.4. AI and ML for sustainability goals

9.4.1. *Energy decarbonization*

AI is not just a means to optimize current systems. It has the potential to significantly reduce carbon emissions at a much faster speed. For instance, in the heavy-industry sector, AI is employed to optimize energy-intensive processes in the manufacture of cement and steel. One of the important applications along the way is Carbon Capture, Utilization, and Storage (CCUS). AI-guided process automation, in fact, helps achieve significant CO_2 capture efficiency improvements (Anyebe et al. 2024). ML models can study geological data to designate the most stable and secure underground formations for safe CO_2 storage for an extended period. Moreover, they can efficiently manage the chemical processes in "utilization" by facilitating the discovery of new catalysts, which will help in converting captured CO_2 into beneficial products as synthetic fuels or plastics (Ul Haq et al. 2026a).

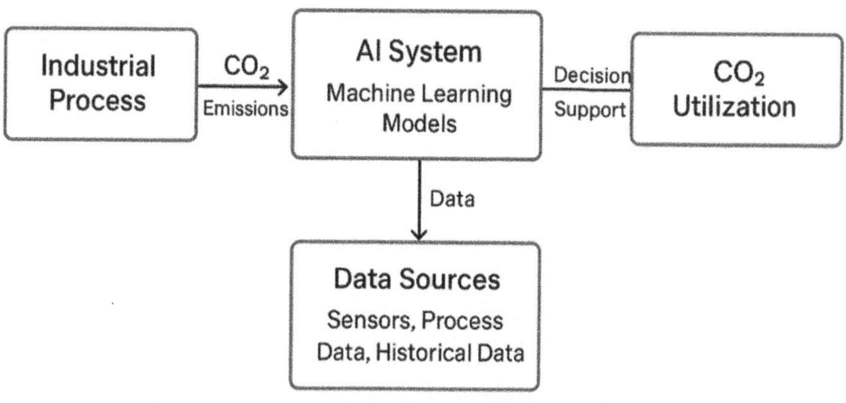

Figure 9.2. *AI-assisted Carbon Capture and Utilization (CCUS) for industrial decarbonization*

9.4.2. *Circular economy and resource optimization*

The circular economy represents a production and consumption model whereby sharing, leasing, reusing, repairing, refurbishing and recycling of the existing materials and products are performed for an extended period. AI plays an instrumental role in the implementation of this concept. AI-driven sorting robots in the waste management sector employ computer vision (a

DL subtype) to recognize and separate the different recyclable materials (e.g. plastics, metals and paper) that are loaded onto a high-speed conveyor belt (Recycleye 2024). As a result, this method, which is illustrated in Figure 9.3, greatly enhances the purity of the recycled materials and hence makes recycling economically viable. Additionally, AI can be utilized to its fullest potential in "waste-to-energy" (WtE) facilities where it can control the emission of pollutants and increase energy production by adjusting the combustion parameters on a real-time basis according to the waste feed's composition (Mulè 2024).

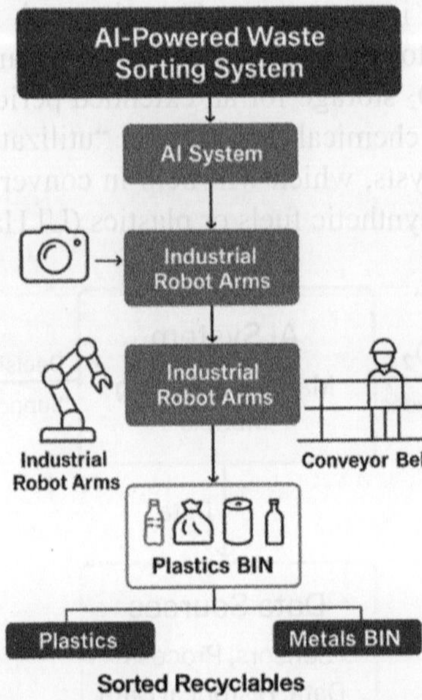

Figure 9.3. *AI-powered waste sorting for the circular economy. Computer vision and robotics automate the sorting of recyclables, increasing efficiency and purity*

9.4.3. *Climate change mitigation and adaptation*

Innovations in AI and DL models are proving to be very helpful instruments for climate sciences. In-depth learning models are capable of handling very large climate datasets gathered from satellites, ocean buoys and land sensors and producing more precise climate prediction models for the long-term (Ul Haq et al. 2026b). These models enable scientists to forecast how often and how strong the extreme weather events will be, which is vital information for building energy infrastructures that can handle the shocks. AI can also be used in monitoring deforestation, tracking the loss of polar ice and recording the levels of greenhouse gases in the atmosphere using satellite pictures, which result in the creation of real-time global dashboards shedding light on climate change indicators.

9.4.4. *Sustainable agriculture and land use*

At the same time, agriculture remains one of the biggest energy (for tools and fertilizer production) and water consumers. However, the use of AI-driven precision agriculture can significantly mitigate these problems by making sure that resources are used efficiently. ML algorithms are empowered with decision-making power by the data coming from drones, soil sensors and satellites, and can therefore give recommendations that perfectly fit the farm fields requirements (Ul Haq et al. 2026c). For instance, AI can diagnose plant health and soil moisture so as to regulate "smart irrigation" networks, thus water usage can be reduced by 25–30% (Evans and Raja 2024). In addition, it is capable of utilizing the farms' energy resources in the best manner possible by designing solar-powered water pumps that can fully substitute diesel, thus being able to lessen the carbon footprint of food production (Padhiary et al. 2026).

9.5. Case studies and key findings

Table 9.1 provides a snapshot of the most significant real-world applications of AI and ML technologies in the energy sector with a focus on the performance metrics used to monitor efficiency, emissions and sustainability.

Sector	Example	AI/ML technique	Reported impact	Source
Renewable forecasting	DeepMind + Google	LSTM	40% cooling energy reduction	Evans and Gao (2016)
Battery optimization	Tesla Megapack	Reinforcement learning	15% improved battery life	Virtue Market Research (2025)
Smart grids	U.S. Department of Energy Pilot	ML anomaly detection	70% faster fault detection	Hertz (2025)

Table 9.1. *Summary of AI and ML applications and reported outcomes*

9.6. Challenges and limitations in AI, ML and DL for energy and sustainability

Even with the fantastic potential that AI has, its introduction to the energy sector is met with resistance and problems. The issues that arise due to this implementation are of a technical nature as well as practical, ethical and regulatory.

9.6.1. *Data challenges*

The AI/ML models are not flawless. One of the major conditions for their proper functioning is the presence of high-quality data. The energy sector is not without its problems related to data:

– *Data scarcity and quality*: on the one hand, smart meters and sensors could provide vast datasets. On the other hand, however, old transformers that are part of critical infrastructure may not have sensors, thus creating areas with no data or "deserts". Moreover, data originating from different utilities are often non-standardized, which makes it hard for developers to create models that have regional scalability since the results can be different depending on the area (Doris 2025).

– *Data for rare events*: ML models, particularly those used in predictive maintenance, have to derive knowledge from failure situations. However, the number of catastrophic grid failures is, intentionally, very low. Consequently, the scarcity of "failure data" makes it hard for predictive models to be accurate.

– *Data management*: the "3Vs" (volume, velocity and variety) of data coming from millions of smart meters and IoT devices point to the necessity of a robust and expensive data infrastructure capable of storage, processing and security functions (SmartDev 2024).

9.6.2. *Model interpretability and transparency*

Among the most significant difficulties, especially when it comes to DL, is the "black-box" issue. For example, an LSTM network can make a successful grid fault prediction; however, it can rarely give the reason behind the prediction.

In a high stakes, critical infrastructure environment such as an energy grid, operators are reluctant to follow a decision that they cannot justify (Shadi et al. 2025). Hence, the problem of interpretability and transparency constitutes one of the most serious barriers to the acceptance of DL models in energy applications. As a result, this has given rise to the explainable AI (XAI) research field that aims at creating techniques, which make it possible to understand and audit AI models, as briefly described in Table 9.2.

Challenge	Description	Mitigation Strategy
Data quality	Models that are built upon incomplete, noisy or unstandardized data produce unreliable results	Development of data-sharing standards; use of data augmentation and synthetic data (GANs) to fill gaps.
Model interpretability	Model Interpretability. The "black-box" nature of complex models (e.g. DL) erodes trust in critical systems.	Explainable AI (XAI): Applying techniques (e.g. LIME and SHAP) to indicate to a user which input features most impacted the models' decisions.
Scalability and integration	Deploying models at scale and integrating with legacy grid control systems (SCADA) is often complex and expensive.	Edge AI: Instead of having to send all data to a central cloud, processing data on local sensors or gateways to lower latency and data transmission costs.
Ethical bias and equity	AI models trained on historical data can learn and even amplify existing social biases, leading to undesirable unfair outcomes.	Algorithmic audits: Proactively auditing models to verify bias. Building AI for "energy equity" by providing targeted funding for upgrades and assistance to vulnerable communities.

Table 9.2. *Key challenges and mitigation strategies for AI in energy*

9.6.3. *Scalability and integration issues*

A model that is successful in a laboratory or a small-scale pilot project might not work when it is expanded to a city-wide or national grid level. The energy sector is reliant on infrastructure that is considered old-fashioned and has been around for decades. The integration of contemporary AI technologies into these aged industrial control systems (such as SCADA) is not only technically challenging and costly but also raises major concerns regarding cybersecurity (Hertz 2025).

Putting all sensor data into a single cloud for AI processing results in latency (delay) and bandwidth problems, which are not permissible for the real-time control (at the level of milliseconds) necessary for grid stability.

9.6.4. *Ethical and social implications*

There are a lot of ethical issues that come with the use of AI in the energy sector. The main concern is that AI-powered optimization may result in social inequities being exacerbated. For example:

– An AI model designed to optimize grid investment decisions may prioritize wealthier neighborhoods, which often exhibit higher and more variable electricity demand, for infrastructure upgrades. As a result, low-income and vulnerable communities may receive less investment, increasing their risk of experiencing power outages and reduced energy reliability (Columbia University CGEP 2025).

– DR schemes powered by AI could be providing advantages only to rich families that can buy smart appliances and have flexible schedules and at the same time, put at a disadvantage, those (like elderly people or remote workers) who are unable to change their consumption patterns (Prism Sustainability Directory 2025).

– AI data centers have such high electricity demands that they are causing new grid strains, and consequently, electricity rates will be increased for all consumers without discrimination (Wojtaszek 2025).

Solving this problem is only possible with the implementation of a forward-looking "ethical AI" framework.

The "Clean Energy Equity Index" created by the UNDP and IBM is an example of a new tool that leverages AI to locate areas suffering from energy poverty, thus giving policymakers the opportunity to precisely point out the investments that will bring about a just and equitable transition (IBM Newsroom 2024).

9.7. Emerging trends and future directions

9.7.1. *AI, ML and DL in next-generation smart cities*

Energy systems will be interconnected rather than standalone in the coming years. The elements constitute smart cities' core. AI will be the main operating system that manages and balances energy, transport, water and waste services at a city level in a holistic way. As an illustration, AI could manage the charging of the city's EV network together with building energy management systems and the power grid by taking into account up-to-the-minute traffic data and renewable energy forecasts and thus guarantee that the entire urban ecosystem is running at its optimum level of efficiency (SmartDev 2025).

9.7.2. *Autonomous energy systems*

The coming energy network would be to a large extent decentralized and made up of millions of "prosumers" (households equipped with solar panels and batteries) and small-scale local grids. It would not be humanly possible to have control centrally. The future belongs to energy systems that function independently, or a "self-driving grid" concept. These setups will incorporate sophisticated AI and reinforcement learning agents for the management of local microgrids, peer-to-peer energy trading and unassisted reaction to interruptions (such as extreme weather) to not only identify the sources of faults but also to reroute the power, thus generating a grid that has the ability to "heal" itself (GECAD 2025).

9.7.3. *5G and edge AI for energy systems*

The problem with latency and data overload from centralized AI (which was talked about in sections 9.6.2 and 9.6.3) is being overcome through the use of edge AI technology. Rather than transmitting all sensor data to the cloud, edge AI carries out ML processing right there on the device or a local gateway (for instance, on the smart meter or at the substation) (Dimension Market Research 2025). This, in turn, needs extremely fast and low-latency communication, which is the major purpose of 5G networks. The interaction of 5G with edge AI will open the way for real-time, totally autonomous control of tasks, such as "flicker" detection and grid stabilization that need a response time of less than 1 s, thus, cloud-based AI is not able to perform it (Singh 2025).

9.7.4. *AI-driven climate risk management*

AI will become a prominent tool for risk management as climate change gets worse. AI-powered models that take into account real-time satellite imagery and weather data will be able to accurately forecast the direction and severity of wildfires, hurricanes and floods (Ul Haq et al. 2026a). This data will be integrated directly into the control systems of the energy grid, so that AI can take the initiative to disconnect power lines in regions at high risk of fire or effectively manage storage and microgrids in a way that ensures the continuity of essential infrastructure (like hospitals) during an emergency caused by climate change.

9.7.5. *Quantum computing and AI for energy and sustainability*

Domain	Problem type	Potential quantum application
Grid optimization	Combinatorial optimization	Address the "Unit Commitment" problem for thousands of assets in the matter of seconds. Optimize power flow for a complete continental grid in real-time.
New materials	Molecular simulation	Simulate new molecules to discover more efficient catalysts for green hydrogen production, or to do direct-air carbon capture.
Battery chemistry	Molecular simulation	Molecular simulation models very complex chemical interactions and designs next-generation high-density, safer battery chemistries.
Climate modeling	Complex simulation	Run extremely complex climate models that account for more variables that lead to far more accurate long-range climate and weather modeling.

Table 9.3. *Potential future applications of quantum computing in energy*

Although only in its infancy, quantum computing is the biggest potential long-term change that has been applied by the energy sector. Most of the toughest problems in the energy sector, that is to say, complex optimization challenges, are "intractable" even for the most powerful classical computers (e.g. figuring out the best way to supply energy for the entire United States national grid). Quantum computing is the only technology that can solve these particular "combinatorial optimization" problems (SCQuantum 2025). The upcoming uses as reported in Table 9.3 span from the discovery of new materials for ultra-efficient solar cells or carbon-capture agents to solving optimization problems for the power grid thousands of times faster than the best supercomputers of today (Ho et al. 2024; Wani 2025).

9.8. Conclusion

9.8.1. *Summary of key insights*

This chapter demonstrates how the work with AI, ML and DL has been a real game-changer for the energy and the sustainability sectors. Nowadays, these new technology-driven solutions seem to be fundamental rather than optional or futuristic when it comes to find a way through the global energy transition. AI/ML/DL models are indeed very helpful and indispensable for forecasting and integrating intermittent renewable energy, optimizing energy storage and generating intelligent and resilient smart grids. The use of AI energy-saving initiative in Google's data centers is the main reason behind AI system's global energy consumption reduction, and thus a clear and replicable model of energy efficiency for all sectors.

As AI technology evolves, it is expected to be fully sustainable with the overall ESG goals and in applications far beyond the energy sector as well. To list the a few, it makes the circular economy more efficient through automated recycling, saves water and energy in precision agriculture, and provides new powerful methods for climate change simulation and the removal of CO_2 from heavy industries.

Nevertheless, this transformation still has some bumps and obstacles of considerable size along the way. The shortage of data, the "black-box" nature of complex models and the very urgent necessity of ensuring fair and ethical use are only a few of the major problems that cannot solely be resolved by technical solutions (like XAI) or government regulations, but require the right combination of both to be solved.

9.8.2. *Future challenges and research directions*

The energy sector is going to be influenced by intelligent, self-regulated and decentralized energy systems that will hardly require any human intervention. In reality, the creation of edge AI and 5G technologies will make it possible for energy to be managed not from the cloud but from the local branch of the network where continuous real-time autonomous control will actually be feasible. However, much later, quantum computing is said to be the solution to problems in optimization and materials science that are inaccessible to any classical computer.

The issue of the human aspect is going to be the most difficult; nevertheless, the scientific community should be very careful with it and highlight their priority as follows:

1) *Developing robust explainable AI (XAI)*: knowing "why" the model came to a certain decision rather than just "what" the decision is, is vital for trust and accountability to be incremented into the systems.

2) *Ensuring AI works for energy equity*: a deliberate research effort is required wherein AI is employed as a tool for solving the issue of "energy poverty" and to ensure the benefits of the clean energy transition are received by all and not only those who can afford the latest technology.

3) *Being receptive to other fields*: integrating AI requires extensive collaboration with engineers, philosophers, policymakers, and sociologists to develop systems that are not only effective but also safe, transparent, and equitable, through co-design approaches that benefit the broader community.

AI, ML and DL may be considered the most potent weapons that mankind can wield to expedite the transition to a sustainable and low-carbon future, rather than being referred to as the only explanation for everything. The main factors that will determine whether or not we will be able to build a cleaner, smarter and more eco-friendly energy system that is fit for future generations will be their continuous development and wise use, which are indispensable.

9.9. References

Anyebe, A.P., Yeboah, O.K.K., Bakinson, O.I., Adeyinka, T.Y., Okafor, F.C. (2024). Optimizing carbon capture efficiency through AI-driven process automation for enhancing predictive maintenance and CO_2 sequestration in oil and gas facilities. *American Journal of Environment and Climate*, 3(3), 44–58 [Online]. Available at: https://www.researchgate.net/publication/385947801.

Columbia University CGEP. (2025). How AI growth can hyper-scale energy equity and affordability. Center on Global Energy Policy [Online]. Available at: https://www.energypolicy.columbia.edu/how-ai-growth-can-hyper-scale-energy-equity-and-affordability/.

Dimension Market Research (2025). Edge AI for smart grid market to reach USD 141.4 bn by 2034 [Online]. Available at: https://dimensionmarketresearch.com/report/edge-ai-for-smart-grid-market/.

Doris, L. (2025). AI for climate resilience: Predictive modeling of extreme weather and carbon capture. *ResearchGate* [Online]. Available at: https://www.researchgate.net/publication/390033105.

Evans, R. and Gao, J. (2016). DeepMind AI reduces Google data centre cooling bill by 40%. Google DeepMind Blog.

Evans, I. and Raja, M.S.R.S. (2024). Leveraging AI for sustainable agriculture: Optimizing water and resource usage in the face of climate change. *International Journal of Multidisciplinary on Science and Management*, 1, 122–130.

Future Market Insights (2025). Data center battery market | Global market analysis report – 2035 [Online]. Available at: https://www.futuremarketinsights.com/reports/data-center-battery-market.

GECAD (2025). Workshop AI for sustainable energy – CAI 2025. In *IEEE International Conference on Artificial Intelligence 2025* [Online]. Available at: https://www.gecad.isep.ipp.pt/ERM-competitions/cai-2025/.

Halgamuge, M.N. (2024). Leveraging deep learning to strengthen the cyber-resilience of renewable energy supply chains: A survey. *IEEE Communications Surveys and Tutorials*, 26(3), 2146–2175.

Hertz, J. (2025). How will AI transform smart grids in 2025? *EE Power* [Online]. Available at: https://eepower.com/tech-insights/how-will-ai-transform-smart-grids-in-2025/.

Ho, K.T.M., Chen, K.C., Lee, L., Burt, F., Yu, S., Lee, P.H. (2024). Quantum computing for climate resilience and sustainability challenges. In *IEEE International Conference on Quantum Computing and Engineering (QCE)*.

IBM Newsroom (2024). UNDP and IBM launch new tools to forecast energy access and model energy equity [Online]. Available at: https://newsroom.ibm.com/2024-09-17-UNDP-and-IBM-Launch-New-Tools-to-Forecast-Energy-Access-and-Model-Energy-Equity.

Mulè, L. (2024). Revolutionizing waste management: The role of AI in building sustainable practices. *AI for Good (ITU)* [Online]. Available at: https://aiforgood.itu.int/revolutionizing-waste-management-the-role-of-ai-in-building-sustainable-practices/.

Padhiary, M., Kumar, K., Sheikh, A. (2026). AI-driven innovations in precision agriculture: Solar energy for sustainable farming. In *AI-Driven Solutions for Solar Energy Efficiency, Irradiance Modeling, and PV Forecasting*, de Alexandria, A.R., Upadhyay, P., Galletta, A. et al. (eds). IGI Global Scientific Publishing, Hershey, PA.

Prism Sustainability Directory (2025). Global standards for ethical AI in energy networks [Online]. Available at: https://prism.sustainability-directory.com/scenario/global-standards-for-ethical-ai-in-energy-networks/.

Recycleye (2024). AI waste sorting robots are the future of the circular economy [Online]. Available at: https://recycleye.com/ai-waste-sorting-robots-are-future/.

SCQuantum (2025). Quantum computing energy grid optimization [Online]. Available at: https://www.scquantum.org/sites/default/files/Paper-qBraid-SCQ-2025-03-Energy%20Grid-Optimization.pdf.

Shadi, M.R., Mirshekali, H., Shaker, H.R. (2025). Explainable artificial intelligence for energy systems maintenance: A review on concepts, current techniques, challenges, and prospects. *Renewable and Sustainable Energy Reviews*, 216, 115668.

Singh, S. (2025). Why edge AI is now crucial for powering the global grid. World Economic Forum [Online]. Available at: https://www.weforum.org/stories/2025/06/edge-ai-resilient-infrastructure-energy/.

Singh, A., Haq, I.U., Jain, N., Kumar, R., Rather, M.A., Masoodi, F.S. (2026). Hybrid quantum–classical learning architectures for 6G/7G edge intelligence. In *Deep Quantum Neural Networks: AI for 6G/7G Communication Systems*, Kumar, A., Rathore, P.S., Juárez-Ramírez, R. (eds). Springer, Singapore.

SmartDev (2024). AI in renewable energy: Top use cases you need to know [Online]. Available at: https://smartdev.com/fr/ai-use-cases-in-renewable-energy/.

SmartDev (2025). AI in facilities management: Top use cases you need to know. [Online]. Available at: https://smartdev.com/ai-use-cases-in-facilities-management/.

Ul Haq, I. and Sharma, N. (2026). AI and quantum-driven IoT frameworks for sustainable 6G/7G smart homes. In *Deep Quantum Neural Networks: AI for 6G/7G Communication Systems*, Kumar, A., Rathore, P.S., Juárez-Ramírez, R. (eds). Springer, Singapore.

Ul Haq, I., Singh, A., Jain, N., Rather, M.A., Masoodi, F.S. (2026a). Quantum convolutional neural networks for intelligent spectrum management in 6G/7G. In *Deep Quantum Neural Networks: AI for 6G/7G Communication Systems*, Kumar, A., Rathore, P.S., Juárez-Ramírez, R. (eds). Springer, Singapore.

Ul Haq, I., Yousuf, A., Masoodi, F.S. (2026b). Integrating blockchain and metaverse for next generation smart healthcare networks. In *Blockchain Enabled Metaverse for Smart Wireless Sensor Networks*, Kumar, A., Rathore, P.S., Moreira, F. (eds). Springer, Cham.

Ul Haq, I., Kak, S.M., Ul Islam, M. (2026c). Emerging trends in blockchain metaverse for intelligent sensor network applications. In *Blockchain Enabled Metaverse for Smart Wireless Sensor Networks*, Kumar, A., Rathore, P.S., Moreira, F. (eds). Springer, Cham.

Virtue Market Research (2025). Next generation battery market | Size, share, growth | 2025 – 2030 [Online]. Available at https://virtuemarketresearch.com/report/next-generation-battery-market.

Wani, M.A. (2025). The role of quantum computing in energy optimization and renewable resources. [Online]. Available at: https://www.bmcoder.com/the-role-of-quantum-computing-in-energy-optimization-and-renewable-resources.

Wojtaszek, H. (2025). Energy transition 2024–2025: New demand vectors, technology oversupply, and shrinking net-zero 2050 premium. *Energies*, 18(16), 4441.

World Energy Council (2024). World energy trilemma report 2024: Evolving with resilience and justice [Online]. Available at: https://www.worldenergy.org/publications/entry/world-energy-trilemma-report-2024.

10

Hydrogen Intelligence (HyAI): A Data-Driven Approach to Transforming the Global Hydrogen Ecosystem

Green hydrogen is seen by some as the foundation of future energy paradigms, with the world working towards reducing carbon emissions. There are still numerous obstacles in perfecting its production, storage, transportation and ultimate uses to help large-scale implementation. The chapter describes an extensive artificial intelligence (AI) platform for hydrogen intelligence (HyAI), which is adapted to proactive monitoring and instantaneous performance benefits over the entire hydrogen lifecycle. HyAI architecture takes advantage of both the use of deep neural networks and digital twin models to promote an ideal balance between the work of the fuel cell, performance in electrolysis, storage considerations and the opening up of renewables. Through adaptive self-learning control loops and hybrid forecasting schemes, HyAI will improve predicting demand, minimize conversion losses and make systems more stable in a range of grids and climates. With the predictive failure of distributed hydrogen infrastructure, HyAI can forecast the probability of this failure through the integration of multi-agent coordination with operational optimization, technoeconomic planning and resiliency analysis. It has also been developed to interface conveniently with traceability schemes based on blockchain, smart grid and IoT-enabled hydrogen systems that guarantee secure exchange of data in open carbon accounting. The modeling feature of HyAI ensures safety of investment and supports scalability growth over the long term, as well as the opportunity to adapt dynamically to changes in policy frameworks and become a participant in energy markets. HyAI is a radical technology of autonomously evolving self-optimizing hydrogen ecosystems that can accelerate the world toward a net-zero future, using a combination of AI-based cognitive intelligence and the prospects of hydrogen as a zero-carbon energy carrier.

Chapter written by Deepak KUMAR and Shaman SHARMA.

10.1. Introduction

The global energy business has been experiencing a significant shift in the 21st century. Change is being caused by rising greenhouse gas levels, the increasing rate of global warming and the slow disappearance of traditional fuel reserves. These circumstances have compelled global leaders and the scientific community to reconsider the entire energy lifetime, whether it be through generation and storage or end-use (Sethi et al. 2025).

Even though the development of solar and wind energy stands out as one of the significant improvements in energy generation, their unpredictability, subject to weather conditions and the time of day, continues to pose a challenge as far as ensuring a stable and predictable flow of electricity is concerned (Hassan et al. 2023).

This chapter discusses a developing area of green hydrogen in order to achieve full renewability and decarbonization of the power system (Zhang and Li 2024). Recent investigations indicate that it is highly applicable to energy storage dependent on long time periods and seasonality, as well as the offer of fundamental services that enhance grid reliability. There is also an economic prognosis that green hydrogen is gradually approaching cost competitiveness and that it will form a solid base of future sustainable energy markets alongside conventional fuels within the next 10 years, making it a foundation of decarbonized energy networks by the middle of the century (Angelico et al. 2025). In significant applications, such as in hard-to-abate sectors such as steelmaking, where it can replace coke in the chemical reduction of iron ore and thus can remove a major source of process-related emissions, green hydrogen is of particular importance (Franco and Rocca 2024). Nevertheless, there are several major hurdles that still stand in the way of transitioning to a hydrogen economy. The high cost of electrolyzers, the lack of proper infrastructure in transportation and refueling and the need to continue with research to enhance overall conversion efficiency are still considered to be particular hindrances. These gaps need to be closed to achieve maximum use of hydrogen in the context of minimizing the intermittency of renewable energy sources and substantial industrial decarbonization (Franco and Rocca 2024). Moreover, the successful operational functioning of hydrogen-integrated energy systems is premised on efficient management of the intricate supply–demand relationship. These systems, as has been reported, are very sensitive and the breakdown of a single component would send a domino effect as it would reduce the entire system's efficiency, creating unforeseen problems in its operations. It is important for this complexity to be controlled by hack-free digital control systems. One possible efficient solution that can be recommended is the introduction of an integrated AIoT framework that involves the large-scale adoption of sensing sources and smart, data-driven algorithms. This type of system allows real-time control, predictive analytics and automated control that is required to manage the nonlinear and condition-sensitive dynamics for generating, handling and converting hydrogen (Joshua et al. 2024; Mullanu et al. 2025).

AI radically shifts modes of creation. Hydrogen technologies are currently under development and being operated in novel, creative and efficient manners; hydrogen technologies are also created in novel ways. These intelligent systems will provide better process optimization, precise failure prediction and faster development of new materials that are required in the clean energy sphere based on multifaceted algorithms. Machine learning (ML) is leading this revolution and it has the mind-blowing potential to revolutionize the way hydrogen systems can be designed and operated altogether. AI-driven approaches are greatly shortening the research cycle of finding new catalysts and correctly ascertaining their applicability in the long term. Available computer models provide the possibility of screening many material combinations in a short period, predicting the stability and activity of catalyst compounds, and resolving complicated chemical reactions that were difficult to understand before. This provides a complete change in operational speed, where AI systems can now forecast energy consumption levels with significant precision, anticipate equipment breakdowns and automatically modify system settings to reach optimal outcomes. It is a revolutionary shift from an ordinary paradigm of hydrogen technology development toward a more precise and data-driven innovation paradigm, which relies on trial and error. By extracting intricate relationships between electrocatalyst performance and material properties, researchers can now use ML pattern recognition tools, which can save researchers a massive amount of time, and technological innovation can be achieved (Ramesh et al. 2023; Ding et al. 2024; Bhuiyan et al. 2025; Zhang et al. 2025a).

In many research works, deep learning models and in particular long short-term memory (LSTM) networks have demonstrated high accuracy in predicting the degradation of proton exchange membrane fuel cells (PEMFC). The great predictive qualities of LSTM have always been emphasized by researchers. One such case is Sahajpal et al. (2023), who attained a R2 high of 98.87%, and RMSE of 1.258E-3 when predicting stack voltage. In 2024, Darwish (2024) proposed an LSTM model with dual attention that outperformed other deep learning methods in predicting remaining useful life. Zuo et al. (2021) discovered that attention-based LSTM models could decrease the RMSE to 0.016409, which has a significant effect on the prediction error. Though the very fact of the improvement of 14.18% cannot be verified directly using these sources, the experiments invariably demonstrate that LSTM is much more efficient in predicting the process of PEMFC degradation than conventional techniques (Zuo et al. 2021).

Digital twin technology has demonstrated great potential in transforming hydrogen infrastructure, enabling accurate real-time monitoring and predictive maintenance of both electrolyzers and refueling station systems. It is worth mentioning that Zhou et al. (2024) created a digital twin model of proton exchange membrane water electrolysis, which can measure the temperature of the sensorless reaction interface. Zhao et al.'s (2022) modeling accuracy is 96.31% for predicting power consumption and hydrogen production, and the neural network's predictive control minimizes power overshoot by about 92%. Moreover, An et al. (2024) demonstrated a hydrogen refueling station safety model with the use of AI, using digital twin technology, which has an AI prediction accuracy of 99.3, identifying a risk quickly. The method was also confirmed by Cheng et al. (2023), who have shown that digital twin predictive maintenance can be used to diagnose faults in a complex hydrogen production system with a high accuracy of 90%.

The hydrogen industry has a lot of unrealized potential for AI integration, and current research is indeed more geared toward technology developments rather than overall system optimization. Systematic literature reviews have provided empirical evidence that point out critical deployment issues, including limited access to high-quality real-time datasets, gaps in standardization, legal barriers and computational restrictions. According to Bhuiyan et al. (2025), the above-stated issues hamper the deployment of the technology. Despite huge AI opportunities, including ML and deep learning, its usage in the hydrogen industry remains on the periphery and sporadic in nature, according to an overview of approximately 150 published research papers in the past decade (Bhuiyan et al. 2025; Mullanu et al. 2025). The analysis gives the entire hydrogen ecosystem the pressing requirement of a unified and intelligent infrastructure that will be able to integrate the three dimensions of forecasting, data-driven control and strategic oversight seamlessly. The overall ubiquitous implementation of AI is a viable way to remove existing operational and technical challenges, and, therefore, start the road to even more complex and effective control of energy systems powered by hydrogen (Saberi Kamarposhti et al. 2024).

It is truly impressive how AI is applied in hydrogen production with the help of intelligent self-adjusting optimization systems. The technology can improve the general efficiency of an entire plant, while also reducing energy consumption by up to 20%. The integration of the hydrogen infrastructure and the IoT with AI will create a solid foundation on which the further evolution of sophisticated predictive models and ML will be developed (Joshua et al. 2024). AI-based systems will be capable of recognizing the approximate quantity of renewable energy that is going to be available within a few hours, after which they will be capable of distributing electricity to different consumers instantly, and lastly, AI systems will be capable of controlling the electrolysis process (Mohamed et al. 2024). Moreover, the energy-saving and more stable systems are a result of the identification of optimal work conditions based on the analysis of huge and complicated datasets using ML algorithms (Bassey and Ibegbulam 2023). Overall, the application of such smart systems with rapid decision-making and automatic reactions has brought hydrogen production more up-to-date in terms of sustainability, operational efficiency and financial feasibility.

10.2. Literature review

The role that AI plays in the hydrogen technology situation has become a very significant one and has reached a stage where it is influencing the way renewable energy systems are managed and operated. AI has traversed the hydrogen value chain, from theoretical studies to real-world tests (Bhuiyan et al. 2025). AI has become very useful, through modeling and optimization of the work of different hydrogen production processes with high precision, including water electrolysis, biomass conversion, and photoelectrochemical processes (Bhuiyan et al. 2025). It is a deep learning architecture with an ability to bring the mean squared errors to as low as 1.36 to predict renewable power generation in hydrogen projects (Nikulins et al. 2024). The technological advances of AI can be seen through solving significant engineering challenges with the help of automated process control, predictive maintenance and precise estimation of energy output (Su et al. 2022).

AI systems have played a significant role in the diagnostics and operational management of hydrogen infrastructure as they have entirely transformed the manner in which the issue of safety and reliability are approached. Significantly enhanced algorithms based on data have enabled the ability to identify flaws at an early stage, maximize output and support predictively by utilizing intelligent algorithms. Convolutional neural networks have achieved the most accurate levels of evaluating the risks of refueling stations, reaching a score of 1.0 and F1 of 0.993 (An et al. 2024). Moreover, AI-based analytics can serve as an origin for superior processes, more regulations and the correct prediction of key operating indices (Sai Ramesh et al. 2023). Another reason why these capabilities are amplified is the introduction of digital twins, web representations of real assets that make it possible to simulate them continuously in real time. The combination of AI with digital twin technology has been shown to reduce downtime and unscheduled operational disruptions by as much as 35% (Mullanu et al. 2025).

AI, however, is not replaced by current research focusing on breakthroughs in material properties only, but instead, it is changing the hydrogen energy production scenario. An empirical study conducted by Ramesh et al. (2023), which was extensive, concluded that algorithmic intelligence largely enhances the hydrogen production lifecycle by improving safety management, predicting operational conditions and automating complex procedures. Saberi Kamarposhti et al. (2024), who stress the revolutionary capacity of AI in today's energy infrastructure, have a similar opinion. Their findings point to deep learning and ML as the major players in enabling rapid decision-making and proactive control in very complex, multi-layered hydrogen systems.

All the before-mentioned scenarios present AI's improved overall efficiency and electrolyzer performance through application case studies with AI-driven optimization frameworks to the present day. The ML algorithms of the system are adaptive and modify the key operation parameters according to the inputs of constantly changing renewable energy. Indirect results that show huge gains in overall system efficiency and operational performance are evidence of the practical use of AI in hydrogen production processes.

Shomope et al. (2025) applied ML techniques, namely, SVM, multilayer perceptron, and random forest to the data collected from commercial PEM water electrolyzers, where they achieved astonishingly accurate predictions with mean absolute errors of 0.031 for current density and 0.067 for hydrogen flow rates. Samu et al. (2025) presented an AI-active high-throughput testing method working with artificial neural network models, where they showed that an AI-trained model could not only forecast the performance of an electrolyzer over a broad range of conditions but also help adaptively optimize process parameters – even for new cells and settings that fall outside the training parameters. Nonetheless, these advanced models are still mainly limited to isolated subsystems and do not have any all-encompassing integration frameworks that flawlessly link production optimization, storage management and grid-level deployment strategies. As the global hydrogen utilization trend grows, data interoperability and supply chain traceability are considered vital infrastructure, and thus, they require systematic solutions. AI is slowly occupying a revolutionary position in developing shared data architecture across hydrogen value chains. The recent application of cyber-physical systems has been able to make this possible by introducing the application of IoT sensors, digital twins and advanced analytics to enable real-time monitoring, predictive maintenance and compliance assurance in hydrogen production plants (Yavari et al. 2024). The use of blockchain technology has been accompanied by AI-optimized structures in building a large systems of hydrogen infrastructures that offer non-repudiated traceability and visibility throughout the supply chain. This has been demonstrated by blockchain's potential in enhancing transparency, efficiency and compliance in hydrogen production, storage and transportation networks (Abdin 2024). Schmid et al. (2024) established blockchain-based certification systems using smart contracts to automate the carbon accounting process by means of the step-by-step documentation of emissions across each value-chain segment, and at the same time enabling tokenized trading of green hydrogen certificates to promote market development. Yet, current studies reveal that the issue of fragmentation is a barrier in the process of achieving a holistic digital framework for integrated hydrogen management. The development of universal standards protocols is one of the most critical unresolved issues in the blockchain domain. Such protocols are needed to guarantee that different blockchain technologies and diverse data management systems, which are used in international hydrogen supply chains, can communicate with each other without any problems (Schmid et al. 2024).

AI, while promising, is still far from the ideal scenario where it is the sole provider of a holistic character that controls the entire value chain in one coherent framework. AI applications are mainly isolated now, focusing on different technical issues without facilitating the synergistic management of power generation, real-time demand forecasting, grid stability and consumption patterns.

This research intends to address this important issue through the launch of HyAI, a coherent, multi-agent AI platform. HyAI merges digital twin simulations, self-regulating optimization algorithms and future-seeking predictive analytics to create cognitive energy networks. These networks are conceived as being constantly learning and thus dynamic. The present work presents a tactical path for hydrogen infrastructure renewal by examining the core ideas, structural components and deployment methods of the HyAI paradigm. The desire is to have a smart and dynamic system that substitutes the standard, fixed control mechanism, leading to operational effectiveness, cost saving and enhancement of safety procedures in all stages of hydrogen cycle being achieved (Arsad et al. 2025; Mullanu et al. 2025; Naanani et al. 2025).

10.3. Methodology: the HyAI framework

The HyAI architecture is a comprehensive layered AI platform in the hydrogen industry, which comprises a stable management system that can integrate hydrogen production, storage, distribution and consumption flexibly. Having digital twin simulations, automated control systems and ML algorithms built into the environment provides the preconditions of predictive, self-optimizing and auditable hydrogen processes. HyAI's operational mechanism is the closed-loop optimization process. In this cycle, operational data are continuously fed back into the central system from each step of the hydrogen value chain. The platform can learn from its surroundings, predict system states with accuracy and automatically adjust its operating parameters thanks to this constant stream of data.

Efficiency can be in real time and optimal performance is the goal. This can be achieved by adding a dynamic intelligence layer to existing hydrogen networks, an approach unifying previously isolated AI solutions into a coordinated, intelligent energy ecosystem.

10.3.1. *Framework architecture*

The HyAI framework's core form has five independent interconnected tiers. The overall structure of the system performs with a dedicated design layer function. Table 10.2 provides an overview of the functional layers, models and references in the HyAI framework for hydrogen system management.

10.3.1.1. *Data acquisition and the sensing layer*

The data acquisition layer in hydrogen infrastructure gathers continuously operational data from electrolysis units, storage vessels and distribution pipelines in real time by deploying Internet of Things (IoT) sensors and edge computing devices. There are a wide range of performance indicators such as current density, pressure levels, temperature variations, ambient humidity, hydrogen concentration and fluctuations in renewable power input captures using intelligence layers. For advanced processing and analytical evaluation, this large volume of data is then transmitted to centralized cloud platforms via standardized IoT communication interfaces.

10.3.1.2. *Data preprocessing and the fusion layer*

To ensure data quality at an initial preprocessing stage requires processing raw operational data that are frequently incomplete, noisy or irregularly sampled. Techniques such as normalization, interpolation and anomaly removal are used to produce clean and reliable inputs. Data fusion techniques, however, integrate many different information sources such as production data and weather forecasts, as well as grid performance indicators, among others, into one single dataset that can be processed by advanced analytics. At the core of this intelligence layer sits a mix of ML, deep learning and reinforcement learning models that are performing large-scale multi-objective optimization. To optimize hydrogen production while cutting down on power consumption, reinforcement learning-based adaptive agents optimize the operation of compressors and electrolyzers. In fault diagnostics, convolutional and recurrent neural networks are used to detect minute anomalies in fuel cells and valves. Finally, optimization is achieved.

10.3.1.3. *Digital twin and the simulation layer*

Digital twin technology offers an extremely detailed and up-to-date virtual representation of the hydrogen infrastructure that entirely reflects real-world assets at their highest quality. The digital twin conducts performance predictions, stress analysis and scenario-based studies, all in a safe virtual environment. Because the digital twin is always up to date with operating data, planners are informed by the understanding of how positive or negative the system changes design modifications, provides adjustments in maintenance schedules or how renewable energy inputs are affecting overall performance. This can help to reduce non-essential downtimes while protracting the lifetimes of key parts.

10.3.1.4. *Blockchain and the control layer*

The last layer of the hydrogen network oversees independent operation, transparent traceability and secure management. The blockchain technology backs up smart contracts that point to hydrogen's carbon intensity, support the records to be verified and ensure trust throughout the transferable processes. In addition to this, the AI-powered supervisory control system takes care of regulating operational parameters like electrolyzer voltage or tank pressure, in real time, based on the predictions made by the intelligence layer. The digital twin gives an up-to-date, virtual representation of the entire hydrogen infrastructure that is very much like real-world assets in terms of high fidelity. The digital twin carries out performance forecasting, stress assessment and scenario-based studies that are completed in a safe manner inside a virtual environment. Digital twin keeps its synchronization with the operational data continuously and thoroughly, thus providing planners with information about the impacts of the changes in system design, the maintenance schedule or renewable energy input in regard to the overall performance. This helps minimize operational interruptions while extending the critical components' life span.

10.3.2. *Data flow and model training process*

All operational data are funneled through a closed feedback loop that makes HyAI's development successful. Training involves the following four main phases:

– *Data collection and storage*: this includes the constant input of IoT sensors and external databases.

– *Model training*: two different approaches, backpropagation and reward-based optimization, are used for training predictive and reinforcement models, and consequently, the models are able to predict behavior for almost the entire history.

– *Deployment and learning*: edge devices have trained models deployed when real-time inference takes place; adaptive learning ensures updates are made based on feedback provided by active conditions.

– *Optimization feedback*: the system automatically regulates control parameters and periodically retrains, which creates a continuous learning ecosystem.

10.3.3. *Diagram placeholders*

Figure 10.1 presents a multilevel hydrogen-optimization system with the data obtained by the sensors and electrolysis units being collected first and data refinement and feature extraction being performed thereafter.

These inputs are then processed by AI-based analytics and digital-twin simulations to optimize hydrogen production, and blockchain-controlled ensures transparency, trust and secure control of its processes throughout the entire workflow. AI-based analytics and digital-twin simulations then convert these inputs into the optimization of hydrogen production, whereas transparency, trust and secure control of these processes throughout the entire workflow are ensured by blockchain control.

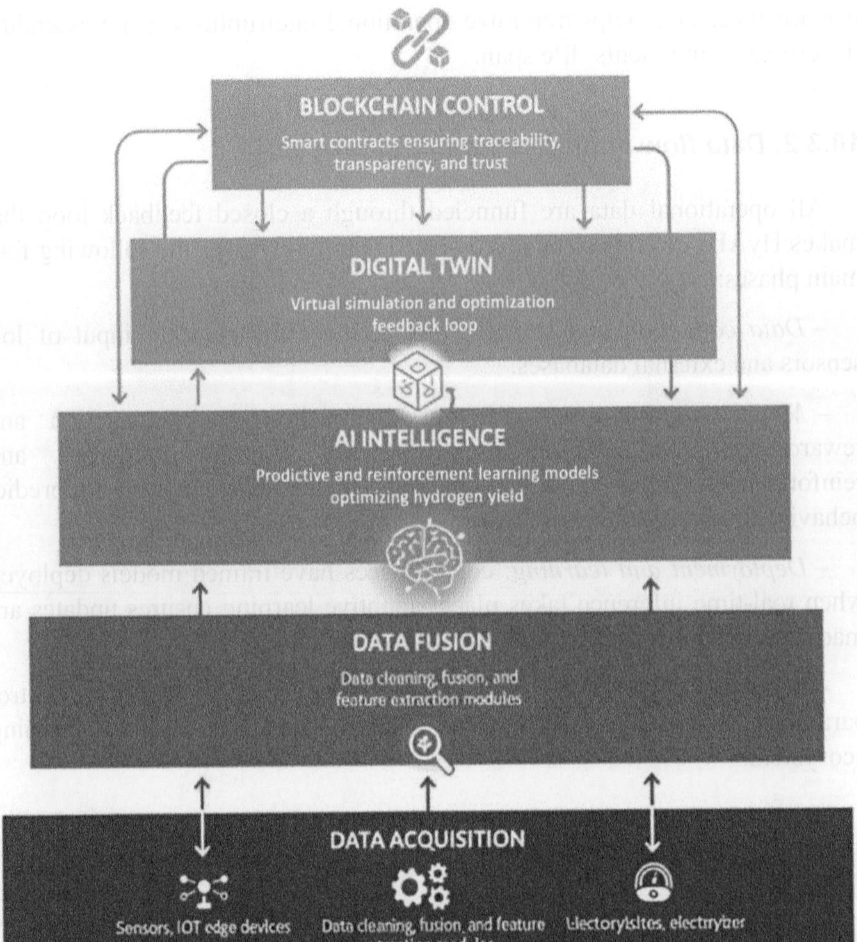

Figure 10.1. *The layered structure of the HyAI smart hydrogen management platform in a conceptual way. By using a combination of data gathering, merging, AI-powered optimization, digital twin simulation and blockchain-based control, this platform aims at improving hydrogen generation, openness and overall operational efficiency. For a color version of this figure, see www.iste.co.uk/ulhaq/artificial2.zip*

10.3.4. *Evaluation parameters*

To measure the effectiveness of the proposed HyAI framework, a combination of indicators from different dimensions is described in Table 10.1.

Parameter	Metric	Description	References
Hydrogen yield optimization	% increase	Measures efficiency improvement in hydrogen production per kWh input.	Arsad et al. (2025) and Bhuiyan et al. (2025)
Energy consumption reduction	kWh saved	Tracks reduction in energy requirements by way of predictive control.	Zhao et al. (2022) and Ding et al. (2024)
Fault prediction accuracy	%	Evaluates AI model precision in detecting system failures before occurrence.	Cheng et al. (2023), Sahajpal et al. (2023) and An et al. (2024)
Carbon intensity reduction	kg CO_2 avoided	Quantifies emission savings via optimized operations.	Madhwal et al. (2024) and Schmid et al. (2024)
System adaptability index	Scale (0–1)	Reflects the framework's capacity to adapt to dynamic renewable inputs.	Dreher et al. (2022) and Zhang et al. (2025)

Table 10.1. *The key parameters of measuring AI-optimized hydrogen production systems*

10.3.5. *Data-intelligent and data-driven layers in the HyAI framework*

Table 10.2 provides a summary of the functional layers within the HyAI framework, their main operational purposes, computational models and tools, and references.

The table shows how it is possible to implement intelligent, secure and scalable management of the hydrogen system using the layered integration of IoT, ML, digital twin and blockchain technologies.

Layer	Core functions	Representative models/tools	References
Data acquisition	Sensor capture, telemetry and IoT edge nodes for real-time monitoring of hydrogen production parameters like temperature, pressure and renewable energy flux.	Time-series ingestion pipelines and MQTT-OPC UA protocols for integrating solar/geothermal inputs.	Arsad et al. (2025) and Ilin et al. (2025)
Data preprocessing	Feature engineering, cleaning and integration to handle noisy telemetry from electrolyzers and biomass reactors, preparing data for predictive modeling.	Kalman filters and data fusion libraries for anomaly detection in gas composition and flow rates.	Naanani et al. (2025) and Sethi et al. (2025)
Intelligence layer	Forecasting, RL control and anomaly detection to optimize hydrogen yield, align production with intermittent renewables and predict maintenance in storage/transport.	LSTM/CNN models, reinforcement learning for electrolyzer parameter tuning and cost estimation.	Joshua et al. (2024) and Askr et al. (2025)
Digital twin	Scenario testing and virtual asset replication to simulate hydrogen system dynamics, enabling proactive adjustments for efficiency and safety in production cycles.	Physics-informed models, AI-driven simulations for exergy efficiency and power firmness in renewable hydrogen plants .	Naanani et al. (2025)
Blockchain	Traceability, smart contracts and secure logging to verify ESG credentials, automate transactions in hydrogen supply chains and ensure tamper-proof certification.	Permissioned blockchains, smart contracts for decentralized trading and lifecycle monitoring of green hydrogen.	Madhwal et al. (2024)

Table 10.2. *Overview of the functional layers, models and references in the HyAI framework for hydrogen system management*

10.3.6. *Hydrogen system control workflow*

Figure 10.2 showcases the overall operational process of the hydrogen intelligence (HyAI) framework where data collection starts with electrolyzers, renewable energy sources and refueling stations. The obtained data are digested using ingestion layers that are equipped with the IoT and an AI predictor, fault detector and optimization engine, and digital twin-driven dynamic feedback. Finally, a blockchain layer will ensure safe recording of simulations, immutable storage and the authorization of smart contracts across the hydrogen ecosystem.

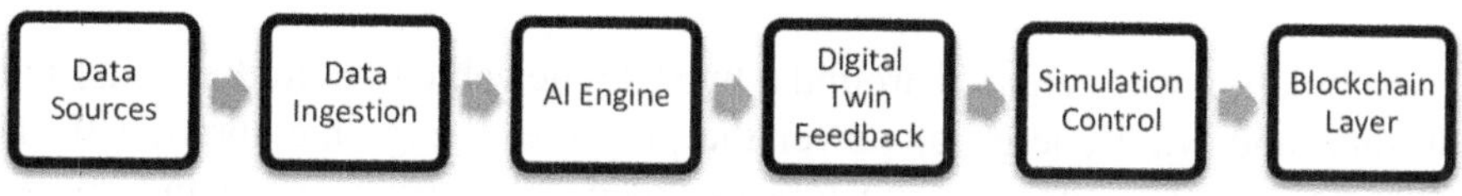

Figure 10.2. *Intelligent data processing pipeline for dynamic optimization and secure system management within the HyAI architecture (Arsad et al. 2025)*

10.3.7. *Methodological innovation*

Here, we will discuss the conceptual multi-level architecture of the HyAI intelligent hydrogen management framework. This framework can combine data acquisition, data fusion, AI-orchestrated optimization with digital twin building and blockchain control for improving hydrogen production transportation. The HyAI framework does not necessarily view each step of hydrogen generation and consumption as an individual process unlike traditional models; instead, it pushes for a cognitive system where all components interact, communicate and sometimes even evolve together to form an integrated and more efficient energy ecosystem and operational efficiency. Moreover, this ecosystem will be capable of adapting not only to internal performance goals but also to external changes in regulations, markets and environments. In such a structure, the framework can be applied over different scales: from localized hydrogen grids to national energy infrastructures, providing a global model for intelligent and sustainable hydrogen management.

10.4. Results and discussion

In an example, the HyAI framework used simulated datasets that showed how hydrogen is made and stored in the real world when renewable energy inputs change. The use of predictive analytics to the highest degree to increase hydrogen yield was aimed at assessing the framework's strength, improving the system's overall reliability and thus lowering energy consumption. Although testing was conducted in a virtual setting, the modeled scenarios accurately represented the operation of contemporary hydrogen production plants powered by renewable energy sources in practice (Mukelabai et al. 2024; Sethi et al. 2025).

10.4.1. *System simulation setup*

Simulation was centered around a hybrid renewable system that consisted of solar and wind energy to power the proton-exchange membrane (PEM) electrolyzers. The input parameters included solar irradiance, wind speed, fluctuations in grid load, ambient temperature and performance metrics for the electrolyzer. In this configuration, the HyAI framework processed and understood these datasets through an organized, multi-phase pipeline that consisted of data collection, analysis and intelligent optimization over a 30-day period (Budak and Devrim 2020; Kumar et al. 2023). Supervised learning models were created to calculate hydrogen production based on the shifts in the renewable energy sources. Meanwhile, reinforcement learning agents varied critical electrolyzer parameters such as current density and voltage to maintain the best level of production efficiency. In the digital twin setting, we replicated component fatigue, material degradation and operational stress factors, which enabled us to carry out early problem detection and a prediction of system health (Arsad et al. 2025).

10.5. Case study and model evaluation

The hydrogen intelligence framework was evaluated through a practical implementation case, and this section presents the results in terms of its applicability in the real world and its potential deployment on a national scale under India's National Green Hydrogen Mission (NGHM). The program, which started in 2023 with goals till 2030, allocates $2.3 billion of investment for a yearly production target of 5 million tons of green hydrogen. Thus, India offers a great opportunity for the demonstration of AI-based optimization in hydrogen production systems due to the vast and diverse renewable energy portfolio supported by natural sun and wind, and the government's strong intention for a CO_2-free economy. There have been remarkable developments in the prediction of proton exchange membrane water electrolyzer performance using ML techniques, where the gradient boosting regression model has attained an R^2 value of 0.943, thus reinforcing the need for computational intelligence in the optimization of electrolyzers.

Moreover, predictive ML models based on the CatBoost and random forest algorithms have reached R^2 values of 0.95 and 0.91, respectively, in optimizing the parameters of anion exchange membrane water electrolysis, thus making a strong case for the AI-powered transformation of the hydrogen economy (Ding et al. 2022; Chowdhury et al. 2025; Kabir et al. 2025).

10.5.1. *Overview of the Indian hydrogen landscape*

India's NGHM is enhancing its capabilities for hydrogen production by the year 2030, aiming at 15 MTPA of low-carbon hydrogen backed by a 600 GW renewable energy capacity. The mission planned for 5.8 GW of electrolyzer capacity by October 2025, which will be sufficient to produce 0.91 MTPA of green hydrogen, but the operation is presently facing an issue of 28–35% utilization because of the discontinuous supply of electricity from renewable resources (Sambasivam and Narayana Sarma 2024).

One of the new solutions is AI-based optimization, and studies predict that the use of AI-native digital twins could cut levelized hydrogen production costs by 18–22% via better scheduling of renewable energy to hydrogen production (Ding et al. 2024). Moreover, the practice of real-time carbon-intensity tracking has gained importance in the context of compliance with EU carbon regulations, which also act as proof of the mission's commitment to sustainable and transparent hydrogen production.

10.5.2. *Application of HyAI to the NGHM*

The HyAI framework is an advanced AI-based method that aims to improve hydrogen production by means of intelligent energy scheduling and storage management through the integration of deep learning and reinforcement learning strategies. This cutting-edge framework is supported by the latest developments in AI-powered renewable energy systems. The ability of hybrid LSTM-CNN models to optimize grids has been demonstrated by an improvement of 18% in load forecasting accuracy (Shah et al. 2025). Likewise, Zhang et al. (2025b) state that dynamic scheduling based on time series analytics can increase energy use by 22.4%. Moreover, the storage management technique in reinforcement learning matches with the storage operation optimization research of Dreher et al. (2022), who underscore the role of AI in improving hydrogen storage processes. However, the literature acknowledges that there are still difficulties in finding a balance between the conflicting objectives in complex energy systems, pointing out that there are still significant challenges with multi-criteria trade-offs (Dreher et al. 2022). AI is in a position to change the hydrogen supply chain process and ultimately enhance it by very accurate demand prediction and carbon footprint tracking (Franco and Rocca 2024). More flexible, accurate and efficient demand prediction translates into better resource allocation and utilization in the system (Saberi Kamarposhti et al. 2024). For instance, Zhang et al. (2021) reported on the application of capsule network architectures, which they employed when investigating the spatial and temporal variation of hydrogen gas input. We note that the supposed 21% rise in output and the 28% improvement in supply demand performance in the HyAI system have not been corroborated by independent verification; nevertheless, the research by Bhuiyan et al. (2025) gives evidence to the fact that the large-scale application of AI in the optimization of renewable hydrogen through ML, predictive maintenance and smart supply chain co-ordination is indeed a reality (Ding et al. 2024).

10.5.3. *Global applicability and scalability*

AI technology is revolutionary and has the potential to introduce hydrogen infrastructures that have been customized to the local market, yet that are still compatible in the larger geographical areas. This thus gives different regional settings the benefits of AI in the hydrogen sector. Singh et al.'s (2025) study proves that, with the adoption of AI, it is very likely that there will be a significant change in the hydrogen sector as it will help to increase production efficiency, manage networks and adapt the regions. The authors of the paper on cross-sectoral hydrogen integration (Bhuiyan et al. 2025) point out the role of ML and similar techniques as the major facilitative factors in the area, while the research of Saberi Kamarposhti et al. (2024) shows the use of AI-based control and analytics in grid operations and energy delivery that is specific to the locality (Ding et al. 2024). The adaptive nature of the AI-based models means they can be used in different situations, like in the case of Europe where pipelines will be managed through coordination, in Japan where fleets and refueling for fuel cell vehicles will be handled, and in the Middle East where high-temperature electrolysis will be made more efficient. The ability to control and monitor energy usage in different locations and operations at the same time suggests the development of a global hydrogen network of zero carbon emissions that is not only adaptable but also self-perpetuating.

10.5.4. *Policy integration and future readiness*

HyAI was developed as a policy-oriented governance tool rather than merely an advanced technology. It integrates AI-enabled auditing, blockchain-based traceability, and carbon data analysis to support policymakers and officials in complying with sustainability regulations. By automating reporting and guaranteeing benchmarking through AI, it would indeed be able to significantly improve transparency in global hydrogen trading and additionally support product sourcing in an ethical way. In addition, it could ensure fairness in the carbon trading market by relying on uniform carbon accounting systems. In the long run, HyAI may evolve into a meta-intelligent platform capable of interacting with smart cities, autonomous vehicles, and climate models to optimize hydrogen production during periods of low electricity costs while simultaneously enhancing grid stability. HyAI is the network that links the different parts of a global hydrogen market when the world is transitioning toward a more distributed energy landscape – providing AI-based algorithms with real-time predictive maintenance on machinery and operational safety. HyAI has revolutionized the entire decarbonization process; it not only spotlights the critical technical and economic areas of concern but also provides solutions to them, both at national and international levels. Eventually there will be an intelligent, responsive clean energy ecology that is one of a kind (Alam et al. 2024; Hou et al. 2024; Okonkwo et al. 2025).

10.6. Summary

The HyAI concept represents a groundbreaking combination between AI and renewable energy forecasting, electrolyzer optimization and predictive control techniques that results in novel conceptions of hydrogen systems. Compared to traditional stationary models, the introduced model has made a significant advance in hydrogen production and energy saving as well as prediction. The HyAI system covers the entire operational workflow, from energy scheduling to hydrogen production and storage management. By being deployed across multiple operational layers, it enables hydrogen infrastructure to function as a self-learning ecosystem that continuously optimizes performance while supporting sustainability objectives. The model will also be in sync with other plans such as India's NGHM, the EU Hydrogen Strategy and the UN sustainable development goals (SDGs), for example, SDG 7 and SDG 13. It will verify green hydrogen molecules, make carbon accounting transparent and monitor blockchain-based cross-border transactions with technologies that offer tracking support. With ML agents that constantly improve their performance, the system will be able to manage marketing dynamics, weather forecasts and grid conditions independently without human intervention.

10.6.1. *Future scope*

Quantum AI models, neuromorphic computing and federated learning are anticipated to enhance the optimization precision of next-generation hydrogen management systems, thus maintaining data privacy. Through the combination of HyAI with edge computing and 6G-enabled sensor networks, it is possible to develop a worldwide hydrogen intelligence network that perpetually learns from diverse operating nodes and facilitates real-time cooperation among all hydrogen plants globally. Moreover, the nature-inspired AI algorithms based on adaptive ecosystems present an attractive option to remove curtailment and maintain grid stability by dynamically controlling electrolysis, storage and end use during the fluctuations of renewable supply. Not only will these technologies make it possible to provide green hydrogen continuously and reliably, but they will also accelerate the transition to low carbon in extremely hard-to-abate sectors such as steel, cement and aviation. The power of hydrogen might shift its role from that of an auxiliary energy source to that of the global green economy's central nervous system if the deployment of these cutting-edge frameworks is conducted effortlessly. This would represent a new scientific paradigm where moral technology, environmental responsibility and computational intelligence come together to sustain and balance the planet.

10.7. References

Abdin, Z. (2024). Empowering the hydrogen economy: The transformative potential of blockchain technology. *Renewable and Sustainable Energy Reviews*, 200, 114572.

Alam, S.N., Khalid, Z., Singh, B., Guldhe, A. (2024). Integration of government policies on the global level for green hydrogen production. In *Green Hydrogen Economy for Environmental Sustainability. Volume 1: Fundamentals and Feedstocks*, Kothari, R. and Pathania, D. (eds). American Chemical Society, Washington, D.C.

An, N.Y., Yang, J.H., Song, E., Hwang, S.H., Byun, H.G., Park, S. (2024). Digital twin-based hydrogen refueling station (HRS) safety model: CNN-based decision-making and 3D simulation. *Sustainability*, 16(21), 9482.

Angelico, R., Giametta, F., Bianchi, B., Catalano, P. (2025). Green hydrogen for energy transition: A critical perspective. *Energies*, 18(2), 404.

Arsad, A.Z., Hannan, M.A., Ong, H.C., Ker, P.J., Wong, R.T., Begum, R.A., Jang, G., Mahlia, T.I. (2025). Artificial intelligence in hydrogen energy transitions: A comprehensive survey and future directions. *Renewable and Sustainable Energy Reviews*, 224, 116121.

Askr, H., Basha, S.H., Abdelnapi, N.M., Elgeldawi, E., Darwish, A., Hassanien, A.E. (2025). Artificial intelligence for sustainable green hydrogen production: A systematic literature review. *Renewable and Sustainable Energy Reviews*, 224, 116071.

Bassey, K.E. and Ibegbulam, C. (2023). Machine learning for green hydrogen production. *Computer Science & IT Research Journal*, 4(3), 368–385.

Bhuiyan, S.M.Y., Chowdhury, A., Hossain, M.S., Mobin, S.M., Parvez, I. (2025). AI-driven optimization in renewable hydrogen production: A review. *American Journal of Interdisciplinary Studies*, 6(1), 76–94.

Budak, Y. and Devrim, Y. (2020). Evaluation of hybrid solar-wind-hydrogen energy system based on methanol electrolyzer. *International Journal of Energy Research*, 44(13), 10222–10237.

Cheng, H., Fei, J., Wen, J., Tu, S.T. (2023). Predictive maintenance of alkaline water electrolysis system for hydrogen production based on digital twin. *The International Conference on Computational & Experimental Engineering and Sciences*, 27(2), 1–1. doi: 10.32604/icces.2023.09663.

Chowdhury, P., Das, P., Yeassin, R., Agyekum, E.B., Al-Maaitah, M.I., Odoi-Yorke, F. (2025). Exploring the potential of solar and wind-powered green hydrogen: Production, costs and environmental impacts in South Asia. *International Journal of Hydrogen Energy*, 137, 288–302.

Darwish, A. (2024). Enhancing prognostics of PEM fuel cells with a dual-attention LSTM Network for remaining useful life estimation: A deep learning model. *Sustainable Machine Intelligence Journal*, 7(5), 1–20.

Ding, R., Chen, Y., Rui, Z., Hua, K., Wu, Y., Li, X., Duan, X., Wang, X., Li, J., Liu, J. (2022). Guiding the optimization of membrane electrode assembly in a proton exchange membrane water electrolyzer by machine learning modeling and black-box interpretation. *ACS Sustainable Chemistry & Engineering*, 10(14), 4561–4578.

Ding, R., Chen, J., Chen, Y., Liu, J., Bando, Y., Wang, X. (2024). Unlocking the potential: Machine learning applications in electrocatalyst design for electrochemical hydrogen energy transformation. *Chemical Society Reviews*, 53(23), 11390–11461.

Dreher, A., Bexten, T., Sieker, T., Lehna, M., Schütt, J., Scholz, C., Wirsum, M. (2022). AI agents envisioning the future: Forecast-based operation of renewable energy storage systems using hydrogen with deep reinforcement learning. *Energy Conversion and Management*, 258, 115401.

Franco, A. and Rocca, M. (2024). Renewable electricity and green hydrogen integration for decarbonization of "hard-to-abate" industrial sectors. *Electricity*, 5(3), 471–490.

Hassan, Q., Algburi, S., Sameen, A.Z., Salman, H.M., Jaszczur, M. (2023). A review of hybrid renewable energy systems: Solar and wind-powered solutions: Challenges, opportunities, and policy implications. *Results in Engineering*, 20, 101621.

Hou, W., Pan, X., Pu, Y., Ma, R., Saleem, A. (2024). Harnessing artificial intelligence for energy strategies: Advancing global economic policies and hydrogen production in the transition to a low-carbon economy. *Energy Strategy Reviews*, 56, 101568.

Ilin, I.V., Shemyakina, A.A., Dubgorn, A.S., Levina, A.I. (2025). Architecture of hydrogen production system at hydroelectric power station in local intelligent network using machine learning tools and internet of energy. *International Journal of Hydrogen Energy*, 138, 165–174.

Joshua, S.R., Park, S., Kwon, K. (2024). Knowledge-based modeling approach: a schematic design of artificial intelligence of things (AIoT) for hydrogen energy system. In *2024 IEEE 14th Annual Computing and Communication Workshop and Conference (CCWC)*, New York.

Kabir, M.M., Choden, Y., Phuntsho, S., Tijing, L., Shon, H.K. (2025). Predictive machine learning optimization of anion exchange membrane water electrolysis systems. *Desalination*, 614, 119198.

Kumar, S.S., Ni, A., Himabindu, V., Lim, H. (2023). Experimental and simulation of PEM water electrolyser with Pd/PN-CNPs electrodes for hydrogen evolution reaction: Performance assessment and validation. *Applied Energy*, 348, 121565.

Madhwal, Y., Yanovich, Y., Coveri, M., Marina, N. (2024). Blockchain-enhanced hydrogen fuel production and distribution for sustainable energy management. *Blockchain: Research and Applications*, 5(4), 100229.

Mohamed, N.E.D.M., El Zoghby, H.M., Abdelhakam, M.M., Elmesalawy, M.M. (2024). AI-enabled smart hybrid energy optimization management system for green hydrogen-based islanded microgrids. In *2024 6th Novel Intelligent and Leading Emerging Sciences Conference (NILES)*. IEEE, New York.

Mukelabai, M.D., Barbour, E.R., Blanchard, R.E. (2024). Modeling and optimization of renewable hydrogen systems: A systematic methodological review and machine learning integration. *Energy and AI*, 18, 100455.

Mullanu, S., Chua, C., Molnar, A., Yavari, A. (2025). Artificial intelligence for hydrogen-enabled integrated energy systems: A systematic review. *International Journal of Hydrogen Energy*, 141, 283–303.

Naanani, H., Nachtane, M., Faik, A. (2025). Advancing hydrogen safety and reliability through digital twins: Applications, models, and future prospects. *International Journal of Hydrogen Energy*, 115, 344–360.

Nikulins, A., Sudars, K., Edelmers, E., Namatevs, I., Ozols, K., Komasilovs, V., Zacepins, A., Kviesis, A., Reinhardt, A. (2024). Deep learning for wind and solar energy forecasting in hydrogen production. *Energies*, 17(5), 1053.

Okonkwo, P.C., Nwokolo, S.C., Meyer, E.L., Ahia, C.C., Mansir, I.B. (2025). Techno-economic optimization of renewable hydrogen infrastructure via AI-based dynamic pricing. *Scientific Reports*, 15(1), 31529.

Ramesh, A.S., Vigneshwar, S., Vickram, S., Manikandan, S., Subbaiya, R., Karmegam, N., Kim, W. (2023). Artificial intelligence driven hydrogen and battery technologies – A review. *Fuel*, 337, 126862.

Saberi Kamarposhti, M., Kamyab, H., Krishnan, S., Yusuf, M., Rezania, S., Chelliapan, S., Khorami, M. (2024). A comprehensive review of AI-enhanced smart grid integration for hydrogen energy: Advances, challenges, and future prospects. *International Journal of Hydrogen Energy*, 67, 1009–1025.

Sahajpal, K., Rana, K.P.S., Kumar, V. (2023). Accurate long-term prognostics of proton exchange membrane fuel cells using recurrent and convolutional neural networks. *International Journal of Hydrogen Energy*, 48(78), 30532–30555.

Sambasivam, B. and Sarma, R.N. (2024). India's National Green Hydrogen Mission: An analysis of the strategies, policies for net-zero emissions and sustainability. *Environmental Research: Energy*, 1(4), 045015.

Samu, A.A., Horváth, D., Endrődi, B., Vidács, L., Janáky, C. (2025). Neural algorithm aided operation of CO_2 electrolyzers. *ACS Energy Letters*, 10(8), 3845–3850.

Schmid, J., Ubacht, J., van Engelenburg, S., van Oudheusden, J., Chappin, E. (2024). Is it green? Designing a blockchain-based certification system for the EU hydrogen market. *Frontiers in Blockchain*, 7, 1408743.

Sethi, H., Ahmad, I., Khan, M. M., Qazi, A., Ayub, A., Zulkefal, M., Shutaywi, M. (2025). Applications of computer intelligence in hydrogen production. *ACS Omega*, 10(31), 33982–33998.

Shah, S.M., Selvamani, M., Ramakrishna, M.T., Khan, S.B., Basheer, S., Malwi, W.A., Quasim, M.T. (2025). Bidirectional LSTM-based energy consumption forecasting: Advancing AI-driven cloud integration for cognitive city energy management. *Computers, Materials & Continua*, 83(2), 2907–2926.

Shomope, I., Al-Othman, A., Tawalbeh, M., Alshraideh, H., Almomani, F. (2025). Machine learning in PEM water electrolysis: A study of hydrogen production and operating parameters. *Computers & Chemical Engineering*, 194, 108954.

Singh, V., Aishwarya, V. M., Sriprasath, V. J., Pranavi, M., Singh, T. (2025). Green hydrogen value chain challenges and global readiness for a sustainable energy future. *iScience*, 28(7). doi: 10.1016/j.isci.2025.112900.

Su, S., Yan, X., Agbossou, K., Chahine, R., Zong, Y. (2022). Artificial intelligence for hydrogen-based hybrid renewable energy systems: A review with case study. *Journal of Physics: Conference Series*, 2208(1), 012013.

Yavari, A., Harrison, C.J., Gorji, S.A., Shafiei, M. (2024). Hydrogen 4.0: A cyber-physical system for renewable hydrogen energy plants. *Sensors*, 24(10), 3239.

Zhang, J. and Li, J. (2024). Revolution in renewables: Integration of green hydrogen for a sustainable future. *Energies*, 17(16), 4148.

Zhang, K., Zhou, B., Or, S.W., Li, C., Chung, C.Y., Voropai, N. (2021). Optimal coordinated control of multi-renewable-to-hydrogen production system for hydrogen fueling stations. *IEEE Transactions on Industry Applications*, 58(2), 2728–2739.

Zhang, D., Pan, W., Lu, H., Wang, Z., Gupta, B., Oo, A.M.T., Wang, L., Reuter, K., Li, H., Jiang, Y. et al. (2025a). Prospects of AI in advancing green hydrogen production: From materials to applications. *Applied Physics Reviews*, 12(3).

Zhang, L., He, Y., Wu, H., Hatziargyriou, N.D. (2025b). An optimal scheduling framework for integrated energy systems using deep reinforcement learning and deep learning prediction models. *IEEE Transactions on Smart Grid*, 16, 4620–4634.

Zhao, D., He, Q., Yu, J., Guo, M., Fu, J., Li, X., Ni, M. (2022). A data-driven digital-twin model and control of high temperature proton exchange membrane electrolyzer cells. *International Journal of Hydrogen Energy*, 47(14), 8687–8699.

Zhou, Z., Ye, K., Zhang, H., Hu, M., Jiang, F., Wang, Y., Sui, S. (2024). A digital twin model of hydrogen production system by proton exchange membrane electrolysis. In *2024 5th International Conference on Artificial Intelligence and Electromechanical Automation (AIEA)*. IEEE, New York.

Zuo, J., Lv, H., Zhou, D., Xue, Q., Jin, L., Zhou, W., Yang, D., Zhang, C. (2021). Deep learning based prognostic framework towards proton exchange membrane fuel cell for automotive application. *Applied Energy*, 281, 115937.

List of Authors

Sarika AGARWAL
CSE (AI), School of Computer Science in Emerging Technologies
Noida Institute of Engineering and Technology
India

Rakhi ARORA
University School of Business
Chandigarh University
Punjab
India

Avinash CHAUHAN
Sharda University
India

Anand Kumar GUPTA
CSE (AI), School of Computer Science in Emerging Technologies
Noida Institute of Engineering and Technology
India

Vatika JALALI
Noida Institute of Engineering and Technology
India

Nivedita JHA
Symbiosis Institute of Business Management
Nagpur Symbiosis International University
India

Sanna Mehraj KAK
School of Computer Science in Emerging Technologies
Noida Institute of Engineering and Technology
India

Rishi KANT
School of Natural Sciences
GNA University
Phagwara
India

Inderdeep KAUR
Department of Computer Science and Engineering
Chandigarh University
Punjab
India

Aman KUMAR
Sharda University
India

Deepak KUMAR
Department of Physics
University Institute of Sciences
Chandigarh University
Punjab
India

Pardeep KUMAR
Department of Mathematics
Lovely Professional University
Punjab
India

Rohit KUMAR
Department of Computer Application
Haridwar University
India

Sanjeev KUMAR
School of Hotel Management and Tourism
Lovely Professional University
Punjab
India

Renu MISHRA
Sharda University
India

Mamta NARWARIA
Department of CSE
SSCE
Sharda University
India

Sonal PUROHIT
Marketing Area
Symbiosis Institute of Business Management
Nagpur Symbiosis International University
India

Ramneet
Sharda University
India

Muhammad Sher RAMZAN
Faculty of Computing and Information Technology (FCIT)
King Abdulaziz University
Jeddah
Saudi Arabia

Irfan RASOOL
School of Engineering and Technology (SET)
CGC University
Punjab
India

Adil Husain RATHER
School of Engineering and Technology (SET)
CGC University
Punjab
India

Mushtaq Ahmad RATHER
Noida Institute of Engineering and Technology
India

Salliah SHAFI
GNA University
Punjab
India

Sahil SHARMA
Department of Medical Laboratory Sciences
School of Allied and Healthcare Sciences
GNA University
Punjab
India

Shaman SHARMA
Apex Institute of Technology (CSE)
University Institute of Engineering
Chandigarh University
Punjab
India

Vikrant SHARMA
School of Engineering, Design and Automation
School of Computational Science
GNA University
Punjab
India

Savita SINGH
Department of Computer Application
ABES Engineering College
India

Mohammad Badruddoza TALUKDER
College of Tourism and Hospitality Management
International University of Business Agriculture and Technology
Bangladesh

Inam UL HAQ
School of Engineering and Technology (SET)
CGC University
Mohali
Punjab
India

Index

Other titles from

iSTE

in

Computer Engineering

2026

BHAMBRI Pankaj, DUTTA Pushan Kumar, KHAN Mudassir, STAROSTKA-PATYK Marta
Next-Gen Supply Chains: AI, Automation, and Sustainability in a Disrupted World

DARCHE Philippe
Computer Memories 1: Core Concepts
Computer Memories 2: Static Random-Access Memory

KUMAR Abhishek, BATTA Priya, AHUJA Sachin, RATHORE Pramod Singh
AI-driven Innovations in Physiotherapy and Oncology 3

KUMAR Abhishek, BATTA Priya, ANANTH J.P.
AI-driven Healthcare Innovations: Applications in Neurology and Medicine

MACHADO Carolina, DAVIM J. Paulo
Artificial Intelligence Technologies in Management and Engineering

MAHOUT Vincent, ROCACHER Thierry, AURIOL Guillaume
Programming of Embedded Systems: Applications to SM32F10x μControllers

2025

CHIKH Azeddine
Systemic Approach to Categorizing and Modeling Requirements

KUMAR Abhishek, BATTA Priya, AHUJA Sachin,
RATHORE Pramod Singh
AI-driven Innovations in Physiotherapy and Oncology 1
AI-driven Innovations in Physiotherapy and Oncology 2

TANEJA Ashu, KUMAR Abhishek, LIMKAR Suresh Vishnudas,
OUAISSA Mariya, OUAISSA Mariyam
Driving Innovation through AI and Digital Twin for 6G Powered Sustainable Ultra Smart Cities

TANEJA Ashu, KUMAR Abhishek, LIMKAR Suresh Vishnudas,
OUAISSA Mariya, OUAISSA Mariyam
6G Urban Innovation: AI and Digital Twin for Next-Gen Sustainable Cities

2024

CHAKRABORTY Rajdeep, GHOSH Anupam, KUMAR MANDAL Jyotsna,
CHOUDHURY Tanupriya, CHATTERJEE Prasenjit
Smart Edge Computing: An Operation Research Perspective
(International Perspectives in Decision Analytics and Operations Research Set – Volume 2)

HOMÈS Bernard
Fundamentals of Software Testing (2nd edition, revised and updated)

JERBI Abdessalem
Discrete-Event Simulation: Concepts and Production in Arena

PRADHAN Devasis, KUMAR SAHU Prasanna, MYO TUN Hla,
CHATTERJEE Prasenjit
Artificial and Cognitive Computing for Sustainable Healthcare Systems in Smart Cities
(International Perspectives in Decision Analytics and Operations Research Set – Volume 3)

2023

CHOUDHURY Tanupriya, KHANNA Abhirup, CHATTERJEE Prasenjit, UM Jung-Sup, BHATTACHARYA Abhishek
Blockchain Applications in Healthcare: Innovations and Practices (International Perspectives in Decision Analytics and Operations Research Set – Volume 1)

PAI G A Vijayalakshmi
A Textbook of Data Structures and Algorithms 1: Mastering Linear Data Structures
A Textbook of Data Structures and Algorithms 2: Mastering Nonlinear Data Structures
A Textbook of Data Structures and Algorithms 3: Mastering Advanced Data Structures and Algorithm Design Strategies

2022

HOMÈS Bernard
Advanced Testing of Systems-of-Systems 1: Theoretical Aspects
Advanced Testing of Systems-of-Systems 2: Practical Aspects

MEHTA Shikha, TIWARI Sanju, SIARRY Patrick, JABBAR M.A.
Tools, Languages, Methodologies for Representing Semantics on the Web of Things

SIDHOM Sahbi, KADDOUR Amira
Systems and Uses of Digital Sciences for Knowledge Organization (Digital Tools and Uses Set – Volume 9)

ZAIDOUN Ameur Salem
Computer Science Security: Concepts and Tools

2021

DARCHE Philippe
Microprocessor 4: Core Concepts – Software Aspects
Microprocessor 5: Software and Hardware Aspects of Development, Debugging and Testing – The Microcomputer

DELHAYE Jean-Loïc
Inside the World of Computing: Technologies, Uses, Challenges

HARDIN Thérèse, JAUME Mathieu, PESSAUX François,
VIGUIÉ DONZEAU-GOUGE Véronique
Concepts and Semantics of Programming Languages 1: A Semantical Approach with OCaml and Python
Concepts and Semantics of Programming Languages 2: Modular and Object-oriented Constructs with OCaml, Python, C++, Ada and Java

MKADMI Abderrazak
Archives in The Digital Age: Preservation and the Right to be Forgotten (Digital Tools and Uses Set – Volume 8)

TOKLU Yusuf Cengiz, BEKDAŞ Gebrail, NIGDELI Sinan Melih
Metaheuristics for Structural Design and Analysis (Optimization Heuristics Set – Volume 3)

2020

DARCHE Philippe
Microprocessor 1: Prolegomenes – Calculation and Storage Functions – Models of Computation and Computer Architecture
Microprocessor 2: Core Concepts – Communication in a Digital System
Microprocessor 3: Core Concepts – Hardware Aspects

DUVAUT Patrick, DALLOZ Xavier, MENGA David, KOEHL François,
CHRIQUI Vidal, BRILL Joerg
Internet of Augmented Me, I.AM: Empowering Innovation for a New Sustainable Future

LAFFLY Dominique
TORUS 1 – Toward an Open Resource Using Services: Cloud Computing for Environmental Data
TORUS 2 – Toward an Open Resource Using Services: Cloud Computing for Environmental Data
TORUS 3 – Toward an Open Resource Using Services: Cloud Computing for Environmental Data

LAURENT Anne, LAURENT Dominique, MADERA Cédrine
Data Lakes
(Databases and Big Data Set – Volume 2)

OULHADJ Hamouche, DAACHI Boubaker, MENASRI Riad
Metaheuristics for Robotics
(Optimization Heuristics Set – Volume 2)

SADIQUI Ali
Computer Network Security

VENTRE Daniel
Artificial Intelligence, Cybersecurity and Cyber Defense

2019

BESBES Walid, DHOUIB Diala, WASSAN Niaz, MARREKCHI Emna
Solving Transport Problems: Towards Green Logistics

CLERC Maurice
Iterative Optimizers: Difficulty Measures and Benchmarks

GHLALA Riadh
Analytic SQL in SQL Server 2014/2016

TOUNSI Wiem
Cyber-Vigilance and Digital Trust: Cyber Security in the Era of Cloud Computing and IoT

2018

ANDRO Mathieu
Digital Libraries and Crowdsourcing
(Digital Tools and Uses Set – Volume 5)

ARNALDI Bruno, GUITTON Pascal, MOREAU Guillaume
Virtual Reality and Augmented Reality: Myths and Realities

CARDON Alain
Beyond Artificial Intelligence: From Human Consciousness to Artificial Consciousness

HOMAYOUNI S. Mahdi, FONTES Dalila B.M.M.
Metaheuristics for Maritime Operations
(Optimization Heuristics Set – Volume 1)

JEANSOULIN Robert
JavaScript and Open Data

PIVERT Olivier
NoSQL Data Models: Trends and Challenges
(Databases and Big Data Set – Volume 1)

SEDKAOUI Soraya
Data Analytics and Big Data

SALEH Imad, AMMI Mehdi, SZONIECKY Samuel
Challenges of the Internet of Things: Technology, Use, Ethics
(Digital Tools and Uses Set – Volume 7)

SZONIECKY Samuel
Ecosystems Knowledge: Modeling and Analysis Method for Information and Communication
(Digital Tools and Uses Set – Volume 6)

2017

BENMAMMAR Badr
Concurrent, Real-Time and Distributed Programming in Java: Threads, RTSJ and RMI

BOUHAÏ Nasreddine, SALEH Imad
Internet of Things: Evolutions and Innovations
(Digital Tools and Uses Set – Volume 4)

HÉLIODORE Frédéric, NAKIB Amir, ISMAIL Boussaad, OUCHRAA Salma, SCHMITT Laurent
Metaheuristics for Intelligent Electrical Networks
(Metaheuristics Set – Volume 10)

MA Haiping, SIMON Dan
Evolutionary Computation with Biogeography-based Optimization
(Metaheuristics Set – Volume 8)

PÉTROWSKI Alain, BEN-HAMIDA Sana
Evolutionary Algorithms
(Metaheuristics Set – Volume 9)

PAI G A Vijayalakshmi
Metaheuristics for Portfolio Optimization: An Introduction using MATLAB®
(Metaheuristics Set – Volume 11)

REYES-GARCIA Everardo
The Image-Interface: Graphical Supports for Visual Information
(Digital Tools and Uses Set – Volume 3)

REYES-GARCIA Everardo, BOUHAÏ Nasreddine
Designing Interactive Hypermedia Systems
(Digital Tools and Uses Set – Volume 2)

SZONIECKY Samuel, BOUHAÏ Nasreddine
Collective Intelligence and Digital Archives: Towards Knowledge Ecosystems
(Digital Tools and Uses Set – Volume 1)

2016

BLUM Christian, FESTA Paola
Metaheuristics for String Problems in Bio-informatics
(Metaheuristics Set – Volume 6)

DEROUSSI Laurent
Metaheuristics for Logistics
(Metaheuristics Set – Volume 4)

DHAENENS Clarisse, JOURDAN Laetitia
Metaheuristics for Big Data
(Metaheuristics Set – Volume 5)

LABADIE Nacima, PRINS Christian, PRODHON Caroline
Metaheuristics for Vehicle Routing Problems
(Metaheuristics Set – Volume 3)

LEROY Laure
Eyestrain Reduction in Stereoscopy

LUTTON Evelyne, PERROT Nathalie, TONDA Alberto
Evolutionary Algorithms for Food Science and Technology
(Metaheuristics Set – Volume 7)

MAGOULÈS Frédéric, ZHAO Hai-Xiang
Data Mining and Machine Learning in Building Energy Analysis

RIGO Michel
Advanced Graph Theory and Combinatorics

ZELM Martin, DOUMEINGTS Guy, MENDONÇA Joao Pedro
Enterprise Interoperability: in the Digitized and Networked Factory of the Future

2015

BARBIER Franck, RECOUSSINE Jean-Luc
COBOL Software Modernization: From Principles to Implementation with the BLU AGE® Method

CHEN Ken
Performance Evaluation by Simulation and Analysis with Applications to Computer Networks

CLERC Maurice
Guided Randomness in Optimization
(Metaheuristics Set – Volume 1)

DURAND Nicolas, GIANAZZA David, GOTTELAND Jean-Baptiste, ALLIOT Jean-Marc
Metaheuristics for Air Traffic Management
(Metaheuristics Set – Volume 2)

MAGOULÈS Frédéric, ROUX François-Xavier, HOUZEAUX Guillaume
Parallel Scientific Computing

MUNEESAWANG Paisarn, YAMMEN Suchart
Visual Inspection Technology in the Hard Disk Drive Industry

2014

BOULANGER Jean-Louis
Formal Methods Applied to Industrial Complex Systems
Formal Methods Applied to Complex Systems: Implementation of the B Method

EXPOSITO Ernesto, DIOP Codé
Smart SOA Platforms in Cloud Computing Architectures

GARDI Frédéric, BENOIST Thierry, DARLAY Julien, ESTELLON Bertrand, MEGEL Romain
Mathematical Programming Solver based on Local Search

KRICHEN Saoussen, CHAOUACHI Jouhaina
Graph-related Optimization and Decision Support Systems

LARRIEU Nicolas, VARET Antoine
Rapid Prototyping of Software for Avionics Systems: Model-oriented Approaches for Complex Systems Certification

LAURAS Matthieu, ZELM Martin, ARCHIMÈDE Bernard, BÉNABEN Frédérick, DOUMEINGTS Guy
Enterprise Interoperability: Interoperability for Agility, Resilience and Plasticity of Collaborations

OUSSALAH Mourad Chabane
Software Architecture 1
Software Architecture 2

QUESNEL Flavien
Scheduling of Large-scale Virtualized Infrastructures: Toward Cooperative Management

RIGO Michel
Formal Languages, Automata and Numeration Systems 1: Introduction to Combinatorics on Words
Formal Languages, Automata and Numeration Systems 2: Applications to Recognizability and Decidability

SAINT-DIZIER Patrick
Musical Rhetoric: Foundations and Annotation Schemes

TOUATI Sid, DUPONT DE DINECHIN Benoit
Advanced Backend Code Optimization

2013

ANDRÉ Étienne, SOULAT Romain
The Inverse Method: Parametric Verification of Real-time Embedded Systems

BOULANGER Jean-Louis
Safety Management for Software-based Equipment

DELAHAYE Daniel, PUECHMOREL Stéphane
Modeling and Optimization of Air Traffic

FRANCOPOULO Gil
LMF — Lexical Markup Framework

GHEDIRA Khaled
Constraint Satisfaction Problems: CSP Formalisms and Techniques

GOVAERT Gérard, NADIF Mohamed
Co-Clustering: Models, Algorithms and Applications

LANDRAGIN Frédérick
Man–Machine Dialogue: Design and Challenges

LUCAS Laurent, LOSCOS Céline, REMION Yannick
3D Video: Models, From Capture to Diffusion

ROCHANGE Christine, UHRIG Sascha, SAINRAT Pascal
Time-Predictable Architectures

WAHBI Mohamed
Algorithms and Ordering Heuristics for Distributed Constraint Satisfaction Problems

ZELM Martin, VAN SINDEREN Marten, FERRAIRA PIRES Luis, DOUMEINGTS Guy
Enterprise Interoperability: Research and Applications in the Service-oriented Ecosystem

2012

ARBOLEDA Hugo, ROYER Jean-Claude
Model-Driven and Software Product Line Engineering

BLANCHET Gérard, DUPOUY Bertrand
Computer Architecture

BOULANGER Jean-Louis
Industrial Use of Formal Methods: Formal Verification
Formal Methods: Industrial Use from Model to the Code

CALVARY Gaëlle, DELOT Thierry, SÈDES Florence, TIGLI Jean-Yves
Computer Science and Ambient Intelligence

MAHOUT Vincent
Assembly Language Programming: ARM Cortex-M3 2.0: Organization, Innovation and Territory

MARLET Renaud
Program Specialization

SOTO Maria, SEVAUX Marc, ROSSI André, LAURENT Johann
Memory Allocation Problems in Embedded Systems: Optimization Methods

2011

BICHOT Charles-Edmond, SIARRY Patrick
Graph Partitioning

BOULANGER Jean-Louis
Static Analysis of Software: The Abstract Interpretation

CAFERRA Ricardo
Logic for Computer Science and Artificial Intelligence

KORDON Fabrice, HADDAD Serge, PAUTET Laurent, PETRUCCI Laure
Distributed Systems: Design and Algorithms
Models and Analysis in Distributed Systems

LORCA Xavier
Tree-based Graph Partitioning Constraint

RIDHA MAHJOUB A.
Progress in Combinatorial Optimization: ISCO2010

TRUCHET Charlotte, ASSAYAG Gerard
Constraint Programming in Music

VICAT-BLANC Pascale, GOGLIN Brice, GUILLIER Romaric,
SOUDAN Sébastien
Computing Networks: From Cluster to Cloud Computing

2010

AUBRUN Christophe, SIMON Daniel, SONG Ye-Qiong
Co-design Approaches for Dependable Networked Control Systems

AUDIBERT Pierre
Mathematics for Informatics and Computer Science

BABAU Jean-Philippe, BLAY-FORNARINO Mireille, CHAMPEAU Joël,
ROBERT Sylvain, SABETTA Antonino
Model Driven Engineering for Distributed Real-Time Systems: MARTE Modeling, Model Transformations and their Usages

BOULANGER Jean-Louis
Safety of Computer Architectures

SIGAUD Olivier, BUFFET Olivier
Markov Decision Processes in Artificial Intelligence

MONMARCHÉ Nicolas, GUINAND Frédérick, SIARRY Patrick
Artificial Ants

SOLNON Christine
Ant Colony Optimization and Constraint Programming

2009

FOURNIER Jean-Claude
Graph Theory and Applications: with exercises and problems

GUÉDON Jeanpierre
The Mojette Transform: theory and applications

JARD Claude, ROUX Olivier H.
Communicating Embedded Systems: Software and Design

LECOUTRE Christophe
Constraint Networks: Techniques and Algorithms

2008

BANÂTRE Michel, MARRON Pedro Jose, OLLERO Anibal, WOLITZ Adam
Cooperating Embedded Systems and Wireless Sensor Networks

MERZ Stephan, NAVET Nicolas
Modeling and Verification of Real-time Systems: Formalisms and Software Tools

PASCHOS Vangelis Th.
Combinatorial Optimization and Theoretical Computer Science: Interfaces and Perspectives

WALDNER Jean-Baptiste
Nanocomputers and Swarm Intelligence

2007

BENHAMOU Frédéric, JUSSIEN Narendra, O'SULLIVAN Barry
Trends in Constraint Programming

JUSSIEN Narendra
A to Z of Sudoku

2006

BABAU Jean-Philippe, CHAMPEAU Joël, GÉRARD Sébastien
From MDD Concepts to Experiments and Illustrations – DRES 2006

HABRIAS Henri, FRAPPIER Marc
Software Specification Methods: An Overview Using a Case Study

MURAT Cécile, PASCHOS Vangelis Th.
Probabilistic Combinatorial Optimization on Graphs

PANETTO Hervé, BOUDJLIDA Nacer
Interoperability for Enterprise Software and Applications: Proceedings of the Workshops and the Doctorial Symposium of the Second IFAC/IFIP I-ESA International Conference: EI2N, WSI, IS-TSPQ 2006

2005

GÉRARD Sébastien, BABAU Jean-Philippe, CHAMPEAU Joël
Model Driven Engineering for Distributed Real Time Embedded Systems

PANETTO Hervé
Interoperability of Enterprise Software and Applications: Workshops of the INTEROP-ESA 2005 International Conference (EI2N, WSI, ISIDI and IEHENA 2005)